Geography

D1516632

When geography specialists decide they want to teach, it can be a daunting prospect having to enter the classroom, no matter how much subject knowledge they already possess. *Geography: Teaching School Subjects 11–19* puts the subject into perspective and shows new teachers and student teachers how to make geography accessible and interesting for their pupils.

Divided into three parts, the book examines the theory and practice of teaching geography:

- Part I explores how teachers can frame their own knowledge for classroom practice.
- Part II focuses on geography in the classroom and curriculum development, as well as aspects of pedagogy and lesson design, evaluation and assessment.
- Part III focuses on the teachers themselves and how they can view and work on professional development within their own subject area.

This book tries to guide the intellectually alive teacher into the nature of the subject in its entirety, and how to think about geography when preparing to teach.

John Morgan is senior lecturer in Education at the University of Bristol.
David Lambert is Chief Executive of the Geographical Association, though writing here in a personal capacity as a former teacher and teacher educator.

Teaching School Subjects 11–19 Series

Series Editors: John Hardcastle and David Lambert

Mathematics
Candia Morgan, Anne Watson, Clare Tikly

English
John Hardcastle, Tony Burgess, Caroline Daly and Anton Franks

Geography
John Morgan and David Lambert

Science
Vanessa Kind and Keith Taber

Modern Foreign Languages
Norbert Pachler, Michael Evans and Shirley Anne Lawes

Business, Economics & Enterprise
Peter Davies and Jacek Brant

Geography: Teaching School Subjects 11–19

John Morgan and
David Lambert

Routledge
Taylor & Francis Group

LONDON AND NEW YORK

First published 2005
by Routledge
2 Park Square, Milton Park, Abingdon, Oxon OX14 4RN

Simultaneously published in the USA and Canada
by Routledge
270 Madison Ave, New York, NY 10016

Routledge is an imprint of the Taylor & Francis Group

© 2005 John Morgan and David Lambert

Typeset in Sabon and Bell Gothic by
Florence Production Ltd, Stoodleigh, Devon
Printed and bound in Great Britain by
TJ International Ltd, Padstow, Cornwall

British Library Cataloguing in Publication Data
A catalogue record for this book is available from the
British Library

Library of Congress Cataloging in Publication Data
A catalog record for this book has been requested

ISBN 0–415–32111–5 (pbk)
ISBN 0–415–32110–7 (hbk)

Contents

Series editors' preface   vii
List of abbreviations   xiii

1   Introduction   1

Part I   **The subject**   3
2   Doing geography   5
3   Making school geography   24
4   Geography, knowledge and education   42

Part II   **The classroom**   69
5   Curriculum planning – curriculum thinking   73
6   Teaching and learning geography   97
7   Evaluating geography education   133

Part III   **The teacher**   153
8   What kind of geography teacher?   155
9   Learning professional values and practice: teachers with high standards   172
10   Professional development and developing geography   188
11   Conclusion   200

Appendix   Strengths of the Royal Geographical Society (with the Institute of British Geographers) and the Geographical Association   203

References   207
Index   219

Series editors' preface

This series aims to make sense of school subjects for new teachers at a moment when subject expertise is being increasingly linked to the redefinition of teachers' responsibilities (Furlong *et al*. 2000). We start from the common assumption that teachers' passion for their subject provides the foundation for effective teaching, but we also take the view that effective teachers develop a complicated understanding of students' learning. Therefore, we also aim to offer subject specialists a picture of students' learning in their chosen field.

The central argument of the series as a whole is that teachers' professional development in subject specialisms turns on their growing appreciation of the complexities of learning. In essence, the subject knowledge that new teachers bring from their experiences in higher education has to be reworked before it can be taught effectively to children. Our contention is that it is the sustained engagement with the dynamics of students' learning that uniquely sheds light on the way that existing subject knowledge has to be reconfigured locally if it is to be taught successfully in schools. What teachers know about their subject has to be reworked on site, and such is teachers' agency that they will always have a key role in shaping curriculum subjects.

Teaching involves a critical re-engagement with existing subject knowledge. This occurs chiefly through contact with children and communities. All new teachers have to learn how to make complicated judgements about the selection, ordering and presentation of materials with particular learners, real children, in mind. Teachers, then, are learners too. So, as well as giving a picture of students' learning, the series aims to offer a sufficiently complicated account of professional development for new teachers to recognise themselves as learners as they take on new responsibilities in their schools. Thus, we aim to offer insights into the kind of thinking – intellectual work – that teachers at the early stages are going to have to do.

This series is aimed chiefly at new teachers in their years of early professional development. This includes teachers in their initial training year, their induction year and those in years two and three of a teaching career. In addition to Post-Graduate Certificate of Education (PGCE) students and newly qualified teachers (NQTs) working toward the induction standards, the series therefore also addresses subject leaders in schools who have mentor responsibilities with early career teachers, and Advanced Skills Teachers (ASTs) undertaking subject specialist in-service training and teaching support.

The books in the series cover the training standards for NQT status and the induction standards. They use both the training terminology and structure of the official standards in a way that enables readers to connect the arguments contained in the books with their obligation to demonstrate achievement against performance criteria. Yet the books in the series have the ambition to take readers further than mere 'compliance'. They openly challenge teachers to acknowledge their own agency in interpreting 'competence' and to see their role in developing the subject, shaping their professional identities.

A distinctive feature of the series as a whole is its concern with how the particular school subjects have been 'framed'. The books therefore offer a contrast with much that has been published in recent times, including the well-known *Learning to Teach* series, also published by RoutledgeFalmer. They include substantial material on how school subjects connect with wider disciplines, and are also alert to broad social and cultural realities. Thus, they form a response to what has been identified as a major weakness in training and teacher support in recent years – namely, its preoccupation with generic matters of teaching competence at the expense of paying adequate attention to particular issues associated with subject specialism. The books in the *Teaching School Subjects 11–19* series aim to redress the balance.

Those who believe that there is a general 'science' of teaching have been especially influential in recent years. There is no denying that the Key Stage 3 Strategy, for instance, has had an impact on the preparedness of teachers generally. Further to this, the identification and recommendation of specific teaching approaches and techniques have enhanced new teachers' technical proficiency generally. Recently, much has been made of teaching 'thinking skills', and such initiatives have raised teachers' all-round performance as well as their professional self-esteem. But when push comes to shove, teaching cannot be sustained in this way. Pupils cannot be taught simply to think. They have to have something to think *about*. If this 'something' is trivial, irrelevant or out of date, then the education process will be devalued and students will quickly become disaffected. The Secretary of State recognised something of this in 2003 when he launched his *Subject Specialisms Consultation*:

> Our very best teachers are those who have a real passion and enthusiasm for the subject they teach. They are also deeply committed to the learning of their students and use their enthusiasm for their subject to motivate them, to bring their subject alive and make learning an exciting, vivid and enjoyable experience.
>
> It is teachers' passion for their subject that provides the basis for effective teaching and learning. These teachers use their subject expertise to engage students in meaningful learning experiences that embrace content, process and social climate. They create for and with their children opportunities to explore and build important areas of knowledge, and develop powerful tools for learning, within a supportive, collaborative and challenging classroom environment.
>
> (DfES 2003a, paras 1–2)

The *Teaching School Subjects 11–19* series aims to make practical sense of such assumptions by fleshing them out in terms of teachers' experiences. So, as well as looking at the histories of particular school subjects and current national frameworks, we shall also look at practical matters through case studies and teachers' narratives. We have noted how new teachers sometimes feel at a loss regarding the very subject knowledge they carry forward from their previous educational experiences into teaching. This feeling may be due to their entering a highly regulated profession where it appears that choices concerning what to teach (let alone how to teach it) are heavily constrained. However, much will be lost that could sustain creative and healthy classrooms if the system cuts off a primary source of energy, which is teachers' enthusiasm for their subject. Good teachers connect such enthusiasm with the students' interests. The *Teaching School Subjects 11–19* series engages with just this issue. If it has a single, clear mission, it is to encourage the thought in teachers that they do not merely 'deliver' the curriculum in the form of prefigured subject knowledge, but that they have an agentive role in making it.

What does it mean to 'make' a curriculum? This is a huge question and we do not aim to provide a definitive curriculum theory. However, we note that current accounts of curriculum and pedagogy (e.g. Moore 2000) tend to emphasise the role of competing interests that decide the educational experience of students. They offer a complicated picture of curriculum construction by taking in societal, economic and cultural influences. Plainly, no single interest wholly determines the outcome. Additionally, there is a growing agreement among educationists in England and Wales that 'central government control of the school curriculum must be loosened' to release teachers' energies (White 2004: 189). We adopt a position similar to John White's, which is to 'rescue' the curriculum from central prescription and 'to see teachers having a greater role than now in . . . decisions on the curriculum . . .' (ibid. pp. 189–90).

This is not to say that the government has no role at all. Few educationists would want to return fully to the arrangements before the 1988 Education Reform Act, when the curriculum experience of students was almost entirely in the hands of teachers and other interest groups. It is surely right that the elected government should regulate what is taught, but not that it should prescribe the curriculum in such an inflexible manner that it stifles teachers' initiative. Teachers play an active role in shaping the curriculum. They make professional decisions given, as White puts it, their 'knowledge of the pupils on whom the curriculum will be inflicted'. We argue that it is here, in deciding what to teach and how to teach it, that teachers' knowledge and creativity is of cardinal value. Teaching is quintessentially a practical activity and teachers' performance matters. But we also know that behind the creativity in teaching lies a form of intellectual work. Our starting position is that intellectual effort is required at every stage of teaching and learning if it is to be worthwhile.

Knowledge of the pupils is a fundamental component of curriculum design. Effective teachers are in secure possession of just this kind of knowledge of their pupils where it informs their decisions about the selection of content and the choice of methods. However, the series also makes it plain that knowledge of the pupils on its own is an insufficient basis for working out what to teach and how to teach it. Secure subject knowledge is equally important. Furthermore, we take the view that an essential element of a secondary teacher's professional identity is tied up with a sense of their subject specialism. It is generally true that effective teaching requires a deeper grasp of a subject than that specified in the syllabus. What is more, pupils frequently admire teachers who 'know their stuff'. What 'stuff' means is usually larger than a particular topic or a set of facts. Indeed, the way that an effective teacher makes a particular topic accessible to the pupils and enables them to progress often relies on their having a good grasp of the architecture of the subject, what the main structures are and where the weaknesses lie. You can't mug this up the night before the lesson.

It is widely recognised that PGCE students and early career teachers frequently turn to school textbooks to fill the gaps. This is fine – inevitably there will be aspects of the subject that the specialist has not covered. Many teachers now use the internet proficiently as a rich source of information, data, images and so on, which is also fine. But what teachers also need to do is to make sense of the material, organise it and sift it for accuracy, coherence and meaning. The series helps new teachers to do this by taking them into the relevant subject debates. The authors introduce teachers to the conceptual struggles in the subject and how these impinge on the making of the school subject. Through debating the role of the school subject, and showing how it hangs together (its 'big concepts'), they also show how it contributes to wider educational aims. Such a discussion takes place in the context of renewed debate about the future of school subjects and the subject-based curriculum. Although the series serves the needs of subject specialists, it does not take as given the unchanging status of school subjects, and the authors will take up this debate explicitly.

Current notions of subjects as inert 'contents' to be 'delivered' grate against learning theories, which foreground the role of human agency (teachers and pupils) in the construction of knowledge. For the teacher, good subject knowledge is not about being 'ahead of the students', but being aware of the wider subject. Teachers might ask themselves what kinds of knowledge their subject deals with. And, following on from this, they might also ask about the kinds of difficulties that students often encounter. Note that we are not concerned with 'correcting' pupils' 'misconceptions' about what they get from their lessons, but with what they actually make of what they get.

The series has a broad theoretical position which guides the way that the components of the individual books are configured. These components include lesson planning, classroom organisation, learning management, the assessment of/for learning and ethical issues. However, there is no overarching prescription and the various volumes in the series take significantly different approaches. Such differences will depend on the various priorities and concerns associated with particular specialist subjects. In essence, the books aim to develop ways of thinking about subjects, even before teachers set foot inside the classroom.

We doubt the adequacy of any model of teaching and learning that reduces the role of the teacher to that of the technician. Teachers mediate the curriculum for their students. Furthermore, there is an urgent justification for this series of books.

It is the ambition of the series to restate the role of subjects in schools, but not in a conservative spirit that fails to engage with substantial change and developments. For some commentators, the information explosion, together with the still-quickening communications revolution, spells the death of subjects, textbooks and the rest of the nineteenth-century school apparatus. Although we do not share this analysis, we acknowledge that the status quo is not an option. Indeed, subject teachers may need to become less territorial about curriculum space, more open to collaboration across traditional subject boundaries and more responsive to what have been called 'unauthorised subject stories' – student understandings, media representations and common-sense views of the world. In such an educational environment, we would argue, the role of disciplinary knowledge is even more important than it was a decade ago, and teachers need to engage with it creatively.

The *Teaching School Subjects 11–19* series aims to support new teachers by helping them to discover productive ways of thinking about their specialism. The specialist authors have tried to maintain an optimistic, lively and accessible tone and we hope you enjoy them.

John Hardcastle and David Lambert
London, 2004

Abbreviations

AST	Advanced Skills Teacher
CPD	Continuing Professional Development
DfES	Department for Education and Skills
GA	Geographical Association
GCSE	General Certificate of Secondary Education
GSIP	Geography, Schools and Industry Project
GTCE	General Teaching Council for England
GYSL	Geography for the Young School Leaver
HE	Higher Education
ICT	Information and Communications Technology
KS	Key Stage
LEA	Local Education Authority
Ofsted	Office for Standards in Education
OS	Ordnance Survey
NCSL	National College for School Leadership
NQT	Newly Qualified Teacher
PGCE	Post-Graduate Certificate of Education
QCA	Qualifications and Curriculum Authority
QTS	Qualified Teacher Status
SATs	Standard Assessment Tests
SEN	Special Educational Needs
TTA	Teacher Training Agency

Chapter 1

Introduction

Geography teaching is important, especially when it is done well. What is more, you can have great fun and derive immense satisfaction from teaching geography well. This book is dedicated to help provide, for anyone thinking of becoming a geography teacher, a sound basis for achieving such professional rewards.

In some ways the secret to satisfaction is very simple. Echoing prominent education philosophers of the last century, we think that if you can show how your teaching is relevant, worthwhile and enjoyable, you will be able to motivate and stimulate your students to achieve things they never thought were possible. When any teacher witnesses the penny drop in a student's mind, or the focused buzz of 30 teenagers grappling with a mystery, it is very satisfying, but in geography (we are biased) it is doubly so, because often we are in the business of helping students to make sense of the world as it is, to enable them to see it in new ways and to gain the confidence to believe they could even change it. Learning geography, therefore, is a fine vehicle for education in a world in which issues of citizenship and sustainable development will gain greater prominence during students' lifetimes.

But planning and teaching relevant, worthwhile and enjoyable lessons is not as straightforward as it may sound. For a start, school geography is not often portrayed in such terms, sometimes being caricatured as glorified 'general knowledge', being more concerned with surface 'facts' than deeper understandings. It sometimes feels a little dated, quaint even, in comparison with the rapidly changing world that is brought daily to television and computer screens in virtually every household in the country. Teachers of geography need to be agile and inventive in order to respond creatively to this dynamic. The curriculum, therefore, is best understood as in a state of constant renewal – and it is teachers who are the developers.

These are the reasons why we set out and discuss (in Part I) the nature of geography in some detail, and the ways in which school geography can interact with the wider discipline. In Part II we move to applying the kind of thinking about geography to the classroom – undertaking planning, understanding teaching and learning, and taking steps to evaluate the outcomes of students' attempts at responding to the learning opportunities teachers provide. In Part III we make a powerful case for understanding professional development as a career-long process, and something individuals not only have a right to, but a responsibility for shaping. If you wait for professional development to come to you, you may have to wait too long. And when it comes it may not be what you want.

We have included questions for further thinking at the end of each chapter to promote discussion and reflection. Boxes within the text are used to highlight issues of importance or case studies.

The ethos of this series is based in the need for teachers to recognise and grasp the intellectual basis of their actions. Teachers, like any other professional group, have to get to grips with expert and specialist ways of thinking. If your initial training focuses so heavily on the absolutely essential practical aspects of teaching to the exclusion of the intellectual underpinnings, it seriously undermines your capacity to engage in curriculum renewal and personalised professional development. This in turn will limit the educational potential of students doing geography.

While some teachers will read this book from cover to cover, there will be many more who will dip into the text in a less structured way. Do so frequently, for we think there is a cumulative message which is optimistic and we hope rewarding. But we do not pretend to hold the exclusive 'truth'. The discussions in this book are even more powerful when used in conjunction with materials and guidance from other sources, not least from specialist sources in the wider professional environment which supports you, such as the Geographical Association.

Part I

The subject

This part contains three chapters that consider the relationship between geography as an academic subject and geography as taught and learned in schools. In Chapter 2, we offer an account of the recent development of Anglo-American geography in recent decades. The chapter has two purposes. First, we see it as offering a coherent narrative that can be used by geography teachers to 'frame' their work in schools. Second, the account we offer is constructed to support the larger argument in this book. We present geography as part of a broader conversation about nature and contemporary society. Our account suggests that, at its best, geography contributes to this in a progressive sense.

There are some things we should say about Chapter 2. First, it is impossible to synthesise the huge output written by geographers, so we can offer only a partial account. We have taken care to reference what we see as important sources in their most accessible form. Second, we write as geography educators, who see our role as 'translators' of material into a form that can help teachers make sense of broad changes in the discipline.

In Chapter 3, we offer an account of the ways in which school geography has developed in the last 40 years. While Chapter 2 sees us at our most optimistic about the possibility of realising progressive geography, our analysis in this chapter is more sobering! We argue that school geography has developed in ways that prevent a sustained engagement with many developments in academic geography, and show how, in recent years, geography has been 'made' in ways that are socially exclusive. Reading these two chapters together, we hope, will offer geography teachers the chance to reflect upon how their work in schools is shaped by a range of forces internal to the discipline and from external forces.

The final chapter in this part offers some alternative frameworks for school geography based on what we call 'post-positivist' approaches. We unearth the tradition of critical geography and offer an account of how it has informed some of the debates in geography education. Our purpose in this chapter is twofold. First, we want to do some definitional work, summarising for readers some of the terms – structuralism, postmodernism, post-structuralism – routinely used in contemporary geography, but less familiar in schools. Second, we want to open the door for the more detailed discussions of teaching and learning in the second part of this book. Chapter 4, then, offers an overview of the frameworks we choose to develop in the rest of this book.

Chapter 2

Doing geography

INTRODUCTION

> What most of us too readily treat as a universal discipline – a sort of 'Geography-with-a-capital-G' – is really only one sedimented and situated product of a series of intersecting historical geographies and colliding geographical experiments.
>
> (Barnes and Gregory 1997: 1)

In this statement, Barnes and Gregory are referring to the fragmented and contested nature of geography as an academic discipline. Often, this fragmentation is regarded as a problem because it threatens to undermine the apparent unity of geography as a subject that bridges the human and physical. For example, Haggett (1996) speaks of his wish to see a return to the 'central and cherished aspects of geographical education; a love of landscape and of field exploration, a fascination with place, a wish to solve the spatial conundrums posed by spatial configurations' (p. 17). Similarly, Rawling (1997) worries about the 'reticence to be absolutely clear about the definition and 'heart' of the discipline' (p. 173). These writers seem concerned to 'pin down' what is essential about geography. In this book, we take a different approach, in order to explore how geography teachers in schools and colleges might use the insights of contemporary approaches in geography to develop a 'progressive' (we discuss what this might mean in Chapter 7) understanding of society and space. In doing so we follow Jackson's (1996) argument that:

> Rather than policing our own disciplinary boundaries in an embattled and defensive mood, I would suggest that it is human geography's

encounter with social theory and its excursions into neighbouring social sciences that are the most promising sources for meeting the intellectual and political challenges of the future.

(p. 92)

At this point, readers may have spotted the focus on human geography, so we need to introduce the question of the relationship between the physical and human components of geography. In schools, students are taught aspects of both physical and human geography. Sometimes there are genuine attempts to integrate the two; at other times human and physical themes are studied in their own right. In universities, physical and human geography are increasingly separated. Students specialise in particular fields and find themselves operating in very different historical traditions. This has implications for school geography since new teachers come to education with different conceptions of the subject. We can highlight some of the issues at stake by briefly considering a recent under-graduate text, *Key Concepts in Geography* (Holloway *et al.* 2003). In their preface the editors are refreshingly candid about the difficulty of defining 'the core' of geography: 'Sociologists have society, biology living things, economists the economy and physicists matter and energy. But what is at the very core of geography? What are its key concepts?' (p. xiv).

Their solution is to suggest that, rather than having one central organising concept, geography has many. They identify seven: space, place, landscape, environment, system, scale and time. The organisation of their book is to have chapters written about each of these seven concepts by human and physical geographers. The lack of integration reflects the different treatments the concepts are given in the different sides of the discipline. While this may not satisfy everyone, it at least hints at the possibility of a dialogue or conversation between physical and human geography.

We do not pretend to have an answer to the question of the relationship between physical and human geography, although we return to the issue at various points in this book. At the very least we hope to convince readers that it is important for all geography teachers to think carefully about the way their teaching is 'framed' by an understanding of geography as a subject. In this chapter, we deal with the histories of physical and human geography separately.

HISTORIES OF HUMAN GEOGRAPHY

Each day, geography teachers are charged with the task of introducing geographical knowledge and understanding to pupils in schools. In doing so, they are involved in providing pupils with geographical knowledge and helping them to explore their own values. We believe that the greatest resource teachers have available to support this task is their understanding of the discipline of geography. However, as the quote from Barnes and Gregory suggests, what counts as geography at any point in time is always contested and subject to re-definition. In this chapter, we want to provide a short account of the recent development of geography as an academic discipline. From the start, we want to make it clear that we do not claim to offer a comprehensive account of the history of geography, since this is something of an impossible task, and inevitably involves simplifying and making generalisations about a complex picture. As Heffernan (2003) reminds us, it is important to ask *whose* history of geography is being written. In recent years, there has been a lot of 'heat' generated over the history of geography, which reflects the importance of historical representation. Our view is that such argument is valuable because it can help us see the work of geographers in a new light. Attempts to tell the history of geography are concerned (in part) to clarify and make the case about why geography is important. They are also attempts to intervene in the making of geography. As we write this chapter, we are mindful of the intended audience for this book – geography teachers – and also of what is to follow in the rest of this book, namely, an account of the science and art of teaching geography, a tireless concern to understand and promote learning and the continuous professional learning that characterises good teachers.

One of the most influential accounts of the development of (human) geography is Ron Johnston's *Geography and Geographers: Anglo-American human geography since 1945* (1997). That this book is in its sixth edition since its first appearance in 1979 says something about its influence. Johnston's account tells the story of the subject as a series of discrete episodes or eras in the development of geographical knowledge. He makes use of the idea of paradigms discussed by the philosopher of science Thomas Kuhn. According to Kuhn (1962), the 'normal' business of science is that it is characterised by periods when there is widespread agreement about what is the best way of doing science and understanding its objects of study. These widely accepted approaches are said to be the

7

'dominant paradigm'. Of course, there may be those scientists who have a different view of the field and who seek to challenge the dominant ideas. The history of science, Kuhn argued, is marked by periods of crisis or periodic shifts when the dominant paradigms are challenged and overthrown.

Another example of such an approach is found in Derek Gregory's book *Geographical Imaginations* (1994). Gregory's book is challenging because it draws upon such a wide range of ideas and reading, but it is worth persevering with. In the first half of the book, Gregory provides a schematic plan illustrating the ways in which Anglo-American geographers engaged with ideas from anthropology, sociology and economics in distinct periods (see Figure 1). According to Gregory, geographers engaged with anthropological studies in the study of exotic cultures in the 'era of *exploration*'. As industrialisation and urbanisation took hold in the cities of North America and Britain in the late nineteenth and early twentieth centuries, geographers were influenced by *sociological* debates about the nature of industrial cities such as Chicago. This sociological influence was replaced in the post-war period as geographers drew upon *regional science* and *spatial science* approaches from *economics*. Since then, according to Gregory, geography has revisited these three phases in reverse order. The focus on spatial models was replaced in the 1970s with an interest in Marxist-inspired *political economy* approaches. The focus was widened to embrace *critical social theories* in the 1980s, and returning to engage with *critical cultural theory* in the 1990s.

These accounts are useful as heuristic models (that is, they are helpful in stimulating thought or discussion). However, they risk implying that all geographers have followed the same route through time, and that the phases are clearly distinct from each other. It is possible to argue that elements of all six of Gregory's phases are evident in contemporary geography. Having said that, accounts such as these have been influential in

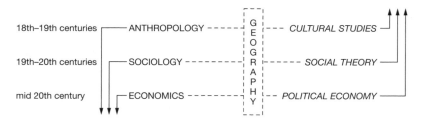

Figure 1 *Maps of an intellectual landscape*

how school geography has been understood. For example, the influential Schools Council Geography 16–19 Project (which still directly underpins and indirectly influences a number of A-level syllabuses) drew upon an eclectic mix of positivist, humanist and radical versions of geography (Naish *et al.* 1987). For the purposes of this chapter, we want to point to the substantial agreement in many accounts of the history of geography that, in the 1950s and 1960s, the methodology and substance of human geography began to change as geographers began to argue for a systematic human geography based on principles of experimentation and quantification.

The shift from the idea of geography as a regional science to geography as a spatial science was linked to the growing prosperity of the post-war period. Cities and regions throughout the developed world were changing and growing in quite new and unpredictable ways. Governments and administrators were faced with solving problems of location, spatial development and transportation and, by the mid-1950s, these were attracting the attention of geographers and economists. It was in this context that the fields of spatial analysis and regional science came together to form a spatial science that sought to identify the regularities (or patterns) of the 'space economy'. In order to develop this spatial science, geographers reached back to an earlier, mainly German tradition of location theory, and 'rediscovered' the works of writers such as Alfred Weber, Walter Christaller and Johann Von Thunen. By the early 1960s, the 'new' geography was becoming increasingly influential, and in Britain was given voice by the publications of Haggett (1965) and Chorley and Haggett (1967), which, as we discuss in Chapter 3, influenced a generation of geography teachers.

We will return to the so-called 'new' geography in Chapter 3, where we consider its impact upon school geography. However, in order to develop the argument in this chapter we want to argue that many accounts of the history of geography suggest that this approach has been largely rejected by subsequent generations of human geographers who have reacted against what they perceive as the de-humanising view of people and place found in the new geography. These geographers have sought to develop a more 'human' approach to the study of geography.

In general terms, many geographers reacted to the excesses of the new geography that sought to develop a discipline that was capable of mapping and predicting human behaviour at an aggregate level, developing models of migration, industrial location, agricultural activity and settlement patterns that denigrated the role of individuals and down-played the ability of people to act as agents and initiators of change. Again it is necessary to simplify a complex literature here, but there were two main responses to this problem. The first was to stress the role of the broad and overarching structures that contained and constrained people's actions. The focus here tended to be on the ways in which the economic system – in the West, this meant capitalism – provided the real backdrop in which people lived and worked. The second approach was to stress the meanings attached to experience by individuals, and that prioritised the thoughts and feelings of individuals. We will briefly consider each of these in turn.

We can illustrate the general direction of the first approach by way of a brief discussion of the work of David Harvey, which has influenced greatly this book. Harvey's first book, *Explanation in Geography* (1969), was an account of the philosophical and methodological issues surrounding positivism. His second book, *Social Justice and the City* (1973), was published four years later and represented an about-turn. In this book, Harvey rejected positivism in geography and turned to Marxism as his method. His concern was the question of whether geography has anything useful to say about the problems faced by people living on the margins in cities. The book is organised into two sections, called 'Liberal formulations' and 'Socialist formulations'. In the first part, Harvey shows how theories such as Alonso's land use model, Von Thunen's rings and Park and Burgess's models of urban structure all tend to describe and explain the status quo. Harvey rejects these and seeks to develop a 'revolutionary theory'. In an often-quoted passage in *Social Justice and the City*, he wrote:

> there is a clear disparity between the sophisticated theoretical and methodological framework which we are using and our ability to say anything meaningful about events as they unfold around us . . . There is an ecological problem, an urban problem, an international trade problem, and yet we seem incapable of saying anything of depth or profundity about any of them. When we do say something, it appears trite and rather ludicrous.
>
> (p. 129)

This is an important passage, since it reminds us that geographical knowledge grows out of and responds to the concrete historical and material context geographers work in. For Harvey, there was something distasteful about the inability (or unwillingness) of geographers to engage with the issues of the day. Harvey's career has been marked by a continued engagement with these issues.

Harvey's major contribution has been to add a geographical perspective to historical materialism. He has maintained his belief in Marxism despite its being unfashionable in academic circles. An important landmark was Harvey's *The Condition of Postmodernity* (1989) which was an attempt to anchor the cultural condition of postmodernity back to what he saw as the material realities of capitalist organisation. Harvey took a lot of criticism for this work, not least from those who suggested that he was unwilling to take on board arguments from other directions, most notably feminism. His later work *Justice, Nature and the Geographies of Difference* (1996) was an attempt to draw together ideas about social justice in relation to environment issues and address questions about how space and places are constructed. More recently, in *Spaces of Hope* (2000a), Harvey urges his readers to get back to analysing the 'crushing realities of capitalist exploitation' (p. 7). His list of the most important concepts include 'fetishism of the market', 'the savage history of downsizing', 'technological change', 'weakened organized labour', and an 'industrial reserve army'. As Barnes (2003) wryly comments, reading this list makes it clear that 'this isn't going to be fun. We need to roll up our sleeves, and be prepared for some serious work' (p. 91).

Having expressed our admiration for Harvey's work, it is perhaps important to offer a critique as well as justification. It is worth making a few points about the geographical imagination his writing provides. In much of his work, Harvey is concerned with the 'big picture'. He is talking about the invisible, abstract, hard-to-grasp structures and forces that operate over our heads. At times, whole landscapes are 'creatively destroyed' in the name of capital accumulation. Although we might agree with the tenor of his analysis, sometimes there seems too little role for human agency in Harvey's writing. People are caught up in the sway of forces that are out of their control. It may be that together these points – the high level of abstraction and the lack of acknowledgement of human agency – explain to some extent the reluctance of teachers to draw from Harvey's work in school. This is a discussion we say more about in the next chapter.

An alternative response to the 'dehumanising' tendencies of the 'new' geography was proposed by humanistic geographers, who were concerned

11

to pay attention to the meanings that individuals give to their experience. Humanism suggests a very different view of geographical knowledge, one that stresses the specificity of meaning and the personal understanding of places. There is insufficient space to engage with the vast literature of humanistic geography (although we do return to it in later chapters), so again we will focus on the work of one influential writer, Edward Relph (our choice is influenced by the fact that his work had some influence in debates within school geography). In *Place and Placelessness*, Relph (1976) argues that a sense of place is important for an individual identity and that this sense of place has been lost or degraded in the modern world. As an aside, it is notable that the idea of the 'sense of place' was included in a volume produced for the Association of American Geographers entitled '10 Geographic ideas that changed the World'. On the first page of *Place and Placelessness*, Relph asserts that 'To be human is to live in a world that is filled with significant places: to be human is to have and to know your place' (p. 1). Relph goes on to distinguish between senses of place that are authentic/genuine or inauthentic/artificial. Authentic sense of place suggests that a fundamental, lasting truth about a place is known, which involves going beyond the ephemerality of the ever-changing modern world. Having this authentic sense of place involves:

> a direct and genuine experience of the entire complex of the identity of place – not mediated and distorted through a series of quite arbitrary social and intellectual fashions about how that experience should be, nor following stereotypical conventions. It comes from a … profound and unselfconscious identity with place.
>
> (p. 64)

You may already be trying to think through for yourself the possible implications of this for teaching geography in schools, and this is the whole point of this section of the book. Our argument is that geography teachers are charged with the task of thinking about how the subject can provide a resource for providing meaningful geographical experiences, and as we will discuss in later chapters, some school geography teachers did try to take on board and engage with some of these ideas. This section has discussed the ways in which human geography took a post-positivist turn in the 1970s. This is not to suggest that empirical/positivist work still did not have a role in academic geography. However, we are suggesting that there was a decisive shift in the work of the majority of human geographers. In the next section, we discuss some of the directions human geography has subsequently taken.

MORE RECENT MOVEMENTS IN HUMAN GEOGRAPHY

We suggested that the so-called 'new' geography, with its concern with spatial science, developed in the context of the post-war boom. In academic geography the limitations of positivism and spatial science were quickly realised, and geographers sought other frameworks for making sense of the world. From the late 1960s and 1970s geographers forged closer links with the social sciences, which were themselves undergoing significant changes in approach. As the long post-war boom spluttered to a halt, uneven development became more marked, and it was clear that poverty and inequality were again on the increase. The 'new models' were those based on political economy (Peet and Thrift 1989). The 1980s were a decade of important shifts in the economic, political, social and cultural systems of North American and Western European countries, and, in this context, geography took a sharp 'left' turn. (We are arriving at the fifth and sixth stages of Gregory's schematic development of geography – see Figure 1.)

If we consider Britain, we can relate developments in the work produced by academic geographers to these broad shifts. Starting with the economy, the 1980s were characterised by important changes in the UK's space-economy. In retrospect, we are likely to attribute this to the transition from a Fordist to a post-Fordist economic system, where indigenous firms were increasingly operating in a global economy, and where governments were faced with the prospect of playing a less regulatory role in economic affairs. These were turbulent times, and economic geographers found that they needed to develop new models to make sense of the changes.

Politically, these economic changes were accompanied by important events. In terms of electoral geography, voting patterns mirrored the 'North–South divide' in economic prospects. Successive Conservative governments that owed their power largely to English and rural voters were deeply unpopular in Scotland and Wales, and as the decade wore on, the question of political union was never far off the agenda. The collapse of the post-war consensus and the pressure on economic resources inevitably meant that social relations were strained. For many, Britain was a divided nation, its social geography scarred by divisions based on class, gender,

13

ethnicity, locality, age and sexuality. No longer could geographical knowledge be seen as neutral, since attempts to understand what was going on and offer possible solutions were necessarily located in debates about desirable futures. The 1980s saw the publication of a whole series of geographical texts that charted the changing economic, social and political geography of Britain. The titles of these are indicative of the mood of many geographers in this period: Hudson and Williams' *Divided Britain* (1995), Lewis and Townsend's *The North–South Divide* (1989), Cloke's *Policy and Change in Thatcher's Britain* (1992), and Johnston *et al.*'s *A Nation Dividing?* (1988). These books can be read as part of the geographical Left's attempt to make sense of the changes that took place under successive Conservative governments.

There were some important changes taking place here. The old Marxist political-economic approaches were rapidly merged with developments in other disciplines that were attempting to account for the decline of Labour politics and the new landscape of Britain. Much of this work was involved in mapping the changes but some geographers were concerned to offer accounts of the changes, a task which meant engaging with social and political theory. These accounts pointed to the fact that the Conservative government inherited in 1979 a country divided in various ways – by class, gender, race and location. They argued that it was to become even more divided in the 1980s. However, these accounts tend to point to the political intent involved in the widening of these divisions. For example, Hudson and Williams (1989), writing at the end of a decade of Thatcher's policies, argued that 'the North–South divide has deliberately been redefined and enhanced as part of the political strategy of Thatcherism. It was and is intimately connected to its electoral prospects' (p. 165).

These texts reflected a concern with four major areas. First, there was a sense of *economic change*. Britain's economy was subject to de-industrialisation and manufacturing decline, which was only partly offset by the development of new types of work. These changes were seen as important because of their uneven impact on regions and localities in Britain. Second, there was a focus on the changing *political relations* of the British state. There was a recognition of the pressures for devolution in the context of heightened economic division, attempts to reassert central political control at various levels of the state, and the moves to reduce public expenditure and open up areas previously dominated by state provision to market forces. Third, there was a focus on the *social effects* of these developments, with a focus on divisions along axes of race and gender. Finally, the *environment* was recognised as an important area of political tension and debate. Together, these amounted to a radical agenda for geographical study, and were a response to the sense that the world had changed:

> For some thirty years from 1945 the economic and social geography of Britain was shaped by a broad consensus comprising, among other things, commitments to full employment, Keynesian techniques of economic management, the welfare state, and a strong regional policy. That consensus has been challenged in the past decade; some challenges have been fundamental, such as the abandonment of any commitment to full employment, while in other policy areas challenges have been partial and less successful (for instance in health care). These changes have had profound effects on the human geography of contemporary Britain and, in order adequately to understand this human geography, an account is necessary of the processes which caused this consensus to break up.
>
> (Mohan 1989: xi)

While there was a tendency in these accounts to chart the 'cartographies of distress' (Mohan 1999), as the decade wore on some geographers began to point to the (partial and uneven) opportunities afforded by these changes. The 'new times' had changed the physical and social geographies in which people lived their lives (Jacques and Hall 1989). New towns and patterns of settlement, new places for consumption such as the mall, and redeveloped town centres in the wake of the decline of manufacturing, new goods and services to consume, the breakdown of established gender relations all offered new opportunities for constituting identities and producing meanings with which to give shape to everyday life.

This renewed concern with the meanings attached to social change led the way for a *rapprochement* between political economic and humanistic geography (Kobayashi and Mackenzie 1989). From the mid-1970s many geographers had expressed concerns about the increasingly structuralist and economistic turn of the discipline. Geographers such as Derek Gregory (1981a) and Nigel Thrift (1983) called for analyses that were more open to the force of human intentionality and sensitive to a variety of political experiences and forms of action. At the same time, there was a growing influence of feminist work that was as much concerned with

15

highlighting the role of gender as class in the production of geographic patterns. Stucturalist Marxism was considered insufficiently open-ended and insufficiently alert to the notion of the human subject to accommodate many of the emerging trends that were now becoming important in the thinking of the academic left. These 'emerging trends' might best be seen as culminating in the so-called *cultural turn*.

Social geographers such as Peter Jackson and Susan Smith (1984) were among those who began to explore 'cultural' issues. They drew upon work in British Cultural Studies which was an explicitly political enterprise concerned with theorising the ways in which 'culture' is a 'domain in which economic and political contradictions are contested and resolved' (Jackson 1989: 1). The 'new cultural geography' began to map these changes. At its best, it seemed to offer a way of thinking about how individuals make sense of the social structures they inhabit. The argument was that many of the social structures that had determined people's life courses had been loosened and this offered new opportunities for individuals to fashion their own identities. This was always and everywhere struggled over. Shurmer-Smith (2002) makes the argument that these new ways of trying to make sense of the world are closely linked to changes in the way that world is experienced. The oil crisis of 1973 and the advent of a new wave of 'neo-liberal' globalisation caused fundamental changes that resonated not just in the economic and political order, but also in the 'recesses of ordinary people's lives':

> Not only in the universities, but also in the media and in private encounters, virtually everyone, everywhere became increasingly conscious of the problem of creating meaning in situations in which so many of the parameters of economic, political and social life had shifted.
>
> (Shurmer-Smith 2002: 1)

The 'cultural turn' – as it became known – marked this new-found attention to the meanings attached to everyday experience, or as one recent book puts it, 'the extraordinary geographies of everyday life' (Holloway and Hubbard 2001). If this sounds like a return to the old humanist geography, we should note that cultural geography is concerned to highlight the problems associated with discussing place. Places both include and exclude, and who belongs or does not is always the outcome of relations of power. This means that human geography in the 1990s is very conscious of difference and who is included and excluded from geographical representations. In the past, it is argued, too much geography has been written from the perspective of the powerful (generally white, middle class, male, middle-aged and straight). In *Geographies of Exclusion*, David Sibley (1995) pointed out that geography has not been very welcoming of those who are 'different'. Consequently, in recent years, geography has been characterised by attempts to make visible those groups previously excluded from geographical research and representation. There has been a focus on the geographies of disability (Gleeson 1999), the geographies of children and young people (Skelton and Valentine 1998), the mentally ill (Butler and Parr 1999) and so on. Holloway and Hubbard (2001: 230) note that 'many geographers are now engaging with the complexity of the world rather than forcing it to fit into established geographic models/theories'.

However, this 'cultural turn' in geography has not been universally welcomed. We have already noted David Harvey's concern that geographers get back to the hard issues of capitalism and exploitation. Others have made similar points; for instance, the economic geographer Andrew Leyshon (1995) asked 'whatever happened to the geography of poverty?' in response to what he perceived as geographers' move away from the study of important social issues. Similarly, Chris Hamnett (2001) launched a blistering attack on the new cultural geography:

> While the new cultural geography has produced some very worthwhile research and scholarship which sheds light on the social construction of the world, a substantial amount of work appears to me to be simply linguistic game playing of minimal relevance to wider economic, social, environmental and political concerns. To this extent, the postmodern turn simply provides a theoretical playpit for academics to amuse themselves harmlessly while politicians and big business get on with their affairs unencumbered by too many awkward or political questions.
>
> (p. 167)

These are important debates, which touch on the crucial question of what geography is for. For some geographers what the cultural turn represents is a loss of faith in the belief that there exists the possibility of a 'better world'. Much of this recent work in human geography is marked by a focus on deconstruction. This is a notoriously complex and difficult term but in simple terms it means to read the world 'against the grain', to show how any account of the world we produce always involves the inclusion of certain perspectives and voices and excludes others. In this book we are trying to explore the implications of these developments for geography teaching in schools. We hope we have conveyed some of our excitement about these debates and that you feel inclined to read more about them for yourself.

HISTORIES OF PHYSICAL GEOGRAPHY

In this section we want to offer an account of the development of physical geography. In writing it we are aware of the old maxim that 'a little knowledge is a dangerous thing'. Neither of us counts himself as an 'expert' in physical geography, but we realise that some of our readers are experts. However, we do want to offer a 'framing' of physical geography that we hope will be useful for all geography teachers. Our advice for teachers is 'don't take our word for it' and read our account in the light of your own reading and experience.

Ken Gregory's (1984) *The Nature of Physical Geography* notes that by 1850 there were clear signs that physical geography was being established in universities. An understanding of the development of physical geography requires an understanding of the wider social and cultural context. Accordingly, the beginnings of modern physical geography date from the developments in scientific thinking that emerged at the end of the eighteenth century. One influential source was the geologist James Hutton's extraordinary *Theory of the Earth* (1795).

Hutton saw the earth as a machine with three parts, which teachers now refer to as the 'rock cycle'. The denudation of continental rocks provided the soil to maintain the earth's fertile mantle, and continental debris was transported seawards by rivers. In a second phase sedimentation took place on the ocean floors and material was converted into new sedimentary rock strata, eventually to be uplifted to form new continental masses in the third and final stage of the process. This pattern was repeated through time. Hutton argued that the origin of the earth pre-dated existing continents. Although this now seems unremarkable to us, Hutton's ideas were controversial because they challenged earlier ideas that relied on biblical interpretations of the creation of the earth and the role of a catastrophic universal flood. It is worth remembering that Hutton's ideas pre-dated Charles Darwin's by many decades.

Hutton's ideas were given support by the concept of uniformitarianism developed by Charles Lyell in his *Principles of Geology* (1830). His idea was that the earth's surface was subject to natural processes operating over long timescales and that many of these processes could be seen shaping the scenery of the present day. Thus the idea is that processes that operate in the present created the landscapes of the past – the present was *the key to understanding the past*. These ideas were given further impetus and in time, authority, by the publication of Darwin's *Origin of Species*, which recognised that the earth's surface 'evolved' or changed through time.

These developments provided the context in which one of the 'founders' of modern physical geography, W. M. Davis, entered the story. Davis worked mainly on the eastern part of the US, and absorbed and developed evolutionary and unformitarian ideas into his explanation of landforms and the cycle of erosion. Davis suggested that after rapid uplift of the seafloor, fluvial erosion (the dominant *process*) would act through time on the underlying geology (*structure*) to produce a landscape described in terms of *stage* of development (youth, maturity and old age). The end point would be a fluvially eroded base-level surface (the peneplain).

The ideas of evolutionary theory became hugely influential and have impacted on other branches of physical geography. Teachers will be familiar with them. For example, in biogeography Clements (1928) explained that the distribution of plant species in space and time was the result of succession as the plant community adapted to sets of environmental conditions or 'controls', ultimately producing a 'climax' community subject to a main control – climate. In climatology, Bjerknes (Bjerknes and Solberg 1922) discussed the life cycle of mid-latitude depressions – using the concepts of cyclogenesis and frontogenesis.

The impact of Davis' work on modern physical geography should not be underestimated. Chorley *et al.* (1973) describe Davis as being 'too important and too prolific to be ignored'. His work became 'established' teaching until well into the 1950s and, as late as the 1970s, school texts such as Small's *The Study of Landforms* (1970) and Sparks' *Geomorphology* (1972) still testified to his influence. However, a criticism of work in physical geography influenced by Davis was that it lacked sufficient knowledge of environmental processes. For instance, in geo-morphology it was pointed out that although the Davisian cycle of erosion embraced structure, process and stage or time the *emphasis* had invariably been on stage with very little upon process.

19

Sims (2003) notes that 'Process studies became very much "The Holy Grail" of geomorphology from the late 60s onwards' (p. 9). In geomorphology the developing science of hydrology gained importance, focusing on drainage basins and catchments. The predominant interest in fluvial processes came from a recognition that many geomorphologists had studied humid temperate landforms without explaining the processes involved, and that techniques were becoming available to establish short-, medium- and longer-term field experiments in which processes and detailed changes in the environment could be studied at a range of scales. There were studies of fluvial processes on hillslopes in small catchments, a renewed interest in channel form and pattern, the solute and sediment loads in rivers and so on. This is the approach to physical geography that tends to be found in schools (see Chapter 4).

The focus on processes became prominent in all branches of physical geography (and perhaps marked it as distinctive from human geography). Thus Pethick's *Introduction to Coastal Geomorphology* (1984) 'attempts to bring coastal geomorphology into the established framework of process studies', Cooke and Warren's *Geomorphology in Deserts* (1973), and Sugden and John's *Glaciers and Landscape* (1976) attempted much the same in their respective fields. The influence of process studies in physical geography has continued, increasing the fragmentation of the branches of geomorphology and leading to an identity crisis for researchers and teachers in higher education (HE) – which is not dissimilar to that in human geography, where links with other disciplines are at least as important as those within the field of geography. The emphasis on process, at least if this is seen as an end in itself, may have led to similar difficulties in schools.

A final theme in this brief review of developments in physical geography is that of increasing concern with the interactions between people and environments. This has become increasingly important over the last 25 years, although it is not new, as evidenced by Jacks and Whyte's *The Rape of the Earth* (1939) that deals with soil erosion and Thomas's *Man's Role in Changing the Face of the Earth* (1956). Particular concerns have been about the relationship between rainfall and run off, the effects of changing land use in river catchments, water quality and pollution issues.

Ken Gregory's more recent discussion in *The Changing Nature of Physical Geography* (2000) notes the need for a 'more global physical geography'. This is a response to the global environmental agenda and Gregory discusses a number of physical geography textbooks that reflect this shift, including Mannion's *Global Environmental Change* (1997), which provides a synopsis of natural and cultural history in the last 3 million years. Roberts' edited collection *The Changing Global Environment* (1994) sought to correct existing texts in physical geography that were 'stuck in the rut of a rather abstract and mechanistic "systems" approach to analysing environmental processes', and Middleton's *The Global Casino: An Introduction to Global Issues* (1999).

In summary, Urban and Rhoads (2003) argue that contemporary physical geography is characterised by a distinctive 'style' that takes for granted appropriate ways of investigating and learning:

- most investigations involve quantification, either in the development of theoretical models or in the analysis of empirical data (from field or laboratory studies);
- the emphasis is on understanding the processes or events that influence the development of biotic, geomorphological or climate systems;
- these studies draw upon background knowledge from a range of ancillary disciplines (physics, chemistry and biology);
- this dependency on knowledge from the 'natural sciences' has led to an implicit acceptance of the philosophical concepts underpinning natural science.

Urban and Rhoads are concerned that this approach to physical geography contributes to a *false division* between society and nature. For their part, human geographers are suspicious of physical geography because they 'are still smarting intellectually from geography's incipient foray into environmental determinism and social Darwinism in the early 20th century' (2003: 224). Their analysis leads them towards an argument for examining the assumptions on which physical and human geography are studied with an eye towards integration. This is a theme taken up by Gregory in his argument for a 'cultural physical geography'. He uses the example of the humanist geographer Yi-Fu Tuan (1976) who wrote his book *Topophilia* 'out of the need to sort and order in some way the wide variety of attitudes and values relating to man's physical environment' (p. v). One of the best examples of the human dimensions of physical change is found in Simmons' *An Environmental History of Great Britain: 10,000 Years to the Present* (2001). This book is notable

21

for its ability to chart the changes that have occurred to a wide range of physical systems and at the same time understand the cultural significance of these changes.

LOOKING FORWARD

Here we want to end our 'whistle-stop' tour of developments in geography. We have covered a lot of ground in a very short time, and we will want to return to some of our 'stops' in future chapters to explain things in more detail. However, before we finish, we want to make some general points that underpin the following chapters.

First, we would emphasise that, as geography educators, we are quite excited about the intellectual foment that characterises geography. We see geographical knowledge as socially produced. What we mean by this is that what geographers choose to study (or not), and how they choose (or not) to study it results from decisions made by a large number of interested parties – at school level this includes policy-makers, syllabus writers, school managers (to some extent), *but most of all by classroom teachers*. But the greater discipline is even freer than this. We suggest that if geographers are choosing to draw upon the insights of disciplines such as politics, cultural studies, art, literature, sociology and seeking to write in more democratic ways, then this reflects a more open approach to the subject. In addition, it reflects a slightly broader social base to the subject as studied at university. Of course, others would argue that this is not 'real' geography, and reflects a lack of 'discipline' on behalf of geographers. In our view, the fact that geographical research and teaching in universities is increasingly making explicit its political and moral basis is to be welcomed, as is the plurality of approaches to the study of geography. The big remaining question – the one that animates this book – is how school geography might be 'opened up' too.

Second, our account of the recent development of geography has necessarily been partial (in both senses of that word). Perhaps the simplest way of summarising the narrative we have constructed in this chapter is expressed in the idea of the shift away from geography to geographies. Geography is not a predetermined pot of knowledge to be 'handed on', but a rich resource that can be deployed to create understanding and insight. To put a little more flesh on that statement we might use Barnes and Gregory's idea that the 'hegemony of spatial science' was based on the 'three C's' of certainty (of empirical observations), coherence (of patterns, forms and processes) and cumulation (of knowledge and discovery). In 1994, Gregory *et al.* emphasised that 'geography's task is now seen to involve dialogue with other disciplines rather than instruction of them, to produce complication as much as simplification, and to issue admissions of doubt as often as declarations of certainty' (p. 5).

Third, in concluding this chapter, we are conscious of representing geography as a subject quite different from that taught in schools. We are aware that we are expecting this chapter to be read by busy teachers who have plenty to occupy them ahead of the task of attempting to keep up with and make sense of an ever-expanding literature that is not written with teachers in mind. The challenge we have set ourselves (and urge readers to engage with) is to convince geography teachers that these developments are of critical and urgent importance in their work in schools and classrooms. For us, geography is a subject that can prompt reflection on the world in which we live, and can provide a resource for teachers who wish to fulfil their role as 'transformative intellectuals'. Part of this role means engaging with the intellectual debates that characterise the subjects we teach. This chapter is intended to provide geography teachers with a starting point for making sense of recent debates in academic geography. In Chapter 3, we turn to the recent history of school geography.

FOR FURTHER THINKING

1 Imagine attending an interview for a job as a teacher of geography. One of the panel, a governor, asks you about geography. 'I loved geography at school,' he says. 'All those maps and pictures of glaciers. A great relief from the really important subjects like maths and science. Why do *you* like geography? Are you a keen traveller?' You think you need to explain geography! How do you answer?

2 Use this chapter to draw up a list of geography's 'big concepts'. For each one, say how it has educational potential (helping young people 'make sense of the world').

3 Do you think that it matters that 'school geography' is very different from geography as studied and taught in universities? Put crudely, do you think theorists and researchers at the leading edge of the discipline are relevant for teachers of geography?

Chapter 3

Making school geography

INTRODUCTION

In this chapter, we want to offer an interpretation of *the making* of school geography based on the idea that it is part of a broader story about the relationship between culture and curriculum. More specifically, we want to offer an account of changes in the practices of school geography that can be read alongside the account of the development of human and physical geography in the previous chapter. Fundamentally, we hope the chapter will help readers construct their own mental maps of where the school subject, geography, has come from and where it may be heading.

In his book, *The Management of Ignorance*, Fred Inglis argues that there is a close relationship between culture and the curriculum. His book was published in 1985, and thus reflects some of the conflicts that characterised that turbulent decade. Inglis argues that the recognition of political change (and he gives a list of issues such as accelerating economic decline, the dislocation of values grounded in images of perpetual prosperity, the dispersal of national identity, and the tendency to a disunited kingdom) has had a profound impact on 'the forms and content of what on earth that nation knows, and thinks it ought to know' (p. 21). At times of 'crisis', he argues, it becomes plain that the curriculum of any society is a product of the history of that society, and that as a history changes, so does a curriculum:

> there has been, in and out of school, a new level of consciousness about the meaning and function of a curriculum, and the dispute about the often conflicting interests a curriculum may be written to serve becomes, as I say, fiercer.

> (1985: 21–2)

Inglis goes on to discuss how teachers have engaged in the discussion of new contents and their relevance to children's and students' needs, and notes that deep-seated changes in curriculum areas (school subjects) and resistance to such changes can be seen as a 'conscious and determined process of cultural reinterpretation' (p. 22). According to Inglis, in the 1980s these changes addressed themselves to questions of national and personal identity as these 'dissolved under the impact of the new world economic order' (p. 22).

This is the very stuff of everyday teaching experience. For Inglis, the crisis in Britain's political economy, the facts of unemployment, of 'riots', of old racial and class hatreds and new poverty, 'require unprecedently thoroughgoing and imaginative responses from deeply tired schoolteachers ... who are trying to build a believable world-picture into a curriculum' (1985: 22). It could be said that the list of crises in the early twenty-first century are now different, but the relevance of the general point made by Inglis 20 years ago remains intact and if anything is now more urgent.

We have chosen to introduce this discussion of the relationship between societal change and geography education because it encourages us to think about everyday teaching experiences in broader terms than we are perhaps used to. It stresses that the curriculum is a human creation, which grows out of and responds to changes in society. Teachers are the agents of this process of producing and reproducing social value, meaning and symbol. As Inglis puts it, 'The curriculum is a message to and about the future' (1985: 23). Other writers have made similar arguments. One of the most famous and influential is that by Raymond Williams (1961) in *The Long Revolution.* His chapter on education starts with the statement that 'There are clear and obvious connexions between the quality of a culture and the quality of its system of education' (p. 145). In relation to the curriculum, the content of education expresses, 'both consciously and unconsciously, certain basic elements in the culture, what is thought of as "an education" being in fact a particular selection, a particular set of emphases and omissions' (p. 145).

We think it is an essential element of being, or becoming, a teacher of geography to 'tune in' to wider debates on society, environment and culture, for without this what are we left with? Is school geography just some kind of 'given', to be administered as palatably as possible to a captive audience? We think the educational potential of the subject is far greater than this and is provided by the creative effort of teachers to identify and refine the selections that are of particular value to students' needs.

HISTORIES OF SCHOOL GEOGRAPHY

In recent years, there have been a number of attempts to represent the history of school geography. Too often, these tend to take the form of 'uncritical narratives' (Ploszajska 2000) which chronicle the 'progressive evolution' of the discipline and the institutions that sponsor it. Writing about the development of geography as an academic subject, Livingstone (1992) argues that these accounts are 'in-house reviews of disciplinary developments for the geographical community' (p. 4), in which the exploits of heroic figures and epic moments in the history of British geography are related to the next generation of scholars (Boardman and McPartland 1993a, 1993b, 1993c, 1993d; Kent 2000; Walford 2000). One of the problems with these accounts is that, written by geography educators for an audience of geography educators, they tend to tidy up much of the confusion and messiness that characterise curriculum change. In addition, they tend to be written by those who have gained a position of authority within the geography education community, and possibly too high a status is afforded these views. However, the biggest problem with these accounts is that they generally fail to unmask the relationship between geography as a subject and school geography. Also, very rarely do they seek to place developments in school geography in a broader cultural context. Our account is intended as an alternative commentary on this well-rehearsed history of school geography.

Our starting point is the work of the educational sociologist Ivor Goodson, whose work has argued that school subjects, far from being the rational entities which some philosophers suggest, are in fact the creations of interest groups whose prime concern has been with maintaining and extending their own status. It is in the interests of each subject group as a whole to preserve strong boundaries between itself and other subject groups. This is done in order to provide a strong identity and act as a base for securing scarce educational resources. This is particularly relevant to the case of geography, where its unstable status as a bridge between the sciences and the humanities has led to a struggle to maintain geography's disciplinary status. A perceived lack of status is a perennial issue for geographers, and in many ways the 'case for geography' becomes one of 'geography for geography's sake', which, though understandable, may be less about educational principles than we imagine.

However, it is important to realise that in many cases the nature of the subject is a matter of fierce debate within the subject community: 'Subjects are not monolithic entities but shifting amalgamations of sub-groups and traditions. These groups within the subject influence and change boundaries and priorities' (Goodson 1983: 3). In writing this chapter, then, we want to highlight the divisions, the selections and omissions, the inclusions and exclusions of geography as it has been constructed as a school subject. Just as, in Chapter 2, we saw that geography should be seen as a 'sedimented and situated product', the same is true of school geography.

FROM REGIONAL GEOGRAPHY TO SPATIAL SCIENCE

Perhaps the most significant event in the recent history of the teaching of school geography was the general acceptance of a move from under-standing geography as a regional study to geography as a spatial science. David Hall (1976) offers an account of how this move developed:

> In 1963 Richard Chorley and Peter Haggett sponsored a summer school for teachers at Madingley Hall, near Cambridge, at which a team of lecturers highlighted what were considered to be significant developments in geography, from geomorphology to urban geography. The importance of geographical generalisation, the assistance which model-building and spatial analysis could provide towards an under-standing of processes, and the place of spatial geometry and of measurement in geographical thinking and the organisation of its data, were stressed in the diverse themes treated. In the epilogue to the publication of the lectures given at that course and at another held in the following year, the editors regarded inertia in education at all levels as a major obstacle to change ... But a group of teachers who departed from Cambridge with enthusiasm developed a quantitative and spatial approach to geography with their pupils; their classroom exercises were exchanged and some dissemination of their work was attempted, mainly in Greater London.

(p. 86)

27

Walford (2000) relates the history of the 'New Model Army' in detail, but the thing we want to note here is that this signalled a shift from geography as a particularistic and ideographic study to a generalising and 'nomothetic' spatial science. It was signalled in 'official' documents such as *New Thinking in School Geography* (DES (Department of Education and Science) 1972) and in new textbook series such as 'Concepts in Geography', which recommended the 'new geography' to teachers in the following terms:

> Teachers are beginning to realise that much of what is taught in our schools is purely repetitive and lacks intellectual stimulus and challenge to the student. Basic to these changes, we feel, is an ability on the part of the student to appreciate fundamental concepts in geography: those concerned with space, location, and interactions through time.
>
> (Everson and FitzGerald 1969: ix)

The key to the development of geography as a spatial science was 'relevance'. From the 1960s, geographers increasingly made claims for their role as spatial planners, providing practical solutions to spatial problems that were well in line with the demands of the corporate state. The answer to solving these 'spatial problems' was planning, to provide a 'more relevant framework for the administration of public decisions' (Chisholm and Manners 1971: 19). Harvey (2000b: 77) has recently commented on the development of this 'pragmatic focus' in academic geography from the 1960s. He suggests that the 'attempt to reconstruct geographical knowledge as instrument of administrative planning in Britain' was linked to the political climate of the time characterised by the Labour Prime Minister Harold Wilson's rhetoric about the 'white heat of technology'. In this context, the goal of rational planning was linked to ideas of 'efficiency of regional and urban planning as a lever of social betterment for the whole population' (p. 77).

There is no reason why developments at the cutting edge of the subject as studied in universities should *automatically* inform the practice of school geography, so it is important to think about the reasons for the adoption of the new geography in schools. Goodson's (1983) discussion of the history of geography as a school subject suggests that the adoption of the 'new' geography in schools reflected the struggle for status and power among subject practitioners. One of the problems of geography as a school subject faced in gaining status within schools was its expansiveness, its tendency to take on ever-new subject matter, with the result that the boundaries of the discipline were ill-defined. The solution to this problem was to hand over power to geographers in universities. Through its newly acquired methodological rigour, geography's position as a 'real' science could at last be assured. New geography, with its respect for 'hard' data, represented a move to the technical rationality of positivist versions of the natural sciences. The 'new' geography stressed the 'scientific' and theoretical side of the subject at the expense of 'field-work' and 'regional studies'. The aspirations of school teachers were about the material gains to be made from having school geography accepted as a fully fledged academic subject able to command more resources and offer better career prospects for teachers. Huckle (1985) argues that the new geography was an elitist exercise, an attempt to render the schooling of a minority of pupils more technocratic and vocationally relevant.

According to this analysis, a version of school geography emerged that reflected the needs and interests of a small minority of the school population. However, the establishment of the 'new geography' with its new-found status gained through the appliance of science is not the end of the story.

HUMANISTIC INFLUENCES AND STUDENT CENTREDNESS

From the 1970s onwards, school geography was influenced by broader developments in curriculum thinking. It was recognised that current curriculum arrangements led to a waste of talent as many working-class children left school at the earliest opportunity without qualifications, a trend that persists to the present day. There were moves to raise the school leaving age and increase participation. In addition, it was increasingly understood that society was changing and that these changes would need to be reflected in a modernised school curriculum. By the early 1960s the Schools Council – set up in 1964 to promote curriculum change – was urging teachers to 'understand and respect the nature of the pupils' . . . experience' (cited in Jones 2001: 47).

Rawling (2001) describes how geography played an important role in this era of curriculum development. For example, initiatives such as the enormously influential Geography for the Young School Leaver (GYSL) project can be read as an attempt to come to terms with the social changes of the 1960s and 1970s. GYSL advocated a shift from 'traditional' to 'child-centred' pedagogies and sought to reflect the multicultural nature of society. This was achieved through the development of an 'issues-based' approach:

> The emphasis was on moving school geography away from regional and descriptive work and focusing more on active learning styles and more relevant thematic content. Some aspects of the 'new geography' were incorporated (e.g. use of models and theories, key ideas) but there was also a strong move into more humanistic, qualitative and issues-based approaches.
>
> (Rawling 2001: 24)

Hall (1976) notes that at the level of content the materials were designed with the needs of 'less able'[1] in mind. There was an emphasis on graphics, photographs and the sparing use of written text. In terms of curriculum design there was a shift away from looking for 'new ways in which conventional geographic material might be taught and transmitted' to 'examining the needs of such children and to ask if there is anything in geography which could be relevant to them'. Pupils' needs were considered to be based on developing an understanding of fundamental issues affecting people in society and having some connection with their own lives as future adults. The project produced three units – Man, Land and Leisure; Cities and People; People, Places and Work. These units were not directly linked to traditional geographical themes and the teaching strategies made reference to a 'geography of feeling'. The approach was closely linked to the ideas of a welfare approach to geography, asking who gets what, where and how (Smith 1975; Bale 1983). Readers will notice that there is less focus on physical geography. This is, presumably, no oversight and based on the analysis of the curriculum planners of pupils' educational needs. On the other hand, it may also reflect the spirit of the times. Today, in the context of environmental concern and 'sustainability' it is less justifiable to ignore physical geography.

A similar question about the relevance of physical geography was raised by another very influential Schools Council project – known as

---

1 For us, a particularly interesting outcome of an historical account such as this is the way in which language has changed, partly as a result of different understandings. A generation ago, when Hall was writing, 'ability' was a more singular concept. It is now more complex and multifaceted, making it more difficult and unconvincing to talk about 'more able' and 'less able' people. Hence our use of 'scare marks'.

The 16–19 Project. This was designed to address the needs of the so-called 'new sixth'. The project responded to educational pressures such as the changing population of the sixth form and the need to provide a relevant educational experience for this group. The project drew upon educational thinking that suggested that conceptual thinking and an understanding of key ideas should take priority over the learning and reproduction of 'traditional' content. The project sought to balance what it saw as two pressures for change. On one hand there was a 'utilitarian' view of education and on the other was a 'concerned' view that recognised social and environmental concerns. The solution to the curriculum problem was a 'people-environment approach' that encouraged students and teachers to inquire into important social and environmental issues (Naish *et al.* 1987).

The overall effect of these changes in educational provision and the nature of geography as a discipline was to increase the diversity of approaches to school geography:

> The 1970s may, with some justification, be described as the decade of curriculum development for geography. Overall, there was a remarkable growth of interest and activity in new ideas in geography, new classroom approaches and new resources and guidelines for the subject, particularly in the secondary sector.
>
> (Rawling 2001: 27)

For example, while in some schools the 'new geography' allowed the perpetuation of a school geography designed for and catering for the needs of a small number of school students, progressivism allowed some geography educators to address the needs of a larger group of students. Writing of the period from the late 1970s to the early 1980s, Huckle (1985: 301) noted that: 'While the majority of school geographers were preoccupied with the "new" geography, others were employing humanistic and structuralist philosophies to design lessons on such topics as environmental issues, global inequalities and urban redevelopment.'

To varying degrees, these approaches had in common a revulsion against the abstraction, dehumanisation and retreat from social relevance that the positivism of the 'new geography' was supposed to represent (Huckle 1983; Smith 2000). This progressive geography drew upon a number of conceptual developments in the discipline linked to behavioural geography, environmental geography, welfare geography and radical geography. These sought to develop a geography education whose content was socially and environmentally relevant and which sought to 'teach geography for a better world'[2] (Fien and Gerber 1988). These approaches sought to provide a counter to the cold objectivity and universal meanings of the 'new' geography.

In addition, some geography teachers sought to develop approaches that made links with the so-called 'adjectival studies' such as World Studies, Development Education, Environmental Education and the like. These were a response to developments in the so-called 'new sociology of education' that emphasised the relativity of school knowledge and questioned the traditional subject-based curriculum. Jones (2001) notes that: 'From the late sixties onwards, other dynamics came into play, and projects of curriculum change became linked to more radical practices and critiques' (p. 48).

Jones notes the development of more 'assertive' curricular practices, especially in some large urban centres. Issues of cultural recognition and social justice found their way into the everyday agendas of classrooms. From the early 1970s, some teachers began to develop curricula that were explicitly anti-racist and anti-imperialist (Gill 1982). These pedagogical shifts reflected social and cultural changes, in response to changed expectations about the education of girls and, in large urban areas, the presence of children of people from the New Commonwealth and Pakistan. As a result, school geography became the site of political struggle over its meanings, and was part of the larger conversation about curriculum and cultural change discussed by Inglis at the beginning of this chapter. These debates about the nature of school geography – its content and pedagogy – are an example of what Inglis called a 'conscious and determined process of cultural re-interpretation'.

Despite the growing diversity of approaches to school geography, it is worth noting that Rawling (2001) ends her discussion of the 'decade of curriculum development' (the 1970s) in geography on a note of caution: 'In retrospect, geography educators were underestimating the increasingly politicised nature of curriculum decision making and the growing influence of the New Right' (p. 27).

It may also be that school geography was becoming too eclectic for its own good. Despite the curriculum renewal of this period, the thinking

---

2 A slightly pompous title for a book, perhaps. The idea of harnessing education 'for a good cause' has received criticism well worth pondering (Marsden 2001), for there are dangers of indoctrination taking precedence over the interest of education.

underpinning it was possibly not hard-headed enough – in a way 'innocent', if not of curriculum politics then of wider political debates. To put this differently, had the organising concepts and the purpose of geography been conditioned and compromised by the buffeting impacts of various 'concerns' and especially an uncritical 'child centredness'? Was an eclectic, but arguably theoretically impoverished, school geography in a strong enough condition to withstand the eddy of every passing 'bandwagon'?

A DIVIDED GEOGRAPHY?

As we noted in Chapter 2, the 1980s were characterised by tumultuous changes in the economic, social, political and cultural geographies of the United Kingdom. In these contexts it is perhaps unsurprising that previous geographical representations favoured within school geography were questioned. For some geography teachers this involved questioning the relevance of much of the school geography curriculum to the lives of children living in increasingly stressed urban areas. The process whereby the geography curriculum becomes a 'message to and about the future' became particularly apparent during the 1980s.

Geography and enterprise

One manifestation of this economic and social 'crisis' was the call for the schools to prepare young people for the 'world of work'. The inauguration of the so-called 'Great Debate' after Prime Minister Callaghan's speech at John Ruskin College in 1976 led to a plethora of initiatives designed to increase the relevance of schooling to the 'world of work'. Thus, in the 1980s many geography teachers became increasingly concerned with the vocational aspects of geography education. For example, Corney (1985) in his introduction to the Geographical Association's collection entitled *Geography, Schools and Industry* discussed the potential for geography education to contribute to school–industry initiatives. There was a feeling that schools should show much greater concern with developing 'economic literacy' among students. This would require the possession of factual knowledge about the national economy, and the teaching of economic concepts, which allow pupils to make balanced and informed judgements about economic matters. This would help pupils appreciate how the nation earns and maintains its standard of living, so that they could properly 'esteem the essential roles of industry and commerce to the process' (DES 1977, quoted in Corney 1985: 10). In short, pupils needed to acquire an understanding of the economic basis of society and how wealth is created.

Corney suggested that geography could provide students with basic skills such as literacy, numeracy and graphicacy, as well as social skills that would equip them for the world of work, such as flexibility, adaptability, working as part of a team, and taking initiative and responsibility. In addition, geography could provide study skills deemed essential for coping with the world of work, such as comprehending arguments, the classification and analysis of data, and time management. In developing economic literacy and developing appropriate skills, there was a need for teaching strategies and assessment procedures that reflect a variety of strategies and develop active pupil participation in the learning process. Corney noted that:

> Modern geographical education increasingly stresses knowledge and ideas which are relevant and up to date, and gives high priority to broader educational aims such as the development of personal skills and capacities. It employs a variety of teaching strategies, emphasising active pupil involvement in learning, and attempts to assess through appropriate techniques the extent to which knowledge and skills can be used in a problem-solving situation.
>
> (1985: 10)

In terms of content, it was argued, geography syllabuses contribute to pupils' developing economic literacy, technological awareness and ability to make informed judgements. For instance, they typically stress the factors that influence the development of industry and economic activities, involve the study of the impacts of changing technology on employment prospects in a locality or region, the influence of economic activity on the quality of life and environment, and an understanding of the planning system. This work is frequently local and involves fieldwork. The Geography, Schools and Industry Project (GSIP) was established with two main aims: first, to identify the contribution of geography teachers in helping pupils to understand the nature of modern industry and its role in society; second, to involve geography teachers together with persons from industry in the development, dissemination and evaluation of activities designed to promote such understanding.

Geography and socially critical education

The calls for geography to play its part in the promotion of an 'enterprise culture' were ironic in the same decade that saw the removal of much of Britain's manufacturing industrial base. As we discussed in Chapter 2, the 1980s saw the publication of a whole series of geographical texts that charted the 'break-up' of Britain. These books can be read as part of geographers' attempts to make sense of the changes that took place under successive Conservative governments, and had their educational corollary in the development of 'radical' school geography. Radical geography educators advocated a form of 'socially critical' education that was less concerned with the defence of geography per se than with the development of a broader social education (Huckle 1983). The flavour of these alternatives can be seen in the issues of the journal *Contemporary Issues in Geography and Education* published by the Association for Curriculum Development between 1984 and 1987. The journal's concerns mirrored those of the geographical left: racism, sexism, wealth and poverty, environmental degradation, war and conflict. In participating in these debates geography teachers were engaging in wider debates about the nature of schooling and how it differed from broader notions of education. For example, Huckle (1987) challenged what he regarded as the complacency of large sections of geography education when he stated that boredom and alienation were the dominant responses of pupils to what was on offer in geography lessons. It is worth noting that these 'assertive' versions of geography teaching were limited in scope and influence.

The approach favoured by socially critical geography teachers was reflected in the journal *Contemporary Issues in Geography and Education*:

> The journal seeks to promote an emancipatory geography; it seeks, in other words, to promote the idea that the future is ours to create – or to destroy – and to demonstrate that education bears some responsibility for building a world responsive to human needs, diversity and capabilities.
>
> (1983: 1)

More specific objectives included:

- to develop a critique of current curricula;
- to explore the assumptions underlying much of geographical education and to make these assumptions explicit;

35

- to examine the ideological content of geographical education in relation to its political content.

Despite these radical aims, for the majority of geography teachers, life in the classroom was 'business as usual'. It is possible that the perceived political project in this movement, aligned to the ideal to 'change the world' (see p. 32), was an inappropriate or at least a poorly expressed one. In any case, in the 1980s – in the midst of profound economic, social and political change – geography continued to provide images and explanations of the world that relied on older models of environmental determinism, neo-classical economics and Whiggish versions of history (Gilbert 1984).

Machon (1987) accounts for the failure of geography teachers to incorporate elements of political education into their teaching as a result of a combination of factors. These included: the enduring and continuing stress on the importance of subject matter (content), and the apparent public acceptance that some issues (politics) are 'not suitable for the children'. Taken together, this means that many controversial issues, explanatory models and radical perspectives are off limits in the geography classroom. This 'slows the pace of change in political, economic and social processes and underwrites the status quo' (p. 39).

Although 'radical' geography was the province of a minority of school geography teachers, it might be argued that it helped establish a climate in which official pronouncements about geography shifted. So far, our analysis suggests that, in the 1980s, school geography was the site of struggle over the purposes of teaching geography. There were those who saw education as a vehicle for social transformation and those who sought to stress its relevance to the economic renewal of the nation. Both these versions of school geography were the subject of critique by the New Right in the 1980s, in the form of calls for the 'return' of traditional subject based teaching.

WHOSE NATIONAL CURRICULUM?

These debates about the purposes of geography education became increasingly heated in relation to the development and implementation of the National Curriculum for geography. Geography had to fight hard to earn its 'place in the sun', and in the process jettisoned most of its (perceived) 'radical' baggage. Ken Jones (2001) argues that 'Conservative education policy in the early 1990s sought to unify the curriculum around nationalist and socially authoritarian themes': 'It asserted the centrality of national history, of European art and music, of the standard form of English; it prioritised "basic skills" and downgraded new kinds of knowledge – most notably, media literacy' (p. 50).

In terms of geography, this 'discourse of derision' (Ball 1994) took the form of an attack on progressive teaching methods that, it was claimed, meant that children no longer knew where places were. The place of geography in the school curriculum had become the subject of public debate in the 1980s when the Secretary of State for Education, Sir Keith Joseph, addressed the Geographical Association (Joseph 1985). In relation to geography the argument was about the extent to which the teaching of content – which meant 'facts' – was being undermined by a focus on values and attitudes. The inauguration and implementation of the 1991 National Curriculum was also linked to wider state concerns and especially the reaffirmation of national identity in a global society. For Ball (1994), the debate about the original National Curriculum was between conservative modernisers, keen to link the curriculum to changing needs of the economy, and conservative restorationists, attempting to reassert a national identity. Ball considered that the balance was tilted in favour of the restorationists, and noted that the curriculum appeared to reposition the UK in 'some mythical golden age of empire':

With its undertones of assimilation, nationalism and consensus around the regressive re-establishment of fictional past glories, restorationist National Curriculum geography isolates students in time and space, cutting them off from the realities of a single European market, global economic dependencies and inequalities, and ecological crisis.

(Ball 1994: 36)

The way in which a school system presents the geography of the nation state carries messages about the relation of that nation to other nations. As Ross (2000) points out, geography as a social subject is all about drawing boundaries between 'us' and 'them'. Similarly, in discussing the original report of the so-called Geography National Curriculum Working Group, Hall (1990) asked:

Why should California feature so strongly, without any requirement to undertake a serious study of China? The naming of the Falkland Islands could be seen as one instance of highlighting detail for its own sake and the re-establishment of Capes and Bays which had taken 50 years of hard campaigning to disestablish in the late sixties; alternatively its inclusion might be seen as a political statement which reifies our Imperial Tradition, which is symbolically out of keeping with our economic future within a European Community. Is Colonel Blimp to haunt us forever either through the specification of factual knowledge as an end in itself, or of particular places which are tombstones of the past?

(p. 314)

The National Curriculum (NC) represented the reassertion of central control over the school curriculum. The National Curriculum was compulsory, with little or no additional training or support for teachers, and yet had a high degree of detailed curricular prescription. Although the process of introducing the National Curriculum was complex and contested, we wish to note that it should be seen as an attempt to overturn the perceived 'progressivism' of teaching in favour of more traditional knowledge-based approaches or what Ball (1994) has called the 'curriculum of the dead'. In the 'discourse of derision' that surrounded the implementation of the National Curriculum, teachers were often criticised for their failure to safeguard standards and were reduced to mere technicians, no longer making decisions about the curriculum but following 'orders' devised centrally. The National Curriculum placed increased emphasis on a particular interpretation of subject knowledge and moved towards central prescription and enforcement of what was to be taught in schools. Despite Roberts' (1994) argument that geography departments have been able to resist the strictures of the National Curriculum 'text' and continue teaching in their preferred ways, we would suggest that it has become increasingly difficult for geography teachers in schools to define and develop their own 'local' curricula. As Rawling (2001) has described, this has been in spite of successive reforms of the 'order' so that in 2000 the NC had a light touch and lay open to local interpretation. It was as if teachers no longer believed in the capacity to decide *the what* and *the how* of teaching geography. If so, this would amount to a calamitous state of affairs.

GEOGRAPHY AND THE NEW OPPORTUNITIES

The New Labour government of 1997 endorsed the management-driven, performance-oriented culture that had developed since 1988. It accepts the National Curriculum, the testing apparatus, the new school inspectorate, the devolution of financial management to schools. It has even increased the central direction of the education system by national government. This is seen in the focus on 'basic skills' through numeracy and literacy, and the implementation of the national Key Stage (KS) 3 strategy for the foundation subjects. There are perhaps few signs that geography teachers will be offered much more control over their own work in this context, although in 2003 the government began to sing the praises of 'subject specialism' and subject associations such as the Geographical Association which has campaigned for 'local solutions' to curriculum and pedagogic issues facing geography.

Thus, there are signs that geography teachers are being encouraged to think more flexibly about curriculum development and to interpret the national curriculum requirements in ways that are innovative and creative. Recent pronouncements relating to the curriculum seem, on the surface at least, to offer more space for a range of alternative representations of the subject. For example, the so-called 'new agenda' offers geographers a role in citizenship education and education for sustainability. Citizenship education, in theory at least, offers an opportunity for the development of rigorous frameworks for geographical studies linking important questions of state, nation and identity (see Lambert and Machon 2001).

In 2003 the government announced the creation of 'humanities' specialist schools – with geography named (with history and English) as one of the humanities subjects. It remains to be seen how many schools choose to take up geography as their specialist focus, but we are convinced that heads of geography should not be too coy about the designation of geography as one of the humanities. There is nothing to stop a geography specialist school celebrating and developing all manner of creative and exciting curriculum links across the humanities, but also across the sciences and the arts perhaps under the unifying banner of sustainability.

The arguments about what geography is will continue – perhaps forever – but with new energy over the next few years because of new opportunities to look beyond the subject barricades. Let us avoid the temptation to merely defend 'our' curriculum turf. We are satisfied that we can more or less agree with enough colleagues that the subject is:

- concerned with both the physical world and human environments;
- about place, space and interaction;

- very interested in the geographies that people acquire, including those developing in students' minds.

This is a powerful basis from which to negotiate curriculum relevance. Or if you like catch phrases, geography is about *what is where, why there and why care?* (Gritzner 2002).

CONCLUSION

Our account is intended to highlight the variety of professional ideologies in which geography teachers can work. Even a cursory reading of this chapter will suggest that school geography has followed a quite different trajectory from that of geography as studied and taught in universities. Alison Lee (1996) states that 'School geography has, on the whole, remained within quite conservative frameworks, although there is significant local diversity as well as multiplicity and competition within particular sites' (p. 31). Whereas in Chapter 2 we showed how geography has responded to economic, political, social, cultural and environmental change, and confronted important questions about the construction of geographical knowledge, these debates have not significantly influenced school geography. Thus, most recent publications written for beginning and practising geography teachers are books about *how to teach* and do not deal with questions of *what to teach* or *why teach* geography. The result is that the gap between the geography taught and studied in universities and schools is wider than ever. The final chapter in this part of the book discusses this 'gap' in more detail. As Gregory and Walford (1989) wrote in their introduction to *New Horizons in Human Geography*:

> The insights of higher education are not, of course, translated directly into the curriculum of the first form of the secondary school. There is a wholly proper re-evaluation of them, and they are subject to transformation through contact with a host of other influences too. Yet any school subject is the poorer without that vital, organic linkage. *If school geography were to become a limited-objective, narrow instrumental study, uninformed by the excitement and potential of contemporary research ... then it would eventually lose its intellectual edge and its capacity to interest students.*
>
> (p. 6, emphases added)

There may be signs that this is already happening. The number of students opting to study geography in public examinations has been declining. What this statement suggests is that it is the proper role of teachers to be active participants in debates over what is to be taught in schools, that our role as a geographical community is to be constantly alert to the relationship between knowledge and the students we teach. In the final chapter of this part of the book, we indicate why this question needs to be addressed and how contemporary approaches in geography dovetail with curriculum debates.

FOR FURTHER THINKING

1 Imagine being involved in a school that had decided to apply for Humanities Specialist School status with geography as the lead subject. The Head asks the geography department, 'With geography in the lead, what distinctive character will this school acquire? How would a visitor see that geography was the lead specialist subject as they walked through the school?'

2 You are at your school open evening. An inquisitive parent comes to you and says, 'Geography seems to have changed a lot, and I am alarmed that my son doesn't seem to know much about the world map! What exactly counts as geographical knowledge these days? And what is a geographical way of thinking?' What is your reply?

3 How would you describe the nature of the relationship between the school subject and the wider discipline of geography?

Chapter 4

Geography, knowledge and education

The supposed neutrality of geographical knowledges has at best proven to be a beguiling fiction and at worst a downright fraud. Geographical knowledges have always internalized strong ideological content. In their scientific (and predominantly positivist) forms, natural and social phenomena are represented objectively as things, subject to manipulation, management and exploitation by dominant forces of capital and the state.

(Harvey 2001: 231)

INTRODUCTION

In Chapter 3 we argued that the purposes of geography education are not fixed. They are the subject of continued debate and revision. For geography teachers, the question of the purpose of geography education is not an arcane question, reserved for the staffroom or Masters' seminar, but is one often posed all too urgently by students who demand to know 'what's the point?'.

In this chapter we explore the question of the purposes of geographical education. We start from the position that all geography education seeks to be relevant to students. Geography education is, in this sense, an application of geographical knowledge. However, the question of relevance is not straightforward. Should geography education be relevant in that it prepares young people for the world of work? Or should it seek to be relevant in preparing them for 'life experiences'? Does relevance refer to individuals or to societal goals? There are, of course, no final and definitive answers to these questions, since they refer to the place of values within the practice of geography education (and, in fact, all education), and as we suggested in the last chapter, questions of curriculum politics. However, we want to make the case that different educational purposes are served by different types of geographical knowledge. This is the point made by Harvey in the quote at the start of this chapter. If Harvey's tone sounds negative, he goes on to say: 'In their more artistic, humanist and aesthetic incarnations, geographical knowledges project and articulate individual and collective hopes and fears while purporting to depict material conditions and social relations with the historical veracity they deserve' (Harvey 2001: 231).

Thus, humanistic geographical knowledge can help us realise our humanity, to have deeper understanding of others and ourselves and of our relationship to the world. Similarly, critical forms of geographical knowledge can 'become vehicles to express utopian visions and practical plans for the creation of alternative geographies' (Harvey 2001: 233).

These observations set the scene for the discussion in this chapter. In what follows we first consider three different purposes of geographical knowledge that imply different educational purposes, and show how they have been reflected in school geography. These are geographical knowledges that promote:

1 an ability to predict and manipulate the world;
2 mutual awareness and understanding of the world; and
3 critical understanding of the forces that structure the world.

We then go on to consider forms of geographical knowledge that threaten to 'interrupt' these ways of understanding. These various knowledges are those associated with various 'posts' – postmodernism, postcolonialism, poststructuralism – which, for convenience, we discuss under the umbrella heading 'postmodernism'. We discuss the possible implications of these developments for geography education. The reader will notice that the chapter focuses largely on these debates as they affect human geography, since it is the case that these arguments have largely been advanced in that part of the discipline. However, we do discuss the ways in which physical geography might also reflect these developments.

Before we start, we should note that we consider this chapter to be an introduction to these issues for geography teachers. We hope that readers will finish the chapter with a sense of some of the important issues surrounding the construction of geographical knowledge and their implications for education, but not to treat the discussion as finished.

HUMAN GEOGRAPHY – PREDICTION, UNDERSTANDING, EMANCIPATION, OR WHAT?

Ron Johnston's (1986) *On Human Geography* contains a chapter enti-tled 'Applied and Applicable' in which he discusses three types of applied geography underpinned by three different approaches to 'science':

- Positivist
- Humanistic
- Realist

Although readers may consider Johnston's analysis to be a little dated, we use it because it serves as a useful heuristic device with which we can begin to clarify our understanding of the purposes of geography educa-tion. In addition, Johnston's work is relatively familiar to geography educators, so serves as a useful starting point for our discussion. In the first part of this chapter we use this framework to analyse the types of geography that underpin teaching in schools.

The first type of applied science identified by Johnston is empiricist and *positivist science*. Empiricist science operates in the world of experi-ence and involves the collection of data by an assumed neutral, outside observer. Positivist science uses the data obtained and structures it into general laws. The goal is explanation. This type of knowledge is linked to an ideology of technical control. Laws can be used to predict events. Johnston considers the application of such knowledge as 'inherently conservative', since it takes the existing organisation of society as given.

Much of the geography taught in schools reflects the legacy of the changes that took place in school geography in the 1970s. The positivist, scientific approach is still strongly present. Models (such as Burgess and Hoyt), spatial theories (such as Weber and Christaller) and quantifica-tion (such as nearest neighbour index and the gravity model) are commonly taught. Human geography as taught in schools is still concerned to identify general laws about people's behaviour (see Box 4.1). Pupils often test hypotheses, use surveys to produce quantitative data, and produce generalisations. The position of positivism within school geography is strengthened by the widespread use of textbooks that share its assumptions about the world and how it can be known. While new themes from behavioural or welfare geography have been introduced, these are generally studied using a scientific methodology.

BOX 4.1 EXAMPLES OF THE LEGACY OF THE NATURAL SCIENCES ON GEOGRAPHY TEACHING

To earn recognition as a spatial science, geography needed to forsake its exceptionalism and become normative, that is, to search for generalisations and to establish scientific laws. To do this it was necessary to establish a theoretical rather than an empirical basis for the analysis of space.

A The physical sciences provided the basis for theoretical models. An excellent example of this is the gravity model, which was used to 'explain' internal migration. Zipf (1949) demonstrated that people's travel patterns are organised so as to minimise the amount of work they must undertake – the principle of least effort. This principle suggests that the greater the distance separating two locations, the smaller the amount of inter-place contact. A second example of a geographical model being derived from the physical sciences was Alfred Weber's (1909/1929) theory of industrial location which used the principle of Varignon frames to determine the least cost location of an industry relying on sources of raw materials and labour.

B Biological sciences provided a basis for models accounting for spatial differences within the residential structure of cities. Sociologists from the University of Chicago developed a theory of urban residential structure using biological concepts. They regarded neighbourhoods as 'natural areas'. The dominance of a particular social mix of people in a neighbourhood resulted from competition for living space with other social groups – a struggle for existence. Neighbourhoods were not static. Like plant communities they were subject to invasion and succession as physical and demographic changes altered the character of areas. Burgess (1925) later developed his ecological model of urban structure based on studies of 'natural areas' in Chicago. He proposed that cities were structured by concentric zones. Objections to the ecological approach have been made on the grounds of the simplistic use of plant ecology comparisons to describe complex patterns of human residential differentiation. These models lacked any consideration of non-economic power and ignored the political power of large corporations, major land owners and the role of planners. However, the neighbourhood idea has remained an influential concept. The point here is that in their borrowing of spatial viewpoints from other disciplines, human geographers were often very selective in their choices.

C   A final example of the ways in which human geographers drew upon explanations in the natural sciences can be seen in the adoption of evolutionary models. An example is Rostow's (1960) modernisation theory which suggested a succession of evolutionary stages to explain social and economic transitions. All nation states were assumed to pass along the same developmental pathway. The end point was the achievement of advanced capitalism, a service economy characterised by full employment and high skill levels and wages. The United States and Britain were provided as examples of this end point. Modernisation, for Rostow, was based on 'Western' ideas of material progress based on industrialisation and urbanisation. Underdevelopment was characterised by 'traditional' cultural values and practices that were labelled 'backward'. Although Rostow's ideas are increasingly recognised as culturally laden, it might be suggested that this type of thinking still underpins much teaching about development in schools. Most importantly, evolutionary models suggest to students that society is moving in one direction. Another commonly used model that relies on an evolutionary approach is the 'demographic transition theory', which explains the modern rise of population as resulting from a substantial fall in the death rates. The model rests upon ethnocentric assumptions about the relationship between development and birth rates.

These approaches, based on models derived from the natural sciences, continue to underpin much of the human geography taught in schools today. Often, teaching in the early years is based on simplified versions of the models taught at higher levels. We pose the questions:

- What are the consequences of understanding human geography in terms of physical sciences, biological concepts or evolutionary theories?
- Are these adequate to helping students make sense of the world?

From the mid-1980s, values and attitudes became part of the national criteria for geography. In theory, this encouraged the development of a more humanistic approach. In practice, different viewpoints are often considered as pieces of scientific evidence to be analysed, rather than being used to explore different meanings. Most school geography textbooks present data of all kinds as objective evidence to be accepted by pupils, rather than as something constructed and selected by people with different perceptions of the world. Many classroom activities demand reproduction of textbook information, analysis and generalisation rather than interpretation of its meaning. Thus, we think it is fair to state that school geography is dominated by positivist approaches (this paragraph owes much to Healey and Roberts (1996)).

Johnston's second type of science is humanistic. *Humanistic sciences* have as their goal the understanding of events, the thoughts behind the actions that produce the world of experience. They seek to appreciate what created the present. The goal of such understanding is both self-awareness and mutual understanding. This is commonly stated as a purpose of geography education. It is about developing respect and toler-ance for other cultures and other ways of life. This is often expressed in terms of developing empathy and a 'sense of place'. In addition, young people are to be helped to understand themselves and their place in the world, and to develop their environmental understanding. This idea of geography as mutual understanding is found in the statement about 'the importance of geography' in the National Curriculum:

As pupils study geography, they encounter different societies and cultures. This helps them realise how nations rely on each other. It can inspire them to think about their own place in the world, their values, and their rights and responsibilities to other people and the environment.

(DfEE/QCA 1999: 14)

Frances Slater (1982) distinguished between 'geography as science' and 'geography as personal response', arguing that 'both have a part to play in developing student understanding through activities based on geography' (p. 1). Geography as personal response directs 'attention to our experiences and interpretations of everyday life whether structured cognitively or emotionally, but more importantly emotionally' (p. 1). McEwen (1986) suggests what a 'phenomenologically based school geography' might entail. It would involve the rejection of all positions that regard people as passive agents who tacitly accept received truths. McEwen saw humanistic geography as a means towards improving the human condition and that it should, therefore, address issues of social

47

concern. Through teaching, geography should not only 'engage' social problems but also aim at a 'conscientious engagement of social problems'. For McEwen, the key word is 'conscientious', since the phenomenological view looks towards the stimulation of the individual's consciousness, in relation to social issues, rather than the imposition of an alien system of concerns.

The starting point should be those areas of the people–environment relationship which are most taken for granted by the students. This might include their perceptions of the local environment, their aesthetic and functional appreciation of the environment. An important theme is *intentionality* since 'intentional students' learning 'intentional geography' will define social problems and issues:

> the need to alleviate the anomie of the post-industrial metropolis, to reinstate meaning to the land through 'the protection of public buildings, preservation of neighbourhoods, opposition to demolition for motorways and public works, and asserting the sanctity of open space' ought to be part of the geography syllabus.
>
> (p. 163)

McEwen stresses that these should all be tackled in a geographical paradigm in which 'fact and value are inseparable and in which intersubjective dialogue between teacher and student, aimed at raising levels of consciousness relating to these problems, is the order of the day' (p. 163).

McEwen makes it plain that *there is a strong relationship between curriculum and teaching approach*. Since a phenomenological stance regards the students' experience and view of the world as central, geography teachers need to teach in ways consonant with that view of the world. McEwen noted that methods of didactic transmission may be inappropriate in this approach and that students' intentionality and intersubjectivity need to be developed through group work and discussion. McEwen's phenomenologically based approach to geography teaching offers a vision that challenges the 'prevailing positivist paradigm'. Humanistic geography is not commonly found in school geography, not least because it would presumably involve handing over considerable responsibility for the curriculum to pupils, although Roberts (2003) notes that a focus on personal geographies is in many ways implied in some versions of geographical enquiry.

Johnston's final type of science is realist. *Realist science* is concerned with providing people with an understanding of the mechanisms and underlying forces that structure the world. The goal is critical awareness, and the outcome is emancipation, releasing people from false ideologies by identifying the mechanisms that constrain people's lives and allow for their removal and replacement. In short, the goal is social change.

An example of how a realist understanding of a geographical issue might be developed in schools is offered here. It draws on a model of political scale developed by the political geographer Peter Taylor. Taylor (1985) offers a trilogy of geographical scales – experience, ideology and reality. The scale of experience is the scale at which we live our daily lives. It encompasses all our basic needs, including employment, shelter and consumption of basic commodities. These day-to-day activities are not all sustained locally. We live in a world system which means that the scale of experience is linked to a much wider sphere of action, the global scale of 'reality'. Taylor asserts that 'in the current world-economy the crucial events that structure our lives occur at a global scale' (1985: 29). This is because it is the scale of accumulation where the world market defines values that impinge on our local communities. However, the links between the global and the local are not direct, since they are mediated through the nation-state – the scale of ideology – which can affect the precise effects of these global processes. Taylor makes clear that it is the scale of accumulation operating at a global scale that represents the motor of the whole system. This is the scale of 'reality' and understanding any event requires an understanding of the processes operating at that scale. Too often however, Taylor suggests, events are interpreted through the scales of experience and ideology, with the result that the nature of reality – the forces that shape the world – is obscured.

A concrete example of this idea is found in an article which appeared in a newspaper (*Guardian*, 1998) and which told the story of Graham Jones who lost his job as a bartender in Whitley Bay. The story relates to the scale of experience. Graham Jones lost his job because there was not enough business to occupy two bartenders in the public bar. At the time the article appeared, things looked bleak for workers like Graham. The pub had lost business because of the closure of the Siemens semiconductor factory on North Tyneside in July 1997. The factory employed 1,100 people and was a major employer in the area. The article hinted that understanding Graham Jones' situation requires knowledge of events happening in the world economy. In 1997 several property companies

49

collapsed in Thailand; property prices and the stock market started to fall. The Thai Baht was devalued. Thai exports became cheaper, and in order to remain competitive, other east Asian countries allowed their currencies to fall sharply. As a result, South Korean firms who needed foreign currency to pay off loans started dumping cheap microchips, forcing a reduction in prices from US$10 to US$1.50. The result was losses for Siemens and the decision to close their Tyneside factory. Thus, it was events at what Taylor calls the scale of reality that explain why Graham Jones lost his bartending job.

Examples such as these can be used in geography lessons as a means of investigating the local experience of employment change in a place. The national context could then be examined, by looking at frameworks for regional policy and, if appropriate, the less tangible aspects of ideology, such as the government's insistence that regions need to be competitive to attract inward investment, and that individuals should insure themselves against such events by being 'flexible', undertaking training and selling their labour. Finally, this could lead on to an understanding of the reality of the global economic system in which large transnational corporations such as Siemens seek out sites for inward investment and operate flexibly across space to maintain profitability. This example suggests what a critical geography might involve. It suggests that what is taught in schools can (in theory) serve to reveal the deeper forces or structures that shape the world.

By way of summary, how does this discussion relate to school geography? Johnston suggests that school geography has become dominated by empiricist/positivist approaches and has 'been linked to the notion of training in the solution of empirical problems' (Johnston 1986: 155).

He continues:

> In school education today geography is unbalanced: just as in higher education, it is empiricist, emphasizing training for problem-solving and despite many good intentions, avoiding understanding. Within human geography it underplays mutual understanding and the important role of place in the constitution of society. More importantly, it fails to explore what it is that produces society, other than variation in the physical environment. By not seeking to understand societies, only describe them, however sophisticatedly, it fails to educate people, fails to help them see what it is that governs their

lives. It is part of the ideology of capitalism, promoting the ruling ideas of that mode of production.

(p. 157)

Although this comment was written some time ago, we think it is still a reflection of how geography is taught in schools. Johnston's analysis is useful in helping geography teachers to think about the values and interests that inform their teaching. It suggests that much of the geography taught in schools serves to offer students a partial and unrealistic view of the world, and prevents them from developing the deeper levels of understanding that might help them make sense of the world.

THE POSTMODERN TURN AND GEOGRAPHY

We want to be clear about what we are doing here. We have been describing the trajectory of human geography in the post-war period. Geography came late to the social sciences and in order to stake their claim geographers went to great lengths to emphasise a particular version of spatial science that focused on models of spatial behaviour (Johnston 2003). As we described in Chapter 3, geographers in schools welcomed the advent of geography as a spatial science, and its influence remains in geography curricula and methods of study. Other geographers quickly declared the 'new geography' a dead-end and looked to other approaches rooted in humanism and Marxist analyses. So far, in this chapter, we have sought to clarify these debates and discuss their relevance to geography education. In this section, we take up the story of the continuing development of human geography.

Barnes and Duncan (1992) suggest that Johnston's book *Geography and Geographers* (1997), which relates the story of the development of post-war human geography, could have had the subtitle 'a tale of three modernisms'. What they mean by this is that despite their apparent differences, positivism, humanism and realism (structuralism) share a belief that there is an underlying 'Truth' and 'Order' to the world and that it can be uncovered. Where they differ is in their view of how that 'Truth' is to be obtained. Barnes and Duncan are writing in the light of what has been called 'postmodernism'. This is a notoriously difficult concept to define and it is now quite fashionable to argue that postmodernism is history. However, Michael Dear (1988, 2000), who was one of the first geographers to confront the 'postmodern challenge', has convincingly argued

51

that postmodernism has had a significant impact on human geography, and in the remainder of this chapter we are interested in the way these ideas have influenced work in geography because their influence may need to extend more fully to school geography itself. Dear identifies seven topical themes within geography that reflect the concern and interest in postmodernism. These are:

1 cultural landscapes and place-making;
2 economic landscapes and cultures of economies;
3 philosophical and theoretical disputes, especially relating to space and the problems of language;
4 problems of representation in geographical writing, in cartography, and in art and film;
5 feminist geography, orientalism and postcolonialism
6 the construction of the individual and the boundaries of the self, including the body and sexuality;
7 reassertion of nature and the environmental question.

This is by no means a complete list, and there are considerable overlaps between different themes. However, it serves to illustrate contemporary geographical interests. At the heart of postmodern debates were developments in feminist scholarship. *Feminist geographers* argued that geography was a male dominated discipline and that its objects of study conventionally concentrated on topics of greater relevance to the lives of men. The result was that women were largely absent as subjects of geographical research. Feminist geographers thus conducted research on a range of issues of immediate concern to women – patterns of domestic work, provision of childcare, mobility and access – and placed women's lives at the centre of more conventional geographical topics such as retailing and urban form. The second 'phase' in feminist geography was concerned with the need to move on from the study of women's lives to beginning to explain the reasons for the differences and inequalities observed. Explanations could not be uncovered by looking at the lives of women alone but had to situate their lives within broader patterns of gender difference. This meant a shift away from the idea of women as a biological category to a concern with gender as a set of socially constructed power relations. This shift in focus was reflected in new directions and topics for geographical research – in, for example, the study of male power in the workplace and the exploitation of women's labour in the household and the relationship between production and consumption. It also involved new theoretical debates concerning the nature of male power and its reproduction within society. A third, more recent phase has sought to break down the universal categories of 'male' and 'female' and focus instead on the diversity and differences within genders. Earlier versions of feminist geography tended to focus on the category 'woman'. However, recent work has stressed the differences that exist within this category. It recognises that women's experiences are influenced by class, race, age and sexuality.

From this research emerged a wider concern with *'positionality'*, which recognised and embraced not only gender divisions in society but also ethnic, racial, national, plus sexual orientation and other dimensions on which individuals' identities are based, such as age and disability (as noted in Chapter 2). It was increasingly argued that geographical knowledge had been produced by a relatively privileged group of academics, who tended to erase their own voices and thus claim to speak for everybody. One of the most striking developments in human geography in the past 15 years has been the increased visibility of a wide range of geographies.

An accessible introduction to postmodern arguments in geography is provided by Cloke *et al.* (1991). They distinguish between the *postmodern* as an object of study ('postmodernity' or 'the postmodern') and *postmodernism* as an attitude. Postmodernity refers to the complex interactions of economic, social, political and cultural processes in the late twentieth-century world. Postmodernism as attitude refers to the knowledge we can acquire about the world, towards the methods we might apply in the process, towards the theories that inform our research, and towards the way in which we represent this knowledge (see Box 4.2).

The postmodern attitude is inherently suspicious of 'grand' intellectual traditions such as Marxism, humanism, structuration and so on, which claim to be able to tell the 'truth' about the world. The postmodern attitude requires that our knowledge claims are more humble, eclectic and empirically grounded. There is a need to think in terms of disorder, incoherence and the lack of a centre determining everything that is 'going on'. There is less concern to identify order and 'sameness' and more attention to 'difference'. This focus on difference:

forces us to respect the myriad variations that exist between the many 'sorts' of human being studied by human geographers – the variations between women and men, between social classes, between ethnic groups . . . and to recognise (and in some way to represent) the very different inputs and experiences these diverse populations have in, and of, 'socio-spatial' processes.

(Cloke *et al.* 1991: 171)

Cloke *et al.* (1991) think that the postmodern attitude appeals to geographers because traditionally the discipline has displayed sensitivity to the specific kinds of differences to be found between different and unique places, district, regions and countries. They suggest that postmodernism is an attitude that insists upon scholarly inquiries being sensitive to the world's geography and thereby perhaps learning from all of the many

---

BOX 4.2 POSTMODERNISM AS ATTITUDE

Cloke *et al.* (2004) point out that postmodernism has become a much maligned and misunderstood term. They consider that it is probably best to see it as a *stance* taken by many academics (including geographers) to questions of what exists in the world and how we can know about the world. Postmodernism as an attitude denies that any one theory can explain how the world works. This goes against the grain of the European Englightenment project which assumes that an understanding can be achieved of how nature works and how humans behave. Postmodernists are suspicious of 'grand theories', which they regard as attempts to dominate by insisting on one interpretation. Instead, postmodernists insist upon a plurality of explanations. This suspicion of grand theory leads to the supposed crisis of representation, whereby it becomes extremely difficult to claim to understand or depict other people and places. A key word for postmodernism is 'difference', which is reflected in the alertness to 'every line or scrap of difference which prevents things, peoples, situations etc., ever being truly the same as one another' (Cloke *et al.* 2004: 233). This alertness leads to a concern with the 'messiness' of the world and rejects the tendency to 'smooth over' the rough edges of phenomena. This is clearly only a brief description of postmodernism. In geography education, there have been few attempts to engage with the question of how postmodernism might be linked to teaching (see Bale 1996).

---

ways in which the discipline of geography has sought to cultivate and to develop this sensitivity over the years.

They note that adopting a postmodernist attitude 'requires us to take far more seriously than hitherto the process of "writing" human geography; the process of representing our findings in words, sounds and pictures' (1991: 197). They note that this is particularly true of the convention requiring that geographers write in a highly 'scientific' fashion, but also in narrative representations, where 'an "unfolding story", a chronology of events, a history of causes and effects – risks imposing order and *in*difference upon the subject-matter being addressed' (p. 198).

If the argument so far is that all knowledge is partial and reflects the positionality of its producers, a second (and connected) theme is to do with the wider politics and poetics of writing and *representation*. In their introduction to a collection of papers, Barnes and Gregory (1997) discuss the 'poetics' of geographical inquiry. The term 'poetics' is used to highlight that all geographical accounts are 'rhetorical constructions' – textual artefacts that seek to persuade us of their claims through an amalgam of 'academic' and 'literary' genres. Geographical writing does not provide an accurate depiction of the world, since language is no longer regarded as mimetic. Words do not merely represent the world: they also create worlds, offer possibilities and produce action. Thus, the linguistic turn challenges the assumption that language is a transparent, self-effacing medium, a means of more or less neutral exchange between the individual pysche and the world. Barnes and Duncan's edited collection *Writing Worlds* (1992) is a useful introduction to these ideas and arguments. Barnes and Duncan argue that:

> Pieces of the world do not come with their own labels, and thus representing 'out there' to an audience must involve much more than just lining up pieces of language in the right order. Instead, it is humans that decide how to represent things, and not the things themselves.
>
> (p. 2)

The work of economic geographer Trevor Barnes is representative of an emergent approach in human geography that is informed by a 'constructivist' approach that denies any possibility of an underlying foundational order to social and economic life. It rejects any view of geographical epistemology that promises to reveal pre-ordained orders and rationalities (such as the types proposed by positivism, humanism and structuralism). As Barnes (1996) puts it:

> there is neither a single origin point for inquiry nor a single logic, spatial or otherwise. The best we can hope for are shards and fragments; there is not one geography but many geographies, not one complete story but a set of fragmented stories.
>
> (p. 250)

This type of post-structuralist argument (see Box 4.3) has a radically unsettling effect on any forms of geography that claim to represent the 'world as it is'. These are challenging ideas, not least because they seem to go against the grain of common sense. However, in this book, we want to suggest that post-structuralist approaches are useful for geography teachers in thinking about their work. As Hubbard *et al.* (2002) point out:

> in a world composed of flows, movements and chaos, post-structuralists suggest that solidity is an illusion. One task for a post-structural geography, therefore, is to expose the practices that maintain this illusion. Crucially, it seems that geography itself is involved in imposing this sense of order on the world, inventing concepts (e.g., place, space, nature) which reduce difference to sameness and potentially fail to do justice to the complexity of things.
>
> (pp. 86–7)

Recent work in geography has provided a clearer idea of what a post-structuralist approach to geography might look like in practice. Such work aims to deconstruct taken-for-granted categories. An example is the term development, where geographers have been concerned with the way that term is understood. As Crush (1995) put it in the introduction to *Power of Development*:

> Rather than asking what development is, or is not, or how it can be more accurately defined, better 'theorized', or sustainably practised, the authors in this volume are generally more interested in a different kind of question . . . The *discourse* of development, the forms in which it makes its arguments and establishes its authority, the manner in

which it constructs the world, are usually seen as self-evident and
unworthy of attention. This book's primary intention is to try and
make the self-evident problematical.

(p. 3)

An example of this type of approach is found in Yapa's (2000) review of
the North American report *Rediscovering Geography* (National Research
Council 1997). The report lists several critical problems where geography
can offer useful knowledge to society. Among these are economic health,
environmental degradation, ethnic conflict, health care and global climate
change. It is assumed that these problems are 'worldly' – that is, they are
'out there', waiting to be investigated by geographers. Geographers, on
the other hand, merely study such problems: their maps and accounts are
assumed to reflect the world as a mirror. Take, for example, the world
map of GNP (gross national product) per capita. This is taken as an

---

BOX 4.3 STRUCTURALISM AND POST-STRUCTURALISM

'Structuralism' is a philosophy which insists that everything occurring in
the human world is ultimately determined in its form and function not by
individual beings but by anonymous structures that lie beyond our own
control and doing. For example, we may be able to speak, but the form
and function of our speech patterns is structured by deep patterns of
language. Or, to offer a more 'geographical' example, we may act and
move around cities as individual men and women, but the nature of our
activities is determined by deeper structures of gender relations that structure our lives.

Post-structuralism shares the view that the human world is 'made' by
structures, but challenges the idea that these are objective entities.
Structures such as class, gender or race are not pre-existent entities, but
are themselves human constructions and, as such, are capable of being
made in other ways. In terms of human geography, what this suggests is
that categories such as 'place', 'space', 'culture', 'nature' and so on, can
no longer be seen as stable and fixed. Instead, post-structuralism would
stress the need to analyse those categories very rigorously, in order to see
how they are constructed in particular contexts.

57

unproblematic 'fact' of the world, a representation of the world. However, the map of GNP per capita is a construction, a specific way of choosing to represent the nations of the world within a certain discursive logic of 'development'. In reading the map in a geography textbook, or seeing it displayed on the wall of a classroom, the reader is being invited to 'buy into' or think in terms of, the discourse of development.

Yapa suggests that this 'lesson' is not lost on school students. They *know* that Bangladeshis or Africans live in 'underdeveloped' nations. They are secure in their own sense of self, that they 'rank' higher than millions of those 'other' people in underdeveloped countries (or LEDCs (less economically developed countries)). He argues that after socialising the young mind into the *hierarchical logic of self and the other* built into the map of GNP per capita, it is difficult to imagine any other possible alternative views or outcomes prevailing. The point Yapa is making is that these school students are not simply learning about a world that is 'out there' like proverbial 'well-known facts'. Rather, their subjectivity is being literally constructed through the same discourse. This is an important argument that should stop us in our tracks.

If we can no longer see the words and images upon which we conduct geographical learning as 'mirrors of the world' but as involved in its construction, geography teachers need to acknowledge the limits to any authoritative singular accounts of the world out there and encourage a critical involvement in meaning making. It includes even the most basic, 'inviolate' geographical concept, scale. We have already seen how the choice of scale can influence how we understand a phenomenon or problem. It is simply worth emphasising here that scale itself is also a social construction.

We set out in this chapter to inquire into the purposes of geography education. We used Johnston's discussion of three types of applied geography to explore the role that geographical knowledge plays in promoting technical control, mutual awareness and understanding, and emancipation. The second part of the chapter went on to explore the 'postmodern challenge'. If spatial science sought to predict and control, humanistic geography sought mutual awareness and understanding, and radical geography promised emancipation, the various geographical knowledges we have just discussed threaten to 'deconstruct' or take apart our taken-for-granted understandings of the world. In the final section of this chapter, we discuss some of the possible implications of these debates for geography education. Before that, however, we turn our attention to physical geography.

THE PURPOSES OF PHYSICAL GEOGRAPHY IN SCHOOLS

What we have been describing in this chapter can be interpreted as the process whereby human geography has distanced itself from its earlier links with the physical sciences and positioned itself as a social science with links to the humanities. This shift is less evident in school geography, where human geography continues to be taught with the methods and assumptions of the physical sciences. We have argued that human geography in schools needs to reflect more fully developments in the social sciences. This has implications for physical geography as taught in schools. In other words, we need to address the question of the purposes of teaching physical geography in schools.

If the purpose of studying geography in schools is to provide a training and preparation for the minority of students who go on to study the subject at university, then the question need not delay us much further. Physical geography in schools ought to be a 'junior version' of the subject at higher levels, providing prospective students with the necessary background in the natural sciences – physics, chemistry and biology – to allow them to study physical systems in detail. Physical geographers in universities have been heard to question the extent to which students come to the university properly trained in this 'basic' knowledge.

However, this argument is not widely accepted by geography educators, even in universities, who recognise that the teaching of physical geography needs to be interesting and relevant to the majority of students who do not go on to study the subject at higher levels. This argument certainly informed curriculum development in the 1970s and 1980s, when non-traditional versions of physical geography were developed. These tended to focus less on the study of physical geography for its own sake and more on the implications of human–physical interactions.

A good example of this argument is found in an article entitled 'Why teach physical geography?' (Pepper 1985). Pepper analysed the London Board's A Level examination syllabus and papers and argued that the physical geography papers did not allow pupils to set knowledge within the context of human society and problems. The physical environment was not seen as a part of a system that also contains human society. Students were encouraged to be analytic rather than synthetic, reductionist rather than holistic. The questions split knowledge into little information 'bits', such as how stream load and discharges are related, or the five stages of coastline development. There was little room for seeing how these bits fit together:

You need neither technical skill nor critical faculty to do the paper; no comprehensive overview, no sense of 'relevance', application or synthesis, and above all no opinions about anything. All you need is the ability to memorise and recall textbook information and recognise what pages of the book you are being asked to regurgitate.

(Pepper 1985: 64)

Pepper asks the question why do we need to know about certain topics, and offers some examples. Knowledge of soil structure, texture, porosity and cation-exchange capacity are important because they are components of long-term soil fertility which are being damaged by modern business farming, perhaps forming the 'deserts' of the future. But in arguing that the physical basis of geography is important to study, Pepper goes on to suggest that without a *social* purpose, there is little justification to teach physical geography. The London examination discussed by Pepper 'fosters an uncritical, atomistic and functional approach to the physical environment which is quite divorced from its socio-economic context' (1986: 69).

The physical geography described by Pepper is derived from dominant models of science education which fail to address the societal context in which decisions are made. This type of education focuses on 'fact' gathering and rote learning, making students puzzle-solvers within a paradigm rather than investigators of the paradigm itself. This critique of the curriculum has been important in challenging the value-free nature of physical geography in schools. In the years since Pepper published his article, school geography has indeed become tied in with debates about the environment, and a major concern of geography educators has been the relationship between physical and human geography. There have been calls to recognise the apparent unity of the subject, which may even sound like a call for a return to tradition. One of the clearest statements of this approach is found in the Schools Council's 16–19 Project, which proclaimed a 'people and environment' motif, and whose first 'knowledge principle' stated: 'People are an inseparable part of the global system within which physical and cultural systems are closely inter-related' (cited in Naish *et al.* 1987: 55).

However, the knowledge produced under the title of this 'people–environment' framework is essentially 'technocratic'. The Project quite openly and purposely refused to align with any particular 'paradigm' of geography, preferring to go for an inclusive people–environment 'approach'. It may be that this left the question of the relationship between people and environment relatively under-theorised, with the result that geography teachers tended to 'default' to the comfortable positivist position.

Thus, although Geography 16–19 may have sought to highlight 'environmental problems' it rarely discussed the fundamental socio-economic processes transforming nature. Instead, it favoured a view of knowledge that leads to policy geared to ameliorating environmental problems without addressing the deeper causes responsible for those problems in the first place. An example of this is the way in which a concept such as sustainable development gets taken up in geography lessons, as an appealing ideal which appears to mean little more than 'business-as-usual'.

So, even in people–environment approaches to geography, in the end it is usually assumed that nature is external to and separate from people, and that nature is something that is unchangeable. Humans might 'destroy' or 'alter' nature, but they cannot make or create nature. Castree (2001), on the other hand, argues how critical geographers increasingly see nature as inescapably social:

> Here the argument is that nature is defined, delimited, and even physically reconstituted by different societies, often in order to serve specific, and usually dominant social interests. In other words, the social and the natural are seen to intertwine in ways that make their separation – in either thought or practice – impossible.
>
> (p. 3)

Geographers have developed the idea of social nature, similar to Pepper's argument, but at school level there is arguably some work to do in developing a curriculum that provides students with the possibility to grasp this potentially very useful idea in some way (see Whatmore 2003).

However, there are of course some potentially serious consequences in taking this forward into schools. Critics say that these ideas are intellectually misguided, and practically and politically disabling. Take, for example, a critical social nature approach to global warming. If global warming is simply a fabrication – a myth cooked up by scientists keen to secure grants for their research – then we are led to conclude that polluting the atmosphere is okay, since we can never know the 'real' climatic effects of greenhouse gases. How can people claim that killing whales or destroying the Amazon is wrong, if we can no longer appeal to nature as a stable external source of non-human values? These are

61

moral questions too. Who are Western European school children (under the guidance of their teachers and textbooks) to argue to Brazilians that they should stop cutting down the forest (for 'environmental' reasons) when forests in Europe were destroyed some centuries ago? Surely geography educators need to engage with such a discussion – or stand accused of *moral carelessness* in teaching dogma, myth and received wisdom (see Box 4.4).

BOX 4.4   ENVIRONMENTAL ETHICS: AN EXAMPLE AVOIDING MORAL CARELESSNESS

In this example we want to explore how ideas about social construction impinge on our understanding of environmental issues and raise questions about the ethics of teaching geography. It is based on an article by James Proctor (2001). What are the ethical implications of social constructionist ways of understanding nature?

Proctor discusses the case of a news story about an environmental issue: 'Some freshwater species are becoming extinct at a rate as fast or faster than rainforest species, but their plight is largely ignored, according to a recent study in Canada.'

Proctor considers the ethical basis of the claims made in the story. The story suggests that people should strive to halt the extinction of North American freshwater species. This is justified on the basis of the facts presented on the rates of extinction, the comparison with rates of rainforest extinctions and noting their impacts on global biodiversity. The story assumes that humans are responsible for these extinctions and that actions could be taken to halt them with few economic costs. The moral foundations are solid in this story: 'There is only one possible reading: biodiversity is important, people have drastically reduced biodiversity in North America freshwater ecosystems, and thus something can and must be done soon' (p. 228).

Proctor suggests that this type of story, and the structure of moral ethics on which it is based, is quite typical of popular environmental ideas. It is perhaps fairly typical of environmental issues in geography education.

He then introduces the idea of social constructivism. He makes clear that he does not see it as arguing that there is 'no such thing' as nature:

Rather, social constructivism reminds us that any descriptive or normative pronouncement people make on nature is never innocent of its human origins. There certainly is a nature 'out there', but we cannot say anything more about it without relying on human modes of perception, invoking human conceptual apparatus, involving human needs and desires – in short, when we speak of nature we speak of culture as well, of the meanings we attribute to nature.

(p. 229)

Social constructivism challenges whether these facts and values – given their social origins – are as solid and unassailable as they are portrayed by many environmentalists. Proctor argues this case by referring to the philosophical tradition of realism. Realism is the position that the world is real and knowable. Facts are not just made up but rather are claims about the real world that are true to the extent that they correspond to this reality. Although realism is primarily a position about facts, it can also be invoked to suggest a similar spirit about values in that they are not just a matter of preference or context. Realism is a philosophy based on universalism: that these concerns are based on facts and values that hold true universally.

Social constructivism challenges the universalism of this realist stance on facts and values. The constructivist challenge to value universalism is less controversial, since most people are willing to admit to some extent that ways of valuing nature are of human origin and may differ from person to person and culture to culture. The challenge to facts is a bit more difficult:

If one views assertions of scientific fact from a constructivist perspective as primarily a human creation, then a serious measure of doubt enters our consideration of whether or not these assertions map faithfully onto reality and are thus true irrespective of who is making or believing the truth-statement.

(p. 231)

Proctor seeks to show that what are regarded as the 'facts' about high rates of freshwater species extinction are decidedly shaky. He asks how the researchers assembled the reams of data to come to the conclusion. They had to *construct* the conclusion out of a vast quantity of other studies and observation, or alternatively extrapolate from certain limited studies. He asks how detailed a model they *constructed* to estimate these trends, and notes that the researchers themselves in their paper admit that their methods of estimating extinctions are 'crude'.

The important point Proctor makes is that the process of discovering facts is actually a process of construction – in order to construct the facts the scientists had to make 'many crucial assumptions and simplifications along the way'. He also argues that this social constructionist distrust of facts-as-simple-representations of reality becomes more and more salient as these facts are more complex – think about global warming, biodiversity loss, acid rain, deforestation and desertification: 'Are they true? The social constructivist would have a hard time forgetting their human origins' (p. 232).

So where does this get us? Proctor argues that there is nothing sinister in trying to simplify vast complexity into something more manageable, as long as we are clear that these are in fact narrative or a story, 'not a fairytale devoid of real content but rather an intentional selection and construction of evidence to bring forth some meaning or moral' (p. 232). From this perspective then, the freshwater species story is not so much untrue as *partially* true, in that it is quite literally made up, constructed or shaped. What it appeals to is the claim of universalism, and this is what social constructivism challenges – it seeks to show how the claims to universal facts and values are, in fact, very particular.

This causes problems for anyone who would seek to invoke people to take action, to act to save the environment. Proctor suggests four resolutions to this stand-off:

- Separation – they do not really contradict each other as long as they keep their own place. Thus the scientist tells us about reality; the constructivist tells us about the social conditions under which truths about reality have been produced.
- Exclusion – in which people choose the side they like best and ignore, or work to disprove, the other.
- Compromise – the two sides are seen as extremes, which can probably be reconciled if they are interpreted in less extreme ways.
- Paradox – this is the option favoured by Proctor and involves recognising that both sides are basically correct as they stand but neither is fully correct without the other.

Proctor concludes:

Let us listen to those who tell us that we must act to save freshwater species, says the perspective of paradox; they have at some level a legitimate and universally binding claim on reality. At the same time let us be prepared to challenge the constructedness of their claims, and the constructedness of our own counterclaims, in the spirit of particularistic limitation.

(p. 236)

We have spent some time on Proctor's argument because it has important implications for the teaching of environmental issues in geography. Just as we would argue that it is morally careless to suggest to pupils that there are 'no right or wrong answers' to complex questions (there are almost always false positions – the difficulty is coming to conclusions that are clear cut), we would also be morally careless to teach as if there were 'answers' at all. The challenge in teaching environmental issues in geography is to avoid dogmatic remedies. Careful teaching will concentrate on thinking strategies so that we can make worthwhile distinctions and decide how to align or attach ourselves to a healthy and sustainable position.

Nevertheless, these powerful criticisms depend on the idea that geographical work on social nature is guilty of an extreme hyperconstructionist view that denies the existence of those things societies define as 'natural'. Most geographical work, not least in schools, does not assume this. But the point is that there is never any way to access, evaluate and affect nature that does not involve socially specific knowledges and practices. The argument is that we have to live with this inability to know nature 'as it really is', while still remaining committed to the idea that some knowledges of, and practices on, nature are better or worse than others.

CONCLUSIONS

The postmodern critique of geographical knowledge has alerted us to the idea that no geographical knowledge can be completely detached from the conditions under which it was constructed and circulated. Linda McDowell (2002: 298) captures this argument:

Scholars from a range of positions . . . insist that knowledge reflects and maintains power relations, that it is partial, contextual, and situated in particular times, places, and circumstances. Representations of these partial truths are produced by authors who are 'raced', gendered, and classed beings with a particular way of seeing the world. Further, these socially produced texts have no necessary or fixed meaning; the reader is implicated in the construction of meaning.

Geography educators have been wary of these arguments, where they have considered them. We hope that one of the contributions of this book will be to discuss these arguments in rather more detail. Our hope is that the theoretical basis for responding to the students' occasional question 'what's the point?' will be more secure, more layered and informed from the structure of the discipline. As a starting point we would argue that one of the advantages of understanding these debates is that it allows us to develop a more sophisticated understanding of geographical issues. Rather than see the messiness or complexity of geographical knowledge as problems to be hidden from students, the recognition of different positions can be the starting point for our teaching. This is the antithesis of the 'answer culture' with its narrow view of 'the right way, the right perspective'. The challenge for scholarly teachers at all levels is to help students understand that the curriculum taught is just one of countless ways of approaching a particular subject matter. This may seem a long way from current ways of thinking about curriculum in geography, where too often students are introduced to a limited selection of knowledge and skills that are sanctioned by curriculum writers and the interpretations of textbook writers, but the arguments for it rest on the idea of academic rigour. This surely must underpin a worthwhile, valued and ambitious education system.

Put simply, teaching that does not explore alternative ways of approaching issues, is not ironical about its own assumptions, is not reflective and self-critical, will tend to produce lower-level cognitive activity and a limited view of the phenomena under study. Radical and feminist perspectives on curriculum remind us that all curricula come from somewhere. They are marked by particular understandings, philosophical assumptions, interpretations of information and cultural inscriptions. This suggests the need to develop a 'self-conscious' curriculum, one that is aware of the power relations that shape it, and the inclusions and exclusions it contains.

This argument implies a high degree of (but not unbridled or unlimited) relativism and involves the rejection of the idea that there is a structure of knowledge that forms the basis of curriculum selection. Indeed, it suggests that there can be no such thing as the curriculum, since it is always a process in the making. The idea of a 'core' curriculum is rejected, at least at the level of 'content'. This recognises that any attempt to 'fix' the geography curriculum is doomed.

In his book on the philosophy of education, *Leaving Safe Harbors*, Denis Carlson (2002) describes in succinct terms the educational implications of this shift in thinking about knowledge:

> The critical shift here is away from an understanding of knowledge or truth as something that exists prior to and independent of the language that describes and represents it. ... a recognition of the formative or generative role of language in producing the world both symbolically but also materially. All of this is linked to a language of paradigm shifts, transformative thinking, and the importance of learning to 'think' the world differently.
>
> (pp. 179–80)

Carlson argues that educators are beginning to move beyond the idea that education is about the transmission of a corpus of knowledge to receptive students, towards the idea that education is a process by which knowledge or truth is actively constructed, that is, a system that values and nurtures the reasoning process. We argue that geography taught and learned well enables people to think about and respond to the world more intelligently. If successful, this enables individuals to live more satisfying lives, with more choices made on the basis of greater understanding and awareness. In Part II of this book, we consider how such a vision of geography education might be realised.

FOR FURTHER THINKING

1 Which do you value more, geography as 'scientific discovery' or geography as 'personal response'? Remember, both are important and this question is not asking you to choose between them. Can you think of geography lessons (or sequences of lessons) that may combine the approaches?

2 In what ways is 'postmodernism' – as an 'attitude' – a useful frame of reference for school geography teachers?

3 Spend some time with a group of colleagues and draw up a list of *purposes* for studying physical geography.

Part II

The classroom

This part consists of three chapters and the overall purpose is to take our thinking about geography and education, and the curriculum manifestation that we refer to as 'school geography', into the classroom.

We start with 'Curriculum planning – curriculum thinking' (Chapter 5). The word curriculum has several accepted meanings: what we refer to is the geography department's plan for geography. In physical terms, this is usually manifest in the form of a document which will contain some kind of statement of purpose which captures the aspirations of the department, followed by schemes of work for each year group. This provides the week-by-week sequence of content and activity – usually referring to resources, field work, ICT, inclusion agenda (responding to gifted students and those with learning difficulties) and assessment plans. It is a working document – somewhat like a road map. A road map, of course, is only useful if you know where you are going. So long as you know that, a map can provide alternatives and choices on how to get there.

The 'map' analogy, though useful in helping us distinguish 'aims' (where are we going?) from 'objectives' (how are we going to get there?), is not perfect. Perhaps it has too 'linear' a feel for geography, as if learning followed a pre-determined path. Perhaps it also fails to acknowledge the students themselves as agents in their own learning. The chapter, with the help of some examples of teaching about development, limestone landscapes, crime and asylum respectively, sets out to clarify curriculum thinking not as a technical fix therefore, but as a supremely creative, human process. When we talk of 'creativity' in education it is so easy to imagine the charismatic classroom 'performance' and students engaged in wacky activity. The really important creative arena, however, is deciding what to teach, and how to do this.

Chapter 6, 'Teaching and learning geography', takes a closer look at what is increasingly referred to as pedagogy. We take a particular line on this, consistent with how we have discussed geography in education throughout the book. We have emphasised the enormous power of recognising and exploring with pupils the constructed nature of geographical imaginations. Not least, we think this emphasis helps teachers assert convincingly the part geography can play in meeting a range of statutory curriculum aims set out and refined in recent years by the government. For example, one of the official aims of the school curriculum (as a whole) is 'to provide opportunities for all pupils to learn and achieve'. It continues, '(t)he school curriculum should contribute to the development of pupils' sense of identity through knowledge and understanding of the spiritual, moral, social and cultural heritages of Britain's diverse society and of the local, national, European, Commonwealth and global dimensions of their lives' (DfEE/QCA 1999: 11).

We feel that a coherent pedagogical approach that encourages a critical reading of evidence, images and text can contribute significantly to pupils' development in these ways – in the context of an uncertain and changing world. We try to provide such an approach, again using examples from geographical classrooms – with extra weight being placed on language, literacies and the use of various media, and in particular through the lens of contested 'environmental issues'.

The third chapter in this part looks at evaluation. The role of evaluation in curriculum planning and in teaching is now well established. It is essential. In the current climate we acknowledge the overwhelming pressure of assessment in the education world, and accept that this is a component of evaluation. We also acknowledge that assessment is very important – for how can teachers get a feel for how successful their teaching has been, or how successful the students have been in their learning, without coming to some form of judgement, based on evidence (usually the work students do – what they are able to show us)? The field of educational assessment becomes ever more sophisticated, and recent developments in 'assessment for learning' are welcome.

But consistent with the theme for this entire book, we choose to place our emphasis in an area that has been deeply neglected in recent years. It concerns judgement, but not (simply) of what has been learned, or even how to improve individual students' learning in the future. The judgement that matters, we argue, is more to do with whether the subject itself is 'making progress', especially in terms of its capacity to contribute to worthwhile and relevant educational experience. We show that that school teachers are essential agents in making and acting on such judgements (for we cannot rely on some kind of trickle down for the research frontier, even if this were desirable). In this sense, Chapter 7 anticipates a deeper discussion on 'professionalism' that follows in the final part of the book.

Chapter 5

Curriculum planning – curriculum thinking

It should be made clear that curriculum design, the creating of educative environments in which students are to dwell, is inherently a political and moral process. It involves competing ideological, political, and intensely personal conceptions of valuable educational activity. Furthermore, one of its primary components is the fact of influencing other people – namely students. Our commonsense thought in education, however, tends to move in a direction quite opposite from moral and political considerations. Instead, spheres of decision making are perceived as *technical problems* that necessitate instrumental strategies and information produced by technical experts.

(Apple 1990: 111)

This statement is taken from Michael Apple's book *Ideology and Curriculum*. Apple is a North American educationist whose major contribution has been to point out the close links between politics and educational knowledge. Who teaches what, to whom, and in what way is never neutral, but always reflects struggles to control the flow of knowledge. The above quote is an important statement of Apple's argument. He reminds us that curriculum design is an intensely human activity, reflecting the values and interests of curriculum planners. However, Apple warns, there is a tendency to forget this and regard curriculum planning as a technical act – or if you like, a practical problem to be solved.

In this chapter we want to illustrate how curriculum design in geography 'involves competing ideological, political, and intensely personal conceptions of valuable educational activity' (p. 111). Our argument is informed by debates about geographical knowledge discussed in the previous section. In what follows we first describe the standard model of curriculum planning that beginning geography teachers are often encouraged to use. We make some criticisms of this model based on arguments about the nature of geographical knowledge. The main body of the chapter uses examples in order to demonstrate the importance of teachers' choices in constructing the curriculum.

RE-THINKING THE CURRICULUM PROBLEM

Most books on geography teaching contain sections on curriculum planning in geography. Since the mid-1970s there has been an established model of curriculum planning in geography, based on Norman Graves' (1975) discussion of the curriculum problem: 'What is the nature of the curriculum problem? It is essentially that of deciding what shall be taught in a school, in what framework, with what methods and how evaluation of the learning may take place' (p. 106).

According to this model, planning consists of three stages:

1 Define objectives.
2 Create the necessary learning situations.
3 Evaluate the achievements of the objectives.

Although this appears to be a linear process, in reality it is not so clear cut and there is an ongoing process of planning, action and reflection. This type of 'rational' curriculum planning is well suited to the epistemological assumptions of empirical and positivist science (indeed, it is no coincidence that rational curriculum planning and the 'new' geography based on positivism and behaviourism found favour at the same time). In other words, it accords with a view of geographical knowledge that asserts that there is an objective world to which we can gain access. It is also suited to the idea that we can search for generalities and key ideas, discover simple orderly causal processes, and represent 'reality' in unproblematic ways. With this view of an easily accessed and stable body of geographical content, planning becomes an essentially technical exercise: a matter of the teacher making selections, finding ways to transfer those selections to the minds of students, and evaluating the outcomes of these educational transactions (for instance, objective testing).

It is useful to consider the view of geographical knowledge that is associated with this approach to curriculum planning. Rational curriculum planning is closely linked to the ideas of educational philosophers such as Paul Hirst (1974). They argued that human beings have slowly differentiated out various types of knowledge. There are forms of knowledge, fields of knowledge and practical theories. The forms of knowledge refer to seven kinds of conceptual structure: mathematics, the natural sciences, the human sciences, moral knowledge, religious knowledge, philosophical knowledge and aesthetics. Peters and Hirst argue that everything we know is within these domains. There is no knowledge outside of them. Fields of knowledge refer to domains where several forms of knowledge constitute a subject, for example, geography.

The liberal view of education insists that all children be introduced to the forms of knowledge. Rational curriculum planners in geography were happy to accept the status of geography as a field of knowledge. In doing so, they accepted the idea that knowledge is best seen as emerging from the natural development of human societies. They rejected the arguments of sociologists of education that knowledge is socially constructed and that what counted as official school knowledge is a reflection of the interests of powerful groups in society. For example, Graves (1975) noted that the new sociologists of education offered an 'illuminating' account of the relationship between the curriculum and powerful interests but rejected it 'because it does not answer the normative question as to the criteria which ought to be used to plan curriculum' (p. 71). Graves' solution was to assume that geographical knowledge (as defined by geographers) was neutral, and that teachers simply needed to make a choice about what to include. It is this pragmatic approach to curriculum planning that this chapter seeks to question. We argue that the processes of selection are crucial.

The influence of this argument about the structure of knowledge is still profoundly felt in education. The power of this idea is that, because it regards the structure of knowledge as 'logical' or rational, it is able to claim that it is above questions of politics or mere human interest. There is, in this account, something rather timeless and fundamental about the logic of the curriculum.

This is the basis from which most discussions of curriculum planning in geography begin. The knowledge to be taught in geography is derived from the structure of knowledge. Students of geography are assumed to have mastered the content of this curriculum and, by the time they become teachers, are assumed to have 'secure' subject knowledge (note that this is assumed in the Standards for Qualified Teacher Status). The task of curriculum planning is to convert this 'pure' formal knowledge into meaningful form for pupils. However, rarely can subject knowledge be assumed as fixed and unchanging. As the first part of this book argued, explanation in geography is dynamic. In terms of curriculum planning, this suggests that the geography teacher is faced with the task of representing a highly unstable world to pupils. It follows that the first step in planning any geographical learning is to examine carefully the nature of the knowledge that is to be the focus of teaching. This may sound obvious, but sometimes, in the rush to plan lessons, it gets overlooked. In this chapter, our approach is to discuss examples of curriculum planning in order to demonstrate the type of *curriculum discourses* we think can lead to a more satisfactory sense of curriculum planning.

WHAT IS DEVELOPMENT?

In the previous section we suggested that often too little attention is paid to the nature of the geographical knowledge that is to be presented to students in lessons. It is not difficult to see why this happens; schools are busy places, teachers are busy people, and often textbooks and other commercially produced material offer 'ready-made' interpretations of the content of the curriculum. We would argue that if such 'stop-gap' approaches persist over a long period of time, teachers risk losing the very basis of their professionalism. In this section, we want to provide a discussion of curriculum planning through the use of the example of 'development', on the grounds that the topic is part of the 'core' of the school geography curriculum.

It is not immediately apparent what a series of geography lessons about 'development' would look like, and a geography teacher charged with constructing a unit of work on 'development' would need to answer for him- or herself the question of what development means. *A Modern Dictionary of Geography* (Witherick *et al.* 2001: 72) defines development as:

In human geography this refers to the state of a particular society and the processes of change experienced within it. Development is generally regarded as involving some sort of progress in four main directions: economic growth; advances in the use of technology; improved welfare; modernization. These dimensions are widely used for distinguishing between the First World and the Third World and between MEDCs and LEDCs.[3] The meaning of Development shifted considerably during the second half of the 20th century. Originally it meant economic development or economic growth. Nowadays the view of development is altogether broader, involving the whole of society and embracing cultural and social as well as economic and technological.

The dictionary offers a view of development that refers to an amalgam of characteristics that are found in particular societies. These are commonly measured by a series of development indicators. Usually, monetary measures of development based solely on economic indicators are balanced with social indicators to produce a Human Development Index. As the definition suggests, the meaning of development is not fixed, but is subject to reinterpretation.

An obvious problem with using development indicators as a way into the topic is that it tends to gloss over and simplify the reality of people's lives. It offers an 'average' statistic. Students come to geography lessons with their own 'mental maps' of people and places, and these would form the basis for starting any teaching about development. Most geography teachers would be unhappy to leave students' commonsense understandings about 'development' (their misconceptions, if you like) unchanged, and would seek to link these 'personal geographies' to the frameworks provided by geography as a discipline. At this stage, an obvious source of information is the representation of the topic offered by textbooks. Although it is risky to generalise about what is quite a large body of texts, we think that they do display a number of common features.

School geography textbooks tend to rely on *modernisation* models or theories of development. Examples of these include the models of Rostow, Myrdal and Freidmann (Rostow was discussed in Box 4.1, pp. 45–6). They share in common a:

strong belief in the power of interventionist economics and the superiority of the current Western model of economic (and by implication cultural) development, as a linear process directed towards the same

3 The terms 'More Economically Developed Countries' and 'Less Economically Developed Countries' are those currently favoured by exam boards in geography – this means that question papers and textbooks adopt the terms and students are encouraged to use them in their written work. This is an interesting example of part of the argument we make in this book, which is about the need to encourage students to take a critical stance to geographical knowledge: Who invented these terms? Why? Whose interests do they serve?

kind of economic, social and political structures which characterized Western Europe and North America.

(Dickenson *et al.* 1983: 15)

There is a danger that unless students are provided with opportunities to examine the assumptions that lie behind these texts, they may come away with a simplistic and Eurocentric view of development. The criticisms of these models and approaches are stated briefly here. During the 1960s and 1970s the *dependency* school developed, which has been characterised as 'the Third World answering back'. An example is Andre Gunder Frank's (1967) idea of 'the development of underdevelopment'. Frank argued that development and underdevelopment are opposite sides of the same coin, and that both are the necessary outcome and manifestation of the contradictions of the capitalist system of development. The condition of developing countries is not the outcome of inertia, misfortune, chance, climate change, and so on, but a reflection of how they are incorporated into the global capitalist system. Dependency theorists argue that the dominant capitalist powers encouraged the transformation of political and economic structures in order to serve their interests. Colonial territories were organised to produce primary products at minimal cost, simultaneously becoming a market for industrial products. Surplus value was siphoned off from poor to rich regions, and from the developing world to the developed world.

Important questions are raised by the realisation that geography textbooks tend to offer teachers and students partial accounts of development. For instance, how do certain representations come to be accepted as the norm? What prevents the discussion of other, more critical viewpoints? Whose interests are served by such representations? Clearly, how a geography teacher answers the question 'What is development?' will have important implications for how they re-present the topic to their students. For example, a teacher using the perspectives of modernisation theory would tend to operate with the view that underdevelopment is a temporary phenomenon. Given the right conditions, such as a stable political system and a government that seeks to develop the shift from primary to secondary industry, and support from the international community, countries are able to undergo development (exam-ples might be selected to illustrate this process). Alternatively, a radical development perspective would be doubtful of this, and an educational experience would suggest to pupils that capitalism cannot or will not promote the development of the Third World; that capitalism alone is ultimately responsible for the world's demographic and environmental ills; that capitalism is incapable of promoting the independent industrialisation of the South; and that the fundamental cleavage shaping the capitalist world system lies between North and South. The point is that it is the decisions made by the teacher, based on his or her own interpretation of the subject, which will influence or frame the perspectives that come through in the classroom.

(Corbridge 1986: 3)

However, as any teacher knows, successful teaching does not depend only on a clear understanding of the subject, but on decisions about how to re-present that knowledge to pupils. This is a precarious task. Teaching geography in the 1990s, one of us (Morgan) remembers teaching lessons about development that drew upon neo-Marxist interpretations of the global capitalist system. I considered that most of the perspectives found in school geography texts adopted neo-Malthusian arguments about the 'limits to growth' and followed 'developmentalist' views. I sought to counter these perspectives with lessons that outlined ideas from political economy. Pupils were always interested in the question of why 'we' are rich and 'they' are so poor, and I used 'Red Nose Day' as an opportunity to raise questions about the efficacy of overseas aid and signal a neo-Marxist perspective on these issues. Although many pupils recognised the logic of these arguments, it troubled me that many pupils, who were genuinely concerned to 'do something' and 'make a difference', found these interpretations quite demoralising and depressing. Indeed, Corbridge (1986) talked about the 'impasse of radical development geography' and criticised it on a number of grounds:

- Radical development geography tends to see things in 'black and white': capitalism either promotes development by definition or it promotes underdevelopment by definition. There is little space for a middle ground.
- Although it rejects the idea of environmental determinism, radical development geography tends to suggest that what happens in a place is the outcome of its location within the structures of a powerful global system.

79

- The world tends to be divided up into distinct blocks, whether by 'North' and 'South', or 'core' and 'periphery'. Again, there is little recognition of the diversity of places.
- Radical development geography has been characterised by an arrogance and contempt for other theories about development. It tends simply to replace one perspective on the world with another.

Looking back to my teaching about development I can recognise aspects of these problems and in response to pupils' reactions to the lessons, tried to incorporate examples that made much of local or 'bottom-up' initiatives drawn from the work of non-governmental organisations. In teaching these lessons, I always felt slightly uneasy, since I felt the focus on small-scale initiatives risked giving the impression that such projects can serve to alleviate the problems that are produced by a global capitalist system. This draws attention to the *choices* that geography teachers have to make about how to represent geographical knowledge. Perhaps the fundamental issue that I faced in planning geographical lessons was that of balancing my own tendencies towards economic determinism and how this risked offering a pessimistic message to the pupils I taught. In such teaching there was a tendency to view people's lives as secondary to the structural forces of the capitalist economy. As an aside, it should be added that geography teachers need to be able to justify and, if necessary, defend the perspectives they present in lessons, not least in the face of those who argue that there is such a thing as 'factual', uncontentious knowledge. It is our belief that having a strong understanding of the way geography as a discipline constructs knowledge is the best way to answer these questions.

What we are describing here is the process whereby teachers decide upon conceptions of 'valuable educational activity'. These issues are not easily resolved. However, the point we are making is that they are a crucial part of the process of curriculum planning that is informed by a scholarly understanding of the subject. What is more, such curriculum planning is always subject to change as the world changes and academic interpretations of the world change. For example, any teaching about development in the present moment would need to be informed by an awareness of debates about post-development. In the *Dictionary of Development*, Sachs (1992) argues for the idea of post-development on the grounds that development involves a new form of colonisation that seeks to bring about a total Westernisation of society. According to this view, development replaces an open-ended historical perspective with the idea of a necessary and inevitable destiny. With a sweep of the hand, development defines: 'the unquestionable inferiority of two-thirds of the world's people, and also defines their only rational societal goal to be a project of catching up with the industrialised societies of the west' (Porter and Sheppard 1998: 111).

Readers might want to re-read the original definition of 'development' in the light of this comment and think about the extent to which it differs from Sach's analysis. In terms of a teacher planning a series of lessons under the heading 'what is development?' these arguments about post-development are quite profound. They demand to be taken seriously, since they suggest that development thinking is destined to leave the pupils sitting in geography lessons with the impression that 'we' are developed and 'they' are not developed. Thus the very language of development serves to situate us within discourses of 'them' and 'us', which are very difficult to shift. This example illustrates what Apple means when he talks of curriculum planning as a moral, ethical and political act. In a Positivist view, teaching about development is a matter of defining development, deciding upon ways to identify it and measure it, then mapping and offering some explanations for its distribution. The outcome is a view of development that takes away the complexity of the experience. More humanist approaches are likely to stress the values and meanings attached to the phenomena. Teachers who adopt the humanistic approach are, of course, making an ethical choice they are deciding to stress that people matter more than statistics – that there is a story behind the figures! What may be less obvious is that to focus on descriptions at the expense of offering explanations is also to make a political choice.

So where does this discussion get us? How should geography teachers plan their lessons based on 'what is development?' Our argument is that, just as geography teachers have rejected texts that relied on environmental determinism to explain differences between countries, they also need to examine the models that replaced them for their underlying assumptions. To put this in the terms we used at the end of the previous chapter: *curriculum needs to be seen as a representational text*. For the geography teacher this would involve asking questions such as the following:

- How are different groups represented in this text?
- What messages about development are offered?
- At what geographical scale are phenomena to be studied? How do local case studies link to ideas about the global scale?

- Does the curriculum allow the voices of people themselves to be heard?
- What theories are used to explain development? Who produced these theories and under what conditions?
- Are there alternative ways of representing this topic?
- What is the relationship between the curriculum as text and actions in the world? Does the curriculum create space for agency and transformation? Or does it offer the message that there is little people can do to change their situation?

We submit that geography teachers who have gone through the process of engaging with questions such as these are more likely to be able to plan learning experiences based on a rigorous and scholarly approach to the topic. They will be skilled at understanding the politics of knowledge production and, rather than accept the representations offered by textbooks at face value, see themselves as engaged in the act of knowledge production. They are less likely to teach lessons that leave students with the impression that there is a single, simple answer to the question 'what is development?'. In addition, such teachers are also likely to be aware of the relationship between the curriculum texts they produce and their readers (i.e. the pupils). This is something we discuss in the next part of this chapter.

TEACHING LIMESTONE LANDSCAPES

In this section we change focus, and discuss a curriculum unit produced by a beginning teacher on limestone landscapes. Mark produced the unit for a year 8 class with the title: 'Why do limestone landscapes need to be protected?'

This unit reflected Mark's own interests in earth science. It had clear links with the National Curriculum (geomorphological processes and their effects on landscapes and people and how conflicting demands on an environment arise and how and why attempts are made to manage environments). The unit would allow pupils to practise geographical enquiry and skills.

In explaining the thinking behind his unit, Mark wrote: 'The unit was designed to follow a broadly thematic line (limestone landscapes) with an issues element (exploitation and management) added to bring some relevance and consideration of values to what may otherwise seem a dry, detached topic.'

Using an enquiry framework, Mark devised a sequence of lessons:

1 Why do limestone landscapes need to be protected?
2 How can we describe the relief of England and Wales?
3 What are the upland areas of England and Wales made of?
4 What is massive limestone?
5 What is special about limestone landscapes?
6 What is distinctive about Cheddar Gorge and Wookey Hole?
7 How are limestone landscapes being changed/damaged?
8 What can be done to manage/protect these landscapes?

There is much more about Mark's unit than can be discussed here. An important focus in his unit was engaging pupils in their work and developing their literacy skills.

Mark used pictures of limestone landscapes taken from the internet and asked pupils to guess the link between them. He then asked them how they thought these landscapes were formed and introduced the terms weathering and erosion. He drew diagrams to explain three different types of weathering.

The next lesson focused on the relief of England and Wales. Key words (relief, uplands, lowlands) were introduced and pupils used atlases and a sheet Mark had prepared to produce a simplified relief map of England and Wales. They then used their maps to answer a true or false exercise about relief, and finally produce written paragraphs to describe the relief.

In the next lesson pupils used atlases to identify and label seven named upland areas on a map of Britain. Having done this, the three main types of rock were revised and Mark provided a simplified account of geological time. They then used a geological column to identify the rocks that make up each of the seven upland areas:

To conclude . . . the pupils were asked to compare the ages and types of rocks in the upland areas with those in the lowland areas. Some made the link between old, hard rocks forming the upland and suggested this could be because they were more difficult to wear down than the younger, softer ones in the lowlands.

The following lesson focused on the formation of limestone and Mark told the story of how Britain was once located near the Equator and covered in a shallow tropical sea. Pupils used the textbook and looked

83

at a specimen of limestone to answer questions about the formation of limestone. A few of the pupils were able to see the effect of acid on a sample of limestone.

Pupils worked in pairs to prepare a presentation on a limestone feature (e.g. dry valley). They used textbooks and previous knowledge to label the feature on a diagram, describe it using technical vocabulary and explain how it was formed and why it is unique to limestone: 'It was pleasing to see that . . . the presenters could recall and correctly use the new, unfamiliar words that they had been explaining, such as stalactites and stalagmites, demonstrating the effectiveness of active learning.'

In the following lesson pupils used tourist leaflets of Cheddar Gorge and Wookey Hole. The class discussed the possible formation of these features. Mark told them that although the images were good they contained no explanations of how the features were formed. Their task was to 'produce an informative leaflet telling people what the features were called and how they were formed'. They selected information from textbooks, their notes and internet sites to produce the leaflets.

Mark produced a high quality series of lessons. His evaluation of the unit focused on the way the lessons went, whether pupils enjoyed the work, how he felt they worked, and the conceptual difficulties they encountered. Mark also noted that it would have been useful to have gone to visit some limestone landscapes as this would have increased the sense of 'awe and wonder'. Videos were in short supply. Mark also noted that it was difficult to ensure the narrative thread through the enquiry questions. Indeed, you may be able to think of an alternative sequence.

In the light of our discussions in the previous chapters, we want now to offer some comments on the type of geography taught in Mark's unit. The question posed by David Pepper – 'Why teach physical geography?' – is especially pertinent here. Indeed, this was a question that was directly posed to Mark during a PGCE session and he went away and devised the unit with this in (the back of his) mind. As a reminder, Pepper stated: 'We need to think more carefully about the reasons for teaching physical geography. There is little point, or interest, in teaching physical geography outside its social context' (1985: 69).

Mark's unit very much falls within the traditional division between physical and human geography. Perhaps reflecting his subject expertise, the emphasis in the unit is on the physical geography of limestone landscapes, and the human geography comes later, almost as an afterthought.

This is not a criticism of Mark's planning, since it is part of the way the discipline has been structured: 'The assumption that everything we encounter in the world already belongs either to "culture" or to "nature" has become entrenched in the division between "human" and "physical" geography' (Whatmore 1999: 4).

In fact Mark does seek to link the two together, by asking whether and how limestone landscapes should be protected. This seems to offer an answer to Pepper's question. Implicit in the question is a statement of value; it is taken for granted that limestone landscapes are valuable and thus worthy of protection. This seems to have come through in Mark's teaching of the unit, and is evident in the work pupils produced about Cheddar Gorge and Wookey Hole, although it might be that there was an opportunity for a more detailed discussion of values (of which more in a moment).

One direction Mark could take the unit in future would be to explore how pupils make meaning out of this landscape. In line with our discussion in Chapter 4 about social nature, limestone landscapes are not objective categories that exist outside human systems of meaning. For example, the very fact that curriculum designers and textbook writers include them as part of school geography is a statement about their worth (less emphasis seems to be placed on granite landscapes; see Box 5.1).

In addition, 'landscape' as a concept is a human construction. One way to explore this is to follow the advice of the American geographer D. W. Meinig (1979: 34):

Take a small but varied company to any convenient viewing place overlooking some portion of city and countryside and have each, in turn, describe the 'landscape' to detail what it is composed of and say something about the 'meaning' of what can be seen. It will soon become apparent that even though we gather together and look in the same direction at the same instant, we will not – we cannot – see the same landscape. We may certainly agree that we will see many of the same elements – houses, roads, trees, hills – in terms of such denotations as number, form, dimension, and colour, but such facts take on meaning only through association; they must be fitted together according to some coherent body of ideas. Thus we confront the central problem: any landscape is composed not only of what lies before our eyes but what lies within our heads.

85

BOX 5.1 THE ROAD TO MALHAM TARN . . .

The seven pages on the study of limestone pavements are an impressive indication of the continuing dedication of geographers to fieldwork. Nevertheless, the article leaves one question unanswered: why study limestone pavements in such detail?

The words used in the analysis – 'massive, flaggy, lumpy' – seem to characterise the whole topic.

Meanwhile, cities are exploding; over 3,000,000 people are unemployed in the UK; wars are fought in the Falklands and the Middle East; people are undernourished in Poland, and the pros and cons of nuclear power become an increasingly urgent issue. All these topics are of burning interest to geographers, to pupils and to the general public. By contrast, limestone pavements occupy far less than 1 per cent of the land area of the UK. Most pupils will never see one. No one lives there. Nothing much happens at limestone pavements except slow solution . . . Limestone pavements probably deserve one lesson, and if you live at Skipton they deserve a visit. But for the rest of us the road to Malham Tarn really is a dead end. By all means let's study pavements, but urban pavements are much more important.

(David Wright, letter to *Teaching Geography* 1983)

Those 'ideas in our heads' are ideologies, and represent very different readings of a landscape. Meinig suggested at least ten (landscape as nature, habitat, artefact, system, problem, wealth, ideology, history, place and aesthetic). Meinig's ten 'ways of seeing' could provide a useful way for Mark's pupils to analyse the question 'why should limestone landscapes be protected?'.

Mark's unit raises another important question in curriculum planning; the extent to which pupils are to be involved. He commented that pupils would see this as a 'dry' topic. Armstrong (1973: 51) refers to a form of authoritarianism hidden in the way we as teachers talk to our pupils, question or praise them. He extends this to curriculum planning:

A theme is chosen, strategies worked out to relate to the pupils' experience and interests, materials prepared, resources mobilized . . . Ironically, by the time the programme is ready to be presented to the pupils for whom it was intended, our own enthusiasm as teachers is often half-spent, or has become so self-absorbing that we cannot appreciate that it will not be shared by anyone else.[4]

Armstrong's warning is timely, not least because it suggests that if we are to take Apple's call seriously, we need to consider the possibility that pupils need to be involved in the planning of curriculum.

CONSTRUCTING CRIME

Our third example focuses on one of the Qualifications and Curriculum Authority's (QCA) published exemplar schemes of work for the geography National Curriculum. It is a good example of Gilbert's (1984) argument that in the selection of 'problems' to be studied in the curriculum, planners generally select frameworks that do not allow pupils to gain a deep understanding of the structures that shape society. This unit of study is entitled 'crime and the local community'. It is expected that in studying the unit, most pupils will:

- understand that there are different categories of crime, that not all crimes are recorded and why committing criminal offences is wrong;
- describe and begin to explain locational patterns of crime in the local area and beyond;
- suggest how to modify environments and make them safer;
- select and use skills and sources of evidence in their investigation of crime;
- suggest plausible conclusions and present their findings.

The 'route for enquiry' for the unit is as follows:

What do we know about crime? Is all crime recorded?
What do we feel about the different types of crime? Is there a fear of crime?
Are there areas of the locality where we can expect more or less crime?
Is it possible to map certain crimes in our locality?

4 Thanks to Jessica Pykett for alerting us to this reference.

Would a better understanding of the geography of crime help people
reduce its occurrence?

Are there patterns of crime nationwide? Is there a difference between
urban and rural crime?

Can international comparisons of crime be made?

The unit is seen as offering a modern and relevant geographical experience. It has clear links with the National Curriculum requirements for
citizenship. The unit is clearly located in the tradition of the 'welfare
approach' to geography and focuses on important questions about quality
of life and who gets what, where and how? As a piece of curriculum
planning, it clearly involves decisions about 'competing ideological, political and intensely personal conceptions of valuable educational activity'.
The decision to include crime within a geography curriculum says something about what a teacher or geography department considers valuable.
However, in our analysis we want to suggest that there are serious limitations to this approach to curriculum planning, precisely because it risks
moving too quickly from the ideological, moral and political elements of
curriculum design to the technical and instrumental elements. In other
words, the question of *why* teach is too quickly answered in the rush to
decide *how* to teach. This can result, we argue, in geographical experiences that are not rooted in a clear understanding of the educational
potential of geography as a subject.

In order to develop this argument, we need to consider how geographers have conceptualised and studied 'the geography of crime'. The
development of a field of study devoted to the geography of crime dates
from the early 1970s, as part of the study of social geography. At the
time, geographers were concerned to stress the 'relevance' of the subject.
In line with the major philosophical orientations of the time, they used
insights from positivism and behaviourism to study the problem of crime.
An accessible introduction to the geographical study of crime is found
in David Herbert's *The Geography of Urban Crime* (1982). Herbert notes
two main approaches to the geography of crime.

The first approach is that of *areal studies*. Areal studies are concerned
with the distribution of offences and offenders. These were most associated with the work of criminologists Shaw and McKay (1942) who
developed hypotheses about the distribution of crimes. They involved
mapping crime statistics and generalising about the observed patterns.
Ecological studies were concerned with the relationships between crime

rates and environmental measures. This involved statistical analysis to identify the factors that explained patterns, such as substandard housing, poverty, foreign-born population and levels of mobility.

While the mapping of crime patterns offered a way for geographers to approach crime, other geographers looked at the nature of the vulnerable environments themselves. That is, the context in which the offences occur. Herbert summarised these as primarily physical – the qualities of design, layout and accessibility of buildings – but might also include the ways in which local space is controlled and observed. For example, in his work on the environment as a conditioner of offence behaviour, Newman (1972) suggested that areas will be well defended if they are visible to possible witnesses, if a community spirit is developed in which neighbours are encouraged to guard neutral territory, if design is such that there is a constant stream of potential witnesses and if private property is clearly demarcated, physically or symbolically.

From his review of the literature on the geography of offences, Herbert identified a number of questions worthy of study:

1 Can urban environments of particular vulnerability be identified and classified?
2 What key elements contribute to the vulnerability of urban environments to different types of offences?
3 What is the balance of physical and social factors in endowing space with levels of vulnerability and how are these related?
4 Can the qualities of these areas be characterised in more subjective terms, both by their occupants and by offenders?

Herbert identifies the need to go beyond areal and ecological studies of the patterns of offender residence in order to ask why these concentrations or 'problem areas' occur. This work reflected dominant paradigms in geography. However, Herbert was aware of the neglect of other levels of analysis. Thus he recognised work on the political economy approach but notes that this 'has produced little research which could be labelled "geographical"'. This is also true of studies of resource allocation and provision, which are concerned with 'the ways in which the economy or social formation begins the process of allocating power and resources'. For example, in this approach questions might be asked about how the police deploy their resources, making decisions about what areas to concentrate resources on, what crimes they seek to pursue, and how their actions have a real tangible impact on communities. In turn, an answer to these types of questions would require an understanding of the role of the police in society, whose interests they represent and so on. While it may have been the case in 1982 that there were few accessible accounts of crime from a political economy perspective, this is less so now (see, for example, Pain 2001). From Herbert's discussion, we can see that the curriculum writers have chosen to focus on particular ways of studying crime. There are a number of points to make.

First, the geography found in the unit is set within a positivist and behavioural framework. The questions and activities it offers involve pupils in much mapping and charting of distributions. There is also a focus on ideas of perception (what are these places like?) as well as an invitation to express how they feel about different types of crime. Having collected and described data on crime in their locality, pupils are to learn 'that certain crimes could be reduced by improvements in the design of buildings and street layout'. The examples offered in the text include CCTV in town centres, redesign of streets and buildings, lighting and changing vegetation types. These ideas are linked to the notion of environmental determinism and set crime within a paradigm of management and control. The list of words that pupils are likely to learn and use in the course of the unit is revealing of the emphasis of the approach. The list suggests that crime is seen as a personal issue, subject to management and control:

crime	police	design and the built environment
vandalism	detection	prevention
fear of crime	target hardening	gated communities
defensible space	victim	offender
neighbourhood watch	CCTV	graffiti
decision making		values and attitudes

Second, and related to the above, is the decision of the curriculum designers to focus on crime as a 'local' problem. In addition, the local is conceptualised as the 'built environment'. This means that the focus is most likely to be on what can be observed and measured. Of course, the local only occurs within relationships with other scales, such as that of the home or of the nation. Local policies to reduce crime are linked to national agendas and strategies. By asking questions about the relationship between scales, different issues arise. The focus on the local scale tends to preclude the broader picture. For instance, what factors lead to the rise of local 'neighbourhood watch' schemes and to what broader forces or trends in society are they related? The QCA unit of work fails to question the social structure in which crime occurs. As such it is susceptible to the criticism made by Peet (1975) who argued that geographers have focused on particular kinds of criminality – namely a form of 'lower-class' crime – which is a surface outcome of more deep-rooted social ills:

> Crime is a surface expression of discontents which lie deeply embedded in the social system. Like any surface manifestation, crime can provide clues to the particular forces which cause it; these, in turn, may be traced to deeper contradictions which churn in the guts of the social and economic system . . . A study which starts, continues and ends at the surface cannot possibly deal with cause.
>
> (p. 277)

In other words, in accepting the official definitions of crime, and treating it as a social evil, crime geographers are effectively supporting the status quo and the elite interests whom it favours. In *The Geography of Urban Crime* (1982), Herbert argued the need for a broader analysis of the problem:

> To the extent that crime rates are related to macro trends and forces in society, such as urbanization, industrialization, the ebbs and flows of economic fortunes and the whole question of equitable distributions of resources, any specific policies related to crime control are likely to have a limited impact.
>
> (p. 105)

The QCA unit 'Crime and the local community' provides a stark example of why a scholarly approach to planning learning is necessary. The unit provides a ready-made answer to the question of what and how to teach about crime. It can be used by geography teachers to construct lessons but does not require them to think about what lessons to construct. It does not offer a rationale for curriculum selection. Without an explicit understanding that geographical knowledge is a social construction, teachers are not in a position to assess and evaluate the geography they are asked to teach, and they are unlikely to find ways to alert students to other ways of making sense of the topic, other ways of viewing the world. The first act of any planning exercise must be problem-posing. In this context, we might consider questions such as the following: What types of crime are to be included? Where is the focus of the study to be? If we focus on the local community, does this lead to a neglect of the national scale? How do we see crime, as an individual issue or as a social problem? How a teacher answers these questions will have a profound bearing on the educational process.

THE RIGHT TO ASYLUM?

Our final example is this chapter was produced by Megs, who was a student teacher on a PGCE course, and is a curriculum unit she produced on asylum seekers for a year 9 class. Megs was asked to plan and teach a new unit of work combining citizenship and geography. She broke the scheme into three parts – a global issue (global warming), a national issue (asylum seekers), and local issue (proposed plan for a new airport).

Megs explained the choice of asylum seekers for the national example:

> Firstly, the issues are very current, and much publicised, likely to become an even greater issue with the aftermath of the war in Iraq. Secondly, the vast majority of year 9 pupils are *Daily Mail* readers, a newspaper that writes extensively about asylum seekers from one viewpoint. Furthermore, it is an issue directly relevant to these pupils, as some refugees have recently joined [the] school.
>
> (Personal communication)

Megs' unit took the form of a structured enquiry that moves from questions of what and where, through explanation and analysis, and eventually to questions of pupils' own opinions and values. In planning the unit, Megs was aware of the need for continuity. The topic linked in with previous work on population distribution and change, and she was able to consolidate earlier learning and provide a 'real world' case study. Megs was also supported in her planning by the fact that the National Curriculum seeks to promote pupils' 'social and cultural development through geography', and political and social issues. Megs was aware that 'pupils were likely to have strong views on the issue and the opinion of many would-be "anti-asylum seekers"'. Her approach was to 'deal with these different viewpoints and misconceptions first, before looking at the facts about asylum seekers': 'I also felt, rightly or wrongly, to put a slight emphasis on the viewpoints that they hadn't been exposed to regarding asylum seekers'.

Another practical issue that Megs faced in planning the unit was that in order to 'teach a balanced view', she had to get hold of and design lots of different resources.

All through this chapter we have been focusing on Apple's statement about curriculum design being a political and moral process, and arguing against the tendency to reduce curriculum planning to a technical problem to be solved. Megs' curriculum unit is a fascinating document. In her PGCE year, she has attempted a brave and challenging piece of planning and teaching. The starting point for her planning has been her personal conception of valuable educational activity. Given some space and encouragement to experiment, Megs chose to engage with a theme that had the potential to cause her some problems as a teacher. Megs received a broad geographical education at university, and was by no means a specialist in this topic. Planning and teaching the unit involved her developing her knowledge of these issues and learning about the topic so that she was able to develop pupils' knowledge and understanding. Megs' example displays other aspects of curriculum planning in Apple's sense. Her unit was designed with the purpose of 'influencing other people – namely students'. This at first may appear unremarkable, but often there is a great pressure on teachers to stick to the 'facts' and remain neutral (it's worth noting that there is also a tendency for many teachers to 'self-censor' their teaching). Megs does not discuss this in her account of the unit, but we suspect she needed to think carefully about her own views and values before and during the teaching of the unit. In the end, Megs decided upon the need to provide a 'balanced view' and offered pupils a range of viewpoints. This is a good example of Megs' developing awareness of curriculum design as a moral process.

There are a number of issues raised by Megs' curriculum design. Again, we should make it clear that these are not criticisms of Megs' planning and teaching. Rather, we see them as examples of the types of curriculum discourse that we are proposing in this book. Indeed, the following comments are examples of the types of discussion we might have with Megs. The first relates to the concepts of refugees and asylum seekers. Megs' unit does start with a definition of these concepts, and thus enables pupils to have some conceptual clarity. However, concepts such as these have quite complex histories, and one of the results of this is that there are fine-grained distinctions between people who are 'travellers', 'migrants', 'asylum seekers' and 'refugees'.

Part of the issue is the problems of categorisation, so that being an 'economic migrant' from certain countries means that access to Britain is denied. Megs' unit does hint at the fact that this is a problem with 'global dimensions', but it might be suggested that her unit focuses on a particular aspect of a much wider issue relating to questions of movement across national state boundaries. Again, this may seem to be over-critical of Megs' unit, but it is part of an important point about how concepts get defined and how they are represented in the school curriculum. It might be argued that Megs' unit focuses on the movements and decisions made by individuals and downplays the broader causes (often linked to wider questions of politics and power) that give rise to the problem.

These debates about the construction of knowledge about refugees and asylum seekers may seem pedantic. However, they have a clear link to the pedagogical implications of teaching about this topic.

> Values are socially specific; they derive from the concepts that we use to legitimate society. To take values seriously implies far more than the liberal manoeuvre of presenting different points of view about the same set of circumstances (e.g. is nuclear power good or bad?) or even of evaluating between alternative sets of circumstances, e.g. is this distributive outcome better or worse than that one? Rather, the issue is to relate these assessments, perfectly valid in their own right, to the wider social framework and discourses which set the parameters (e.g. profitability, human needs, ecological sustainability) within which measures of worth are defined.
>
> (Lee 2000: 886)

In terms of Megs' unit, the activity in which pupils are asked to make a judgement about whether or not individual cases should be granted asylum might be seen as an example of how geography lessons sometimes focus on values and opinions without relating them to wider social frameworks and discourses. For instance, it is assumed that existing legal frameworks for citizenship are immutable and fixed, and that the law exists as a neutral framework for making decisions. In terms of developing her unit, Megs might be encouraged to develop her understanding of some of the debates among political geographers about what citizenship means within the context of a increasingly globalised economy. Developing a deeper understanding of these trends and detailed comparative examples would, we suggest, increase her ability to teach this unit and handle some of the complex pedagogical issues that such a controversial topic throws up.

CONCLUSIONS

This chapter has tried to make one simple point: the starting point for curriculum design in geography should be a rigorous and defensible version of the subject matter to be taught in the light of teachers' knowledge and understanding of the pupils they teach. This may seem obvious, but the examples we have provided show the complexities involved in arriving at rigorous and defensible decisions about what and how to teach. In conclusion, we want to offer some thoughts about the limits and possibilities of developing the type of curriculum thinking highlighted in this chapter.

We start with the QCA's schemes of work. In many ways they are models of curriculum planning, reflecting many of the insights about teaching and learning in geography. They are not compulsory, they offer a fresh (even modern) perspective on geography, and, importantly, they can be made to 'work' in the classroom. However, as our discussion on the unit on 'crime' (and by implication on 'development') suggested, they fail if they are judged on the criteria that they offer a rigorous and defensible account of their educational purposes. It is perhaps indicative of the way the work of teachers is presently conceptualised that these educational materials do not come with any discussion of the geographical thinking that lies behind the units of work (Moore 2004 discusses how the 'good teacher' is imagined in educational debates). Imagine what a different message might have been offered had the unit on crime been prefaced with a short discussion of the ways in which geographers have studied crime, and an explanation and justification of the decisions to focus on positivist approaches to the subject. The same might be true of the QCA unit on 'development', where a frank and honest discussion of the moral and practical issues about teaching development might provide geography teachers with a variety of conceptual frameworks to plan their own lessons. The conclusion to be drawn is that teachers are not to be bothered with intellectual arguments, and are not to be seen as part of a scholarly community involved in constructing geographical knowledge and making interpretative decisions about the purposes of teaching in a democratic society.

We may be speaking too plainly here, but this is because it is our passionate belief that geography teachers should be encouraged to make connections between subject matter and teaching methods. As Kincheloe and Steinberg (1998a: 13) argue:

> the well-prepared teacher is not one who enters the classroom with a fixed set of lesson plans but a scholar with a thorough knowledge of subject, an understanding of knowledge production, the ability to produce knowledge, an appreciation of social context, a cognisance of what is happening in the world, insights into the lives of her students, and a sophisticated appreciation of critical educational goals and purposes.

When it is put like this, it sounds a tall order, but the examples of Mark and Megs in this chapter show that such geography teaching is not impossible. They both show evidence of matching Kincheloe and Steinberg's version of the well-prepared teacher. They are not there yet (none of us is!), but our worry is that they will not find enough encouragement in hectic schools concerned with various strategies and initiatives to continue their reading about geography and education, sit down and think deeply about the conceptual frameworks they use to construct geography lessons, and have exciting conversations about geography and its purposes. Such scholarship in teaching develops over a long period of time and needs to be actively encouraged and nurtured. How we might create such 'communities of practice' is something we discuss in Part III of this book.

FOR FURTHER THINKING

1 The 'curriculum problem' is essentially the issue of choosing what to teach. What are your criteria for guiding you through the curriculum problem in geography?

2 We are assuming you agree with us that the curriculum problem cannot be subcontracted to others. Can you identify the principal reasons why engaging in curriculum thinking is vital for geography teachers?

3 Early in the chapter we quoted Meinig (1979): 'Thus we confront the central problem: any landscape is composed not only of what lies before our eyes but what lies within our heads.' Meinig was discussing landscape, but in what ways is the quotation apt for thinking about curriculum too?

Chapter 6

Teaching and learning geography

Geographical knowledges have the largely unrealized potentiality to express hopes and aspirations as well as fears, to seek universal understandings based on mutual respect and concern, and to articulate firmer bases for human cooperation in a world marked by strong geographical differences. The construction of geographical knowledges in the spirit of liberty and respect for others opens up the possibility for the creation of alternative forms of geographical practice, tied to principles of mutual respect and advantage rather than to the politics of exploitation.

(Harvey 2001: 232)

We have argued for a view of geographical knowledge that stresses how it is socially constructed. In this chapter, we want to suggest how geography teachers might go about developing this approach in practice. We need to restate our view that geographical knowledge cannot be regarded as neutral. A critical geography education begins from the realisation of this fact, and asks questions about how geographical knowledge is selected, who selects it, and for what purpose. It implies that teachers and students need to strive constantly to ask questions about the geographical knowledge that is the basis of their lessons. In the quotation at the start of this chapter Harvey is describing a disposition towards geographical knowledges: one that is not prepared to sit back and accept the 'facts' produced by other people, but that seeks to *interrogate* that knowledge.

This is perhaps the single most important skill that geography teachers can cultivate: the ability to locate and critique geographical knowledge. This takes students beyond a 'reified view of knowledge' or a form of knowledge that is beyond question, that erases the fact that it was produced by humans operating in a particular context with a specific set of values. Geography teachers operating in a critical framework seek to gain an awareness of the subjective nature of knowledge and of the need to deconstruct it in order to appreciate the tacit presuppositions about human beings and the world inscribed within it.

APPROACHES TO TEACHING GEOGRAPHY

If this is our model of teaching and learning, we would suggest that much of the geography that is currently taught in schools is *acritical*. The 'banking model' of teaching remains dominant in many geography classrooms. The banking model (based on Friere 1972) operates on the following assumptions:

- The teacher teaches and the students are taught.
- The teacher knows a great deal and the students know little.
- The teacher thinks and the students are thought about.
- The teacher talks and the students listen.
- The teacher chooses and enforces his or her choice and the students comply.
- The teacher chooses the course content and the students (who were not consulted) adapt it.
- The teacher is the subject of the learning process, while the students are objects.

This is clearly a caricature of the 'banking model'. However, there are other more 'progressive' models found in geography education. One version of progressivism is based on the assumption that nothing can be learned unless it has meaning and is relevant to the experience of the student. Since knowledge is socially constructed, the experiences of the individual are always valuable and valid. The 'received' or 'absolutist' curriculum defined on logical grounds is seen to be 'external to the knower', 'imposed', and having little connection to the commonsense understandings of pupils.

The idea is that students have their private geographies that comprise personal and cultural views of the world and are coloured by intimate and individual environmental meanings. Academic and school geography provide a methodically derived, largely objective and generalised view of the world. Fien (1983) argues that *both* have their place in geography teaching since 'neither can be understood without the other': 'a consideration of our students' private geographies and their environmental needs and interests, *not* syllabus guidelines to course objectives and content, should be the starting point in all our course planning' (p. 47). The approach is learner-centred and requires a change in syllabus and classroom philosophy and practice, since it 'accepts the active private geographies of students as the starting point in curriculum planning' (p. 48).

Madan Sarup (1978) describes the difficulty with this position. He was writing in the heat of the debates about the new sociology of education, which had argued that teaching should not be thought of as a 'commodity' to be consumed, or as something to be 'banked'. He described a student teacher who adhered to the ideas of phenomenology. She believed that the teaching of her colleagues was 'impositional' and did not want to teach in that way. Sarup notes that when he watched her teach, the lessons seemed to consist only of 'chats'. He suggested to her that she was not 'teaching': 'Does not teaching imply a difference between pupil and learner, a difference between what is known and what can be known? Teaching seems inevitably to involve intervention – but how can we prevent it from being seen as impositional?' (Sarup 1978: 99).

Sarup argues that the student teacher had a misguided respect for pupils' ways of constructing reality, and actually prevented them from 'gaining the knowledge that might give them the power to create a less oppressive world' (1978: 99). This example may seem a million miles away from the educational experiences of student teachers today (it is hard to imagine a student teacher planning their lessons as a series of 'chats' around geographical themes!). However, elements of phenomenological thinking remain in curriculum planning. For example, pupils are often asked to record their feelings about a place or an issue in geography. They may be asked to express their values in words or pictures. These ideas are based on a key insight of phenomenology – that pupils construct images and ideas in their minds. Teachers need to recognise and value these constructs. However, the danger is that pupils remain 'experience bound', unable to see issues in broader perspective. They see problems in too personalised and subjective a manner.

We can provide an example here, which comes from *More Thinking Through Geography* (Nichols 2001). The activity involves a structured decision-making exercise. Students are provided with a scenario in which a male worker is offered a job in the north-east of England. This involves moving house and students are set the task of deciding what is the 'best option' for the family. There are various criteria to be considered, and a variety of options. Once they have made their decision, the teacher complicates the situation by providing information about the wishes and feelings of the other members of the family. Invariably, the choice made by the (male) 'head' of the family is not acceptable to the rest of the family and students need to rethink their decision in the light of this new evidence.

The activity is valid, and students would be active participants in the learning process. The question is what would they learn from such an activity? The activity is set within a frame of positivist and behavioural geography. The content of the lesson is about the choices made by individuals about residential location. This is an appropriate theme. However, from a critical perspective we would want to consider the validity of the model that underpins the activity. It is one that seems to ignore the political-economic context in which housing is situated. For example, the historical evolution of the housing market in Britain which favours home ownership over public housing surely provides the context for the family's decision. Taking things further, students might be encouraged to question the way in which housing is often suburban and the separation between home and work, an argument explored by feminist geographers. The point we are making *is that it is the teacher's understanding of conceptual categories drawn from the discipline that is crucial to the type of geographical learning that might result from this activity.*

It may seem unfair to critique this activity, and it might be argued that the activity itself could be a useful way into discussing these issues. However, there is little sense of this in the activity, which is supposed to illustrate the 'big concept' of 'decision-making'. This does not seem an adequate concept for geography teaching. As John White (2002) argues in relation to 'thinking skills' in the curriculum, if pupils are to think, it is surely school subjects that give them *something to think about?* In order for teachers and students to develop a critical approach, students' experiences need to be mediated through conceptual categories. A critical approach to teaching would seek to ensure that students emerge with an analytical approach to problems and with a comprehension of underlying forces. This must come from the knowledge and skill of the geography teacher who has an understanding of these conceptual categories and is prepared to develop that understanding in students. In the following sections of this chapter, we begin to offer some suggestions for how this might be done.

So, then, the type of critical geography we are discussing here starts from the assumption that all 'texts' must be examined with a view to exposing their assumptions and world-views or ideologies. The teacher's role is to bring to students' attention these assumptions, and to promote the idea of the critical reader. An objection here, of course, is that students frequently lack the maturity or levels of intellectual development to allow them to become critical readers (though see Gilbert 1984). The teacher is best off simply teaching them 'the facts' before allowing them to make up their own minds. The problem with this position, as Harvey's comment suggests, is that geographical knowledge can never be divorced from that of the interests that produced it. As he points out, we have not been very good at asking a fundamental question: who produces geographical knowledge and for what purpose? The underlying idea of this chapter is that teachers need to ask that question and find ways of having that type of discussion with their students. In the sections that follow, we continue this discussion and offer some examples of the type of approach we have in mind.

CRITICAL APPROACHES TO LANGUAGE AND LITERACY IN GEOGRAPHY

Why do we want students to write in geography and what do we want them to write? These are fundamental questions at the heart of geographical teaching and learning. In recent years, geography teachers have recognised their role in developing pupils' language and literacy. The Bullock Report, *A Language for Life*, was published in 1975 and urged all teachers to see themselves as contributing to language development. More recently, prompted by the apparent concern that pupils are not developing the skills of reading and writing, schools have been involved with a National Literacy Strategy, and in 2001 a document entitled *Literacy and Geography* was distributed to all schools (DfES 2002). This document includes a number of suggestions for raising awareness of literacy approaches in geography. However, from a critical geographical perspective, it raises a whole set of questions about the role of literacy in geography. In this section, we want to provide a critique of aspects of the document and show how it may in fact limit pupils' geographical knowledge and understanding. Our argument is that one of the major problems with *Literacy in Geography* is that it starts from a literacy perspective and that geographers ought to look to an understanding of the role of writing in geography as a subject to develop its perspectives.

It is striking that *Literacy in Geography* does not attempt to place literacy in its historical context. Neither does it offer a discussion of how geographers have, in the past, and more recently, thought about language and literacy. This is particularly strange since geography literally means 'earth-writing'. The result is that geography teachers are presented with a set of ideas or strategies to work with in classrooms without any real rationale or explanation. One place to start thinking about the purposes of literacy can be found in Jonathan Rose's (2001) book *The Intellectual Life of the British Working-Classes* (see also Box 6.1). His book is about the reading habits of 'ordinary' people and is a testament to the struggles of working-class people to read and define their own reading, often in the face of opposition from the powerful. Rose reminds us that literacy is political. It should prompt us as geography educators to consider what we ask pupils to read.

BOX 6.1 WHY READING MATTERS

In his book *The Intellectual Life of the British Working-Classes* (2001), Jonathan Rose notes how geography was always a 'conspicuously weak subject in English popular schooling'. He provides statistics to show the relatively small number of geography textbooks, atlases and wall maps purchased by schools in the 1850s. In addition, even the most recently published texts contained maps and figures that were up to fifty years out of date. One of Rose's 'autodidacts', a Swindon railway worker, recalled how after leaving school, a chargeman offered him and five friends pennies for answering simple geographical questions:

> During these tests the chargeman was astonished to learn that Salisbury is a country, Ceylon is the capital of China, and that Paris stands on the banks of the river Liffey ... Only one out of six could give the names of six [English] counties ...

Another (from Merthyr Tydfil) reported how school geography lessons made no imprint on him:

> Who cared where France was? We'd never be going there anyway – the furthest we were ever likely to go was Barry; didn't really know

where that was, but the bus driver did. And what about Sir Walter Scott going to all that trouble to find the South Pole, when it wasn't even lost in the first place.

Rose points out that the geography of one country, at least, was taught well and thoroughly to Victorian schoolchildren. The teaching of biblical geography could produce an 'Anglo-Zionism', 'where children conflated contemporary England and ancient Israel to the point where they merged into a common homeland'.

Rose's book, we suggest, is important because it reminds us why reading matters. It lovingly charts the long tradition of ordinary people struggling to learn to read, get hold of books and teach themselves about their own society and the wider world, often in the face of indifference and active opposition from those who wield power in society. As such, it provides an important reminder about why learning to read and write geography is a powerful means of finding a place in the world and acting to change one's reality.

If the authors of *Literacy in Geography* had gone back to relatively recent discussions of language in geography they would have unearthed some interesting ideas (for example, Frances Slater's (1989) edited collection). The wider context for this was the recognition that some groups of students may have had difficulty with the curriculum because of a mismatch between their own cultures and that of the classroom. Geography educators in the 1980s pointed out that language is never neutral. The most obvious examples here are in relation to gender and race. The terms used to describe and explain the world are freighted with meaning, and unless we are careful in our use of language, we risk reinforcing and reproducing social inequalities. This argument was part of a broader critique of the apparent transparency of geographical language. The idea that words used to describe and explain the world are a direct representation of the world has been challenged. Instead, it is suggested that words are in fact constitutive of that world. The words we use are the building blocks for understanding the world.

An important concept to introduce at this stage is *ideology*. Rob Gilbert (1989) argued that:

In the past (and for some even now) there was a view that language was transparent, that it was a vehicle or medium for our observations and thoughts, and that well-intentioned and careful scholarship would reveal the true nature of reality . . . the aim was to rid language of its vagueness, to control its connotations, to limit its interpretations, to make it transparent so that the real business of observing and explaining reality could proceed.

(p. 151)

Gilbert argues against this view of language, stressing that 'as geography teachers we have no transparent access to the world'. The challenge is to take account of the historical specificity of the language we use, how it is produced in situations of conflicting interest and power, and how particular social relations are constructed through it. Gilbert's book *The Impotent Image* (1984) examined the ideologies contained in school geography textbooks, and throughout the 1980s geographers produced a series of ideology critiques. The argument rests upon a materialist understanding of the relationship between language and society, most famously associated with Raymond Williams. Williams' (1958, 1973, 1976) work demonstrated how ideas (as reflected in language, literature and art) can never be seen as separate from the society that produced them. This argument was taken up by Henley (1989) in relation to the language of school geography. Henley argued that the 'nature of the language used by geographers . . . reflects the wider social and economic climate and the dominant ideological formations' (p. 164).

The attainment of a value-free and neutral methodology and language for geography is impossible. Henley looked at the language used in school geography. For example, he cites Bradford and Kent's (1977) widely used textbook as an example of the language of 'scientism'. The language and approach, according to Henley, 'abdicate any notions towards political or social responsibility' (p. 165). The review of urban geography relies on metaphor derived from plant ecology. Migration is a process divorced from its social, political and economic contexts. Terms derived from the natural sciences (boom, slump, trough, competition) are all in common use: 'The language used in geography, although appearing 'distinterested', is in fact infused with ideology' (p. 166).

The problem is not exclusive to scientific language. Humanistic geography is concerned to reconstruct experience and exercises encourage students to examine or write about their feelings or to reconstruct the experience of others. While such activities have potential for developing the student's affective domain, in promoting empathy, and developing consciousness, there are risks that language is used descriptively and relies on an unexamined acceptance of consensus: 'Humanistic approaches in the classroom can develop into "idiosyncratic geography" that never develops beyond the individual's perception and experience' (p. 169).

Henley stressed how the language of school geography tends to neutralise and gloss over much of the emotion of social processes. Feminist geography educators have made similar arguments, most notably Alison Lee (1996) in her detailed discussion of the processes of writing in the geography classroom. Lee showed how the paradigm of scientific geography led to the use of certain forms of language and encouraged specific forms of writing. These were unconsciously drawn upon by the teacher in the study and had the effect of making it difficult for other perspectives to find expression in the classroom. Interestingly, one of the students in Lee's studies did find ways to write about the topic of shifting cultivation in more holistic terms (although she was awarded a lower mark for her essay!).

More recent work in geography has stressed the inherent instability of geographical language and the idea that 'there is nothing beyond the text' (Barnes and Duncan 1992). The implications of these arguments for geographical teaching and learning are important. Significantly they suggest that the type of language used in geography lessons and texts are important in offering students authoritative representations of the world. Close attention to the language we use as teachers can reveal how we construct the world for our students.

With these arguments in mind, we can consider the *Literacy in Geography* document further. The examples and resources selected to illustrate the document are quite revealing. None of them are written by geographers. They are textbook extracts. They offer a partial (and unrealistic) view of contemporary geography in that they are all quite neutral by attempting to appear value-free and avoid controversy. In addition, although the document claims to induct pupils into how geographers speak, read and write, there is a distinct lack of 'authentic' text. This begs the question what we are asking pupils to be literate for? The document itself makes great claims for the power of literacy, arguing that it can lead to 'empowerment'. It is interesting to explore how this might be realised.

In order to start to answer this question, it is worthwhile considering a common classification of types of literacy (McLaren 1988). Functional literacy involves being able to read and write. It means being able to decode the printed into the spoken (and thought) word, and to encode the spoken (or thought) word into the written word. Cultural literacy involves educating pupils to adopt certain meanings, values and views. It is the type of literacy required to replicate genres of writing, such as a 'geographical description', or a 'geographical explanation'. Cultural literacy is what 'enables' a pupil to write what the teacher perceives as a 'good' account, a well-presented argument, a clearly labelled map or diagram, etc. Critical literacy is concerned with the development of independent analytical and deconstructive skills. It involves being able to decode the hidden meanings of texts in order to reveal their selective interests. Moore (2000) explains the implications of the different types of literacy:

> We might say that whereas functional and cultural literacy seek to help the student to succeed within an unchanged society, critical literacy has in mind a different educational agenda, which is aimed at changing society itself in ways that will help everyone to succeed.
>
> (p. 87)

In order to illustrate these arguments about the way in which the language used in school geography can tether students to existing social and economic relations, we can consider a double-page spread called 'Old King Coal?' from a textbook called *Living Geography* (Dobson *et al.* 2001).

The text sets out to answer three questions (What is coal? How is it mined? How and why is the coal industry changing in the UK?). These are eminently sensible. However, a closer look at how these questions are answered reveals some problems. The first half of the text is given over to a broadly technical description of the formation of coal, followed by a discussion of how coal is mined. Although factually correct, it is worth asking about the purpose of such a description. In focusing on technical, scientific and 'non-controversial' themes, pupils are given the impression that geography is essentially a scientific subject. A more subtle reading might focus on the way in which change is presented in the text. The text begins with a process of natural change, and then introduces questions of social and economic change, thus suggesting that change is inevitable and a 'fact of life'. In this way, it might be argued that the text conflates social and natural change.

A closer look at how the textbook represents change suggests that it does so using an underlying metaphor of economy – the text contains many terms which reflect this – 'This makes it cheaper to mine', 'all the coal worth mining has been dug out', 'modern mines use expensive machinery' and so on. It seems reasonable to ask whether this economic explanation of change might be supplemented using other discourses, such as political decision-making.

The text seems to offer the view that society is on an inexorable pathway which cannot be diverted. 'UK production goes down, and some mines close down' – this is an example of what Henley calls 'indifferent language' – language that is substituted for concrete terms that describe and explain how society works. The result is the dehumanising and depoliticisation of social processes. The statistics used in the textbook are revealing in that though they refer to the number of mines and the output of coal, the number of workers is not included, a strategy that serves to avoid much of the human meaning associated with the decline of the coal industry.

What this analysis suggests is that a pupil using this spread on 'Old King Coal?' and doing the associated tasks would maybe develop functional and cultural literacy. They would be able to draw and interpret graphs and write about some of their ideas based on the limited resources provided in the text. However, the text does not invite any criticism and indeed is written in a way that seems to discourage pupils from asking awkward questions. The critical approach we are arguing for would require geography teachers to ask questions about the creation of this account and its effects on pupils' consciousness. It might involve teachers in rewriting this textbook extract or devising ways of using it that allow pupils to develop a critical distance from it.

In the light of these arguments we can consider the document *Literacy in Geography*. It displays little sensitivity to the role of language in constructing pupils' understanding of the world and offers a limited vision of geographical writing. It suggests to students that writing is a technical act, straightforward in describing and explaining the world. It promotes a limited form of functional literacy and encourages pupils to mimic a particular form of 'scientific' geography. In this book we are arguing that geography teachers need to find ways to develop forms of critical literacy with students as well.

MAPPING MEANINGS

According to the old saying, history is about chaps, and geography is about maps. Many geography teachers would agree that maps play a central part in developing students' geographical imagination. There is a wealth of research about how children's map skills develop from an early age. Much of this focuses on how children's mapping abilities develop from simple spatial representations of features in their locality towards an understanding of more formal maps. This is linked to cognitive development in the form of developmental psychology based on Piaget's idea of stages. A good example of this is found in Boardman's *Graphicacy and Geography Teaching* (1983) which provides an appendix suggesting particular competencies that pupils might be expected to achieve at certain ages. Boardman's book is useful for teachers because it offers a range of practical teaching activities that can be used to develop pupils' mapping skills. One of the research findings that appears quite regularly in the literature is that different groups of children display different abilities in terms of mapping. For example, it is commonly asserted that boys develop more rapidly in terms of their ability to handle maps, and Bale (1987) reports studies that suggest that middle-class children have a greater ability in terms of mapping than working-class children. Unless we accept the idea that these abilities are 'innate' and 'natural', this suggests that maps and the ability to use and understand maps is linked to wider cultural factors. This then leads to other questions. For example, it is commonly accepted as evident that all pupils should learn certain skills in relation to maps. But on what grounds? Why is it is important that all pupils are exposed to 'maps at a variety of scales' or that all pupils are familiar with an Ordnance Survey map of their local area? Providing an answer to this question requires us to think about the purposes such exercises serve. As it happens, we personally think these are important, but not simply because of some 'tradition' or because it has always been taught like that.

In this part, we want to draw upon some work that questions the commonsense ways in which maps are sometimes thought about in school geography. This is in some ways a difficult point to grasp. To give an example, one of us (Morgan) recently ran a session on 'graphicacy' with a group of beginning teachers. As luck would have it, that very morning

The Times had a front-page story about the proposal, by the Ordnance Survey (OS), to remove from their maps churches that were redundant or had changed their use and replace the much-recognised spire symbol with a black spot. This was proposed so that the Survey's maps reflected social and cultural change. When I showed the article to the group, their initial reaction was, I think, outrage: How dare the Ordnance Survey tamper with maps in this way? As we discussed their response it became clear that they objected to the idea that maps reflected social and cultural change. Maps were a reflection of what was on the ground. Gradually things began to become less heated, and people began to express what they implicitly understood, maps are always social products. They select certain features and omit others. Some of the teachers began to tell stories about how they had come to love maps as children, and how they collected them and even used them as wallpaper. Again, the point we are making is that maps cannot be seen as separate from the contexts in which they are produced and used.

Simon Jenkins, writing in *The Times* on 9 May 2003, saw this as a sign of the times, another nail in the coffin of a godless age. His article spoke eloquently of the pleasure that maps provided him as a citizen. Maps, he argued, were not just about 'navigation', they played a symbolic role. This example raises some important questions about the social purposes of maps and mapping. Jenkins makes the point that maps are intimately tied up with politics. The Ordnance Survey was established in 1791 and the first maps surveyed the south-east of England, the area most vulnerable to French invasion. These national surveys displayed new dimensions of national unity and centralised authority. The first six inch to one mile survey of Ireland in the 1840s was an exercise in colonial rule. This included the ways in which place names were recorded. In Gaelic-speaking areas, the Ordnance Survey field officers nominated local authorities (such as property owners and the professional middle classes) to provide information on local place names (a process brilliantly drammatised in Brian Friel's (1984) play *Translations*). The original military purpose of the Ordnance Survey gradually shifted to providing maps for economic and planning purposes. In addition, they came to play their part in the development of new ways of consuming the countryside. The increasing trend towards day-tripping to the countryside was aided by OS maps which were made more attractive and colourful. The ability to read and interpret the landscape became a valuable skill, to be developed through education: 'With an inch Ordnance Survey sheet of your

109

selected area you are master of the countryside: it lies symbolically before you' (Batsford 1945–6, cited in Whyte 2002).

In making this argument, we are drawing upon some of the ideas informing recent discussions in cartography. Increasingly, maps, which have been thought of as truthful and accurate representations of 'reality', are understood to be texts that are the products of people who make them for particular purposes and are consumed or 'read' in a variety of ways. Holloway and Hubbard (2001) provide a neat summary of this type of thinking:

> Maps are created by particular groups of people, for particular reasons, so that while most people are familiar with the idea of reading a map in order to find their way, we can also think about reading maps *critically*, examining the conditions in which they are produced. This means that we can read something about a society from the maps it produces and uses. Like other representations maps can tell us about power relations, and about a group of people's ways of understanding the world. By looking at a map and exploring what lies behind it, we can get some idea of how members of that society view the world and their place in it.
>
> (p. 169)

This suggests that, as well as understanding how to read and interpret a wide range of maps, critical geography education should encourage an understanding of the broader political and cultural purposes of mapping. This may sound obvious. However, developing an ability to 'read' maps critically does not come naturally – it requires guidance, practice and reflection. The rest of this section provides some examples of how we can read the maps commonly found in geography teaching before making some comments on the theoretical issues at stake.

Economic space

Since studies of economic geography are a key part of school geography, we start with examples of how economic space is represented in maps and diagrams. A simple point to make is that any map found in texts is the product of choices made by its creator: 'Information conveyed on a map can be given different spins or resonances by the presentation of the map, particularly the title, caption and symbolization' (Black 2000: 62).

For example, consider two maps showing the location of nuclear power plants in Britain. The first map is a low-key affair, simply presenting the location of different nuclear power plants. The second is more dramatic. It is titled 'Radioactive', and uses symbols and colour to give the impression that Britain is a land dominated by nuclear conflict. The size of the symbols is disproportionate, and the clenched fist (to signal demonstrations) and guns (to represent the nuclear police) all act to dramatise the map. The inclusion of railway lines adds to the sense that much of England and Wales is involved in this drama.

While this might seem like an extreme example, conventional maps of economic activity such as those found in atlases also involve choices. In general, such maps tend to favour production over consumption. They emphasise manufacturing industry over services or the financial sector, and heavy manufacturing over light industry. Finally, work, rather than ownership, is mapped. In many ways, these choices are not 'sinister' in that they seek to deceive readers. It is easier to map an activity that occurs on only a few sites (such as steel making) rather than one that is widespread (such as plumbing). However, from a critical perspective, we would want to ask about and be aware of the messages about the nature of economic relations that such maps offer students. For example, it may be easier to map work than ownership, but it might be argued that an understanding of ownership is far more important in making sense of the contemporary world. It may therefore be important to find ways to map flows of capital and money and to have a global spatial sense in order to understand these flows. As geographers, we might also question the extent to which such maps allow for an understanding of cultures of economic activity which do not lend themselves readily to mapping (for instance, the black economy).

Social space

Social issues are harder and more contentious to map than economic issues, in that the choice of topics can be thought of as political. Where there is a reliance on simple models of causation it may be possible to map social patterns (for example, settlement patterns as related to environmental factors). However, as soon as we emphasise people as the crucial element in geographical change and patterns, with concepts and ideologies as important, this leads to a less clear cut and more 'messy' situation.

This is because any attempt to map social issues is underpinned by assumptions that need to be examined. Seager and Olson's *Women in the World Atlas* (1986) contains a map titled 'Job Ghettos'. It uses a range of cartographic techniques to highlight the role of women in the global economy. The mapping technique draws attention to the problems of data collection by leaving unmapped spaces blank. The commentary suggests to readers how the spread should be read, and the range of scales at which data are mapped create the sense of a common problem shared by women the world over. The map therefore has a political message, and the assumptions that underpin the construction of the map should form the basis for discussions in geography lessons. In this case, the claim that it is 'universally true that jobs defined as women's work carry low pay, low status, and little security' is worthy of critical scrutiny, especially when it comes to offering explanations for such conclusions. The point is that *all* geographical data and explanations should be subject to analysis and critique (see Domosh and Seager 2001; Steans 2003).

There is also a problem in assuming that identity exists in a simple one-dimensional form. For example, maps that show the distribution of people from New Commonwealth and Pakistan are problematic because they say nothing about how people identify themselves: what does ethnicity mean to them? They may use such identities flexibly. Such maps serve to fix or reify and homogenise a complex issue, and problems result when these maps are used to imply causality (e.g. comparisons of distribution of ethnic groups with maps of housing quality). The same goes for other axes of identity such as disability or sexuality. While mapping patterns may open up different ways of seeing the world, it also closes down others. One option is to avoid controversy by ignoring these aspects of people's lives altogether, but this seems to be an evasion and denial of the fact that such issues are an important part of understanding the making of geographies. As a solution to this problem, Black (2000) suggests that:

> the obvious strategy is to focus on what seems most meaningful and mappable, and to recognize the resulting bias. The complexity of the relationship between space and society is such that the limits of what maps can convey as analytical texts are reached quite quickly.
>
> (p. 73)

Environmental issues

Towards the end of the twentieth century, the human impact on the environment was of increasing concern, and maps and atlases reflected this. Maps have the potential to offer different messages about environmental issues. Black (2000) gives an example from the *Geographical* magazine, which in 1973 ran two articles on Amazonia. The first was on the Trans-Amazonian Highway and mapped roads, existing, under construction and projected, along with river and state boundaries. The commentary was upbeat: 'The road under construction in the Amazon basin will do much to bring about the taming of this great wilderness bastion.'

The second article concentrated on the problems facing the Brazilian Indians. The map recorded major Indian parks and reservations, and an inset map showed major new roads and Indian cultural areas. The example demonstrates the way in which maps can either bolster or contest particular ideologies or ways of viewing the world, although it is worth noting that both these maps were drawn from the perspective of the Western reader and not the perspective of Amerindians.

During the 1980s and 1990s environmental mapping became more 'in yer face', possibly reflecting the heightened sense of 'crisis'. An example is the map on 'Air Quality' from Seager's *The State of the Earth* (1990). Scary 'gas masks' (black for high levels, grey for medium levels) and 'dust clouds' are scattered around the map. The map has the strapline 'In many cities, just breathing is a health hazard'. The message is writ large, and the map clearly makes an environmental case, which can be contested.

Theoretical issues

Before concluding this discussion of mapping, we want to relate our discussion to the overarching themes of this book. For some readers, the focus in this section on 'deconstructing the map' may be a bridge too far, an unnecessary *destructive* act. In *Maps and Politics* (2000) – a text to which this section is indebted – Jeremy Black considers the arguments of the postmodern cartographers such as Brian Harley. Harley was a cartographer who during his career travelled the rocky road from 'traditional' to 'poststructuralist' cartographer. Harley became interested in taking mapping apart to understand maps and how they represented the

113

world. He looked at the social relations behind map production, the working practices of the cartographer, the politics of power and the surveillance of the state. Some of the points Harley made are simple and more or less accepted. For example, he noted how just by looking at the orientation of a map you can guess who made it. British world maps put Britain in the middle, not for 'scientific' reasons but to demonstrate British supremacy. Geography teachers are used to this idea in relation to the debate about the Peters Projection, which broke the accepted code about how the world should be represented. Harley was also interested in what was not shown on maps – the 'silences' (for a good example of his approach read his essay 'Deconstructing the map' in Barnes and Duncan 1992). Black is critical of Harley and others who, he thinks, were too concerned with the issue of state power and the idea that maps were part of a 'conspiracy'. The moves towards deconstructing the map suffered from a number of problems including a tendency to state the obvious and a simplification of ideas of power and ideology. In relation to school geography, we feel that some of these issues are worthy of discussion with students (and certainly should form part of geography teacher education courses). The question we would ask is to what extent geography teachers help students to understand the processes whereby geographical knowledge (of which maps are part) are constructed. Black favours a 'contro-verted' rather than a 'conspirational' approach in which it is recognised that there are 'multiple meanings of space' and that the challenge is to work with the idea that there is no single cartographic strategy. He argues for a pluralistic approach to mapping that is appropriate for a democratic culture and an intellectual culture. He uses the term politics as a 'metaphor for social processes that provide the context for cartography and mould much of its content and reception' (2000: 28). This is the perspective we share. Throughout this book, and particularly in this section, we are arguing that geography teachers need to critically interrogate the nature of the knowledge that finds its way into classrooms.

GEOGRAPHY TEACHING AND TECHNOLITERACY

In this section, we consider the role of information and communications technology (ICT) in geography teaching. We do not feel we have to re-state the arguments about how ICT can enhance geographical teaching and learning, since these are readily available for teachers. Lambert and

Balderstone (2000) are cautious about the extent to which ICT enhances pupils' learning in geography, reminding teachers that they need to look carefully at the quality of pupils' learning. In this section, we want to offer a different slant on this debate, informed by the underlying approach of this book, which is to ask some questions about the *types* and *purposes* of the geographical knowledge constructed through using ICT. In order to do this, we need to place the use of ICT in geography teaching in a broader perspective.

It is interesting to reflect upon how ICT came to play such a large part in school geography. Maguire (1989) describes the development of the 'quantitative and computer revolutions in geography'. He identifies a number of phases:

- From the late 1950s and early 1960s geography changed from being an 'essentially qualitative and descriptive discipline into one which became increasingly concerned with the development of generalized laws and theories about spatial patterns using mathematical and statistical methods' (p. 3). Computers at this time were expensive, scarce and difficult to use.

- From the mid 1960s more advanced computers became available at a lower price. The uptake of computers was rapid. Computers were used at first for statistical analyses, but later, computer cartography, simulation and remote sensing became important applications.

- In the late 1970s and early 1980s the advent of relatively low-cost microcomputers heralded a 'second computer revolution'.

- By the late 1980s and early 1990s, there were two major problems facing geographers. These were the lack of 'liveware' (i.e. suitably qualified people to maintain computer systems and to teach and develop the geographical applications of computers) and the proliferation of data associated with the information revolution which was precipitated by the technological revolution.

Such accounts tend to regard technology as a neutral tool which can be used to improve the study of geography. Teachers are the 'liveware' who are charged with making this technology work:

Computers are an enabling technology: they are tools which enable geographers to improve their efficacy and efficiency in many ways.

115

> There are two key aspects of computers which assist geographers in this regard. First, computers can be used to collect and store large quantities of data in an organized manner. Second, such data can be quickly manipulated and presented in a whole host of different ways.
>
> (Maguire 1989: 222)

Similar arguments can be found in more recent accounts of ICT and geography teaching. For instance, Hassell (2002) explains why geography teachers should be integrating ICT into their teaching, and refers to both the effectiveness and the pervasiveness of technologies:

> Throughout a huge range of human activity, including commerce and the public sector, ICT is playing an increasing role in decision-making, ranging from locating a road or superstore to the identification of flood or weather hazards. ICT can enable better decision-making as it is possible to take into consideration a wider range of variables, as well as supporting the monitoring of natural hazards and systems to provide greater warning and providing the opportunity to take action to reduce impact. As a result, ICT can provide better and faster tools for decision-making. These changes have an impact in two ways; first, they change the geography we teach, but second, they change the decision-making skills and processes that we should be developing in children. The key issue in this area is how can the subject community ensure that the geography of formal curricula that is taught and examined keeps up with these changes?
>
> (p. 155)

Hassell provides a clear 'vision' of the way in which ICT changes the world geographers study in ways that challenge teachers. The 'issues' that Hassell identifies are essentially how 'geography' (presumably he means geographers) can respond to these 'challenges'. The 'problems' are essentially technical, involving people developing their skills, working together and planning more effectively:

> Obviously, there is not enough money in the system, but there are a number of key initiatives that geographers must make the most of. What is important is for geographers to work together and for there to be some strategy for the future.
>
> (p. 158)

These arguments are fairly typical of the literature about ICT and geography teaching. However, in the rest of this section, we want to suggest that these visions of an ICT-enhanced geography depend on a particular understanding of what 'geography' is, and this serves to exclude or marginalise other 'versions' of school geography. We offer an alternative view of the role of ICT in geography teaching. Consider the following statement: 'In an era in which one reads almost everyday of advances in computer technology and of the applications of computers to new areas of life, it may seem odd to suggest that the history of computers is important' (Curry 1998: 59). Curry's comment brings us to a realisation that there has not yet been written a serious history of the role of ICT in geography education. For example, Walford's (2000) recent history of geography in schools has just two references to ICT, both 'neutral' comments noting the growing importance of ICT in geography teaching. We are not in a position to provide such a history. However, we want to make some comments about how the role of ICT has developed in geography education. It is notable that Maguire, in his discussion cited earlier, regards the development of quantitative approaches to the study of geography and computers as going hand in hand. Thus, in the same sentence he writes about 'the quantitative and computer revolutions in geography'. This alerts us to the question of how we tell the history of school subjects such as geography. As we noted in Chapter 3, the so-called 'new geography' offered the opportunity for a rigorous 'scientific' approach to geography. Since the new geography was concerned with modelling, simulation, prediction and statistical manipulation, computers provided the ready-made technology to support the new geography in schools. The point we want to make here is that the 'scientific' view of geography was underpinned by particular assumptions about the nature of the world. This is a view that assumes that there exists an external world from which data can be collected by detached neutral observers and represented to others through a relatively unmediated and uncomplicated language. In this version, science is a neutral tool to be applied.

Goodson (1983) argues that the adoption of the new scientific geography should be understood as an attempt on the part of some geography teachers to increase the standing of geography in schools and secure status and access to resources. By promoting the subject as a science, geography teachers could promote themselves. This project was, of course, more convincing if geography could lay claim to the new technologies finding their way into schools. It is important to clarify the point we are making here; the fact that the introduction of ICT in geography teaching was so closely wrapped up with a particular form of geographical knowledge has meant that it has been interpreted and used in quite specific ways.

From the start then, the introduction of computers in school geography was closely linked to particular forms of geographical knowledge or particular views of what geography is. Macguire and Hassell, in their accounts of the challenge of technology for geography teaching, both appear to operate with this 'scientific' view of geography, or at least they never make clear to their readers their view of geography as a subject and how geographical knowledge is produced. If they did, we argue, they would have to address important questions about the purposes of geography education.

In order to develop this argument, we want to return to the heuristic device or interpretive schema suggested by Johnston (1986). The value of his approach is that it allows us to 'open up' the question of what we understand by geographical knowledge and begin to think about the implications of this for ICT. As we saw in Chapter 4, Johnston suggests that there exist three main types of 'science': empiricist/positivist, humanistic and realist. Much of the discussion of the use of ICT in geography reflects the idea that geography is an empirical science. The examples provided by Hassell to illustrate 'ICT opportunities to support Geography' are revealing. They include: 'use a presentation package to combine various types of information to argue the case to the class on the new superstore location'; 'investigate the changing traffic pressure in a locality using a mapping package to present flow rates over time from a series of observations of major roads' (Hassell 2002: 153).

There is nothing wrong with these activities per se, and they reflect the type of geography that is encouraged by the National Curriculum. However, the discussion of these 'opportunities' neglects to mention that these approaches reflect a particular view or interpretation of what constitutes geographical knowledge, and one which is not neutral but:

> accepts the basic structure of society, and seeks to manipulate certain aspects of its superstructure only; it accepts the need for a strong state to implement planning; and it realizes that its major contributions are likely to be ameliorative problem-solving only. It is involved in patching-up the future, rather than creating it.
>
> (Johnston 1986: 111)

Again, this is not to decry the importance and validity of this type of geographical knowledge. However, we would suggest that there are problems if teachers and students are not encouraged to analyse and critique the assumptions on which such knowledge is constructed. There is a danger that ICT strengthens school geography's 'alliance with science', and denies students access to other versions of geographical knowledge.

You will recall that Johnston's second type of science is humanistic. The goal of such understanding is both self-awareness and mutual understanding, in order to enrich society by making individuals better aware of themselves, each other and the social and natural worlds. A geography teacher operating with this view of geographical knowledge would ask to what extent ICT might be used to develop pupils' self-awareness and mutual understanding. Imagine a pupil looking at a remote-sensed image of Amazonia. It is interesting to speculate upon the 'sense of place' she or he might develop as a result of such an exercise. While the tendency of ICT to represent the 'world as information' would seem to deny the possibility of the deep understanding of human action demanded by humanistic geographers, we should perhaps not be too hasty in reaching this judgement. There may be potential for forms of on-line communication that can bring together people in different places and foster intersubjective understanding. In addition, while school geography has generally worked with a model of science, it is possible that ICT can be used to promote different forms of literacy focused around the use of text. The point here, of course, is that the potential of ICT depends less on any inherent characteristics of the technology and more on the decisions made by teachers about the purposes to which it is put.

Johnston's third type of science is realist. Realist science is concerned with providing people with an understanding of the mechanisms and underlying forces that structure the world. Critical geographers have tended to stress the ways in which the development of information technologies has been linked to the logics of capitalist accumulation. They have pointed out how technology has been used to maintain existing social relations. For example, Huckle argued that software packages in geography:

> have assumptions about the nature of society and citizenship programmed into them. These assumptions are perhaps more difficult to decode than they would be in a textbook, yet for many teachers and

pupils they probably carry greater legitimacy due to the technology via which they are presented.

(Huckle 1988: 58)

Huckle suggests that geography teachers need to evaluate and use these packages particularly carefully, ensuring that they act as 'vehicles for social literacy rather than social control'. We can illustrate these issues by considering one application designed for use in schools (see Box 6.2).

More generally, it is worth remembering Michael Apple's (1988) warning that reliance on pre-packaged technology can lead to a loss of important skills and dispositions on the part of teachers. There is a risk that critical reflection on the curriculum and teaching is lessened as 'more of the curriculum, and the teaching and evaluative practices that surround it, is viewed as something one purchases' (p. 163). This is compounded if teachers do not have the time to evaluate the educational strengths and weaknesses of the curricular material. More importantly, such software embodies a form of thinking that orients a person to the world in a particular way. Computers involve ways of thinking that are primarily technical: 'The more the new technology transforms the classroom in its own image, the more a technical logic will replace critical political and ethnical understanding' (p. 171). Apple's comments echo those of Mercer (1984) in his discussion of 'technocratic geography'. Technocratic geography is linked with technical thinking that relied on 'data techniques' that 'provide tacit support for certain entrenched social inequalities and views about the world' and serve to 'build a fairly impregnable framework of closed discourse which, in effect, prevented genuinely alternative world views from being aired' (Mercer 1984: 182). So, for instance, Mercer noted that we have the analytical means to find the shortest distance to hospital but fail to ask why so many people become ill. This example reminds us of why it is important to think about the values that underpin our teaching.

We are not educational 'luddites'. However, we are concerned that some important questions about educational aims and values may get swept aside in the 'dash for ICT' in school geography. It is interesting to recall Derek Gregory's warning to geography teachers as long ago as 1981:

the appearance of geographers capable of calling on computer-assisted techniques to solve problems in the subject may have dealt satisfying

BOX 6.2   DOWN ON THE FARM

Down on the Farm is a complex simulation that allows pupils to put themselves in the role of a farmer faced with the problem of how to increase his returns. Pupils select crops for particular fields on the farm and then see how successful their judgements are. In each turn (each year) they can refine their choices, making use of the wealth of data about soil type, acidity, geology and so on. The weather is an important factor in determining their success, and this, of course, is an unknown quantity. The realism of the simulation is enhanced by the existence of a number of levels, which allow pupils to engage in various strategies such as set-aside and land reclamation.

A critical perspective points to the need for teachers and pupils to be alert to the assumptions that underlie software packages such as *Down on the Farm*. It relies on the representation of spatial data. It takes existing social and spatial relations and simplifies them in order to make them manageable. Pupils then rehearse the kinds of decision-making required by farmers. There is a strong element of competition that effectively mirrors the market forces that regulate the farming industry. The software suggests to pupils the image of the lone owner-occupier farmer operating in a highly competitive market. This, of course, does not match the reality of agriculture in Britain, which is dominated by large agrobusinesses.

Of course, it can be argued that the programme is simply an educational tool, and that it involves a necessary simplification of the complexity of the real world. In this case then, a particular view of human behaviour and the operations of an economic system are presented to pupils as a simplification of how the world works – unless we are careful to teach about and unpick the assumptions that structure the simulation, we are likely to leave this view unchallenged. In the case of *Down on the Farm*, it might be argued, the logic of the programme leads to a conservative framework in which human patterns are explained in terms of environmental determinism, and human thought is represented in the form of 'rational economic man'. A pupil using the software would be likely to pick up these implicit messages unless the teacher explicitly seeks to break the circle and introduce critical frames. It is this that makes the introduction of alternatives difficult within the logic of the programmes.

body-blows to the sneerers who can be found in most common rooms, but it certainly did not guarantee that the questions they were asking were any more meaningful or that the answers to them were any more incisive.

(1981b: 142)

MEDIA AND GEOGRAPHY

The so-called 'cultural turn' which we have referred to in this book has led geographers to become interested in questions of representation. An early example can be found in Burgess and Gold's (1985) *Geography, the Media and Popular Culture*:

> The media have been on the periphery of geographical inquiry for too long. The very ordinariness of television, radio, newspapers, fiction, film and pop music perhaps masks their importance as part of people's geography 'threaded into the fabric of daily life with deep taproots into the well-springs of popular consciousness'.

(1985: 1)

The implications of this argument for school geography have long been recognised but have so far received little sustained attention. This section provides an introduction to how school geography and popular culture might be related.

While photographs, slides and videos are part of the everyday tools of geography teachers, often these media are used without a critical understanding of their construction. In *Teaching the Media*, Len Masterman (1985) discusses the role of the media in geography teaching.

First, geography is a subject in which visual images have a particularly prominent place. It is 'the subject of mediated, second hand experiences, dealing primarily with regions of the country or of the world which cannot be brought directly into the classroom' (Masterman 1985: 243). Second, some of the most potent sources of our ideas about our environment are the media:

> Different environments and regions are, indeed, so familiar and natural to us that geography teachers need to acknowledge that whenever they teach about a particular region or country they are competing with

images, often fragmented, but sometimes remarkably coherent, which already exist inside the heads of their students.

(Masterman 1985: 245)

Finally, increasingly geographers question the distinction between the 'real' and the 'representation'. This is particularly the case when we think of the idea of 'landscape as a text', which is a human production, then interpreted and made sense of by readers or viewers.

All of these reasons challenge us as geography teachers to get beyond the idea that the media offers us a neutral and value-free 'window on the world'. It sounds obvious, but the products of the media are 'social constructions'. That is, people have created them for a purpose. Once we understand this, and the implications that follow, it is difficult to use media in geography lessons without considering questions about that process of social construction. An objection to this argument, of course, is that geography teachers are not media teachers. However, we think it can be argued that geographers need to encourage all students, whatever their age or 'ability', to ask questions about the sources of geographical data.

In what follows we offer some illustrations of what it might mean to use the media to develop a 'critical geography' and suggest some practical ways in which to do this.

Musical geographies

Even a subject such as geography can be enriched by drawing upon the popular music of the area being studied. Records from the Third World are now fairly easily available.

(Lee 1980: 171)

If we take seriously Burgess and Gold's argument, it should be clear that music pervades the geographies of everyday life. Indeed, it is argued that music is one of the media by which young people create and re-create their identities. Lee's comment reflects the tendency to see music as a resource with which to enrich and enliven geography lessons (this approach is also found in Lambert and Balderstone 2000). Until recently, there have been few studies of popular music in geography, which probably owes much to the 'cultural elitism' of many geographers who privilege 'serious' artefacts

123

over popular cultural forms, along with a feeling that music is not 'geographical'. However, recent work informed by the 'new cultural geography' has challenged this view, and we would argue that music provides an important means through which to develop students' geographical imaginations (Connell and Gibson 2003; Leyshon *et al.* 1998).

At the simplest level, some of the places studied in geography have distinct musical cultures. Sorting out the soundtrack to the place could be the basis for a useful discussion. This could be an interesting way of discussing how a 'sense of place' gets constructed. For example, the songs of Bruce Springsteen emphasise the relationship between place, community and identity. They tend to be set in place, in small-town United States, notably Astbury Park, New Jersey. There is a politics of place to many of Springsteen's songs which defend the landscapes of blue-collar Americans in the face of deindustrialisation. Other artists do a similar thing, often choosing local names that are evocative of place and history (for example, Ladysmith Black Mambazo, Lindisfarne or Cypress Hill). Of course, we should be wary of labelling musical cultures as 'authentic'. Cultural geographers would remind us that they construct particular narratives about places.

Music and song lyrics provide a means to discuss representations of places. As Connell and Gibson (2003: 71) note: 'Nothing should more closely signify the relationship between music, place and identity than the words of songs.' Rap lyrics – especially those of gangsta rap – are indicative of the harsh realities of urban space. In an earlier time, the songs of Jam described the soulless and dreary landscapes of Britain's suburbs and new towns (for example, 'A Town called Malice' featured in the film *Billy Elliott* and depicts urban life). Geographical celebrations and tensions are played out through music. Many country songs, for instance, simultaneously celebrate the simple and uncomplicated nature of life, yet at the same time point to the disappointments and com-promises that attachment to such places entails (think about Tammy Wynette's 'Stand by Your Man', which is at once a song that regrets the conservatism of rural life, yet at the same time accepts the fatalism of living in a closed community where there is no escape). Steve Earle's 'The Mountain' could be used to initiate a discussion of the way in which resource extraction creates a sense of place (it is set in the Appalachian mountains):

I was born on this mountain a long time ago
Before they knocked down the timber and strip-mined the coal

When you rose in the morning before it was light
To go down in that dark hole to come back up at night

I was born on this mountain this mountain's my home
She holds me and keeps me from worry and woe
Well they took everything that she gave now they're gone
But I'll die on this mountain this mountain's my home

The lyric to this song is a potentially rich source of discussion in the hands of a skilled geography teacher. Lambert and Balderstone (2000) note the comment of a beginning geography teacher who warned that revealing your musical tastes to children is always to invite ridicule, but the challenge is to find ways to engage pupils in discussions about the geographical aspects of music. We can offer some further examples which reflect our own musical tastes, of course.

It may be interesting to discuss the role of music in the construction of the nation. National anthems are an obvious example of this. The playing of national anthems at sporting events and their lyrics can be the prompt for a geographical analysis, but there are other examples. Think about the 1996 football anthem, 'Football's coming home'. There is a particular construction of Englishness at work here, one that is romantic and dewy-eyed about the '30 years of hurt'. Ben Carrington (1998) provides a thought-provoking analysis of the song and the video that accompanied it, which suggests that it offered an 'imagined' representation of England. At the local and regional scale, identities are sometimes constructed and confirmed by music, of course, as in Sheffield United's 'Greasy Chip Butty Song' (You fill up my senses, like a gallon of magnet/ Like a packet of Woodbines, like a good pinch of snuff/ Like a night out in Sheffield, like a greasy chip butty/ Oh, Sheffield United, come thrill me again).

If some music seeks to locate itself in particular places, other music is linked to movement and mobility. For example, Irish folk songs and ballads are replete with reference to exile and emigration. Contemporary songs, influenced by rock as well as traditional music, also concern themselves with emigration. Good examples can be found in the songs of The Pogues. All of their albums, plus the solo work of their principal singer-songwriter, Shane MacGowan, contain references to the experience of exile. Some early examples include 'Transmetropolitan', 'The Dark Streets of London' and 'The Old Main Drag' which reflect on the experience of the Irish immigrant to London, and 'Sally MacLennane', with the following chorus:

We walked him to the station in the rain
We kissed him as we put him on the train
And we sang him a song of times long gone
Though we knew that we'd be seeing him again
(Far away) sad to say I must be on me way
So buy me beer and whiskey 'cos I'm going far away
I'd like to think of me returning when I can
To the greatest little boozer and to Sally MacLennane

The band also covered the traditional song 'The Irish Rover' with the Dubliners, sang of an Irish-American being returned home for burial in 'The Body of an American', and described the experience of travelling from Ireland to London on 'The Boat Train'. The 1988 album 'If I Should Fall from Grace with God' expressed the emigration theme most strongly. The song, 'Thousands are Sailing' draws upon the now 'silent' Ellis Island (the key point of entry of the Irish to the United States in the nineteenth century) to reflect on the migration of the Irish across the Atlantic in the infamous 'coffin ships':

Where e'er we go, we celebrate
The land that makes us refugees
From fear of priests with empty plates
From guilt and weeping effigies
And we dance . . .

The song captures the ambiguity of migration as a cultural experience. A second example is that of Bhangra which was closely tied to the experiences of Punjabi migrants in distant cities. The music maintained connections with Punjabi folk music, but was transformed in Britain (notably Birmingham, 'the capital of Bhangra') by young migrants who retained the traditional instruments but added guitars, synthesisers and drums, and sometimes English lyrics. These changes meant that Bhangra was seen not simply as the music of migrant Punjabis, but was accepted by other South Asians as 'their' music. The music went beyond its ancestral origins to enable first- and second-generation migrants from throughout South Asia to develop a new common identity. As you read about these examples, you may be thinking about how a study of migration in geography could be informed by a study of musical cultures, something that would contribute to the requirement of the National Curriculum that geography should allow pupils to develop their understanding of cultural diversity.

Music, of course, plays an important role in economic life. It would perhaps be difficult to think of a better case study of the processes involved in globalisation than music. The issue of cultural imperialism can be explored through an album such as Paul Simon's *Graceland*, which was controversial because it allegedly appropriated the sounds and skills of southern African musicians and sold them to a Western audience. What better examples can there be of the processes of globalisation (both economic and cultural) than that of global megastars such as Britney Spears and Christina Aguilera?

In a short chapter such as this, it has only been possible to offer a taste of how some of the work done by geographers on music might be used to inform planning and teaching in geography. We have shown our own prejudices here, and expect that readers will be able to find other and better examples of how music and geography are related. We share the view that music can indeed enrich geography teaching. However, we would suggest that this is best achieved if there is a strong geographical rationale for such work. The argument of the work in the geographies of music is that music is linked with important geographical concepts such as place, space and scale. In addition, we also argue that this type of teaching needs to be informed by a critical media literacy approach. What this entails is explained by Shuker (2001) in his book *Understanding Popular Music*.

Films and video

Geography is the subject that makes most use of videos in its teaching. However, often videos are treated as though they are a transparent 'window on the world'. A critical geographical literacy is based on the need to assess the value of the representations of the world found in videos. There has been less discussion of the role of popular films in the teaching of geography, although geographers have become increasingly interested in the way films represent people and places. The British Film Institute has published a report entitled *Making Movies Matter* (1999) which makes the case for the development of 'cineliteracy' in schools. The report was followed up by *Moving Images in the Classroom* (2000),

127

which offers guidance for the study of films in school subjects such as geography. The document contains a number of ideas for teaching geography using films. The ideas for geography in *Moving Images in the Classroom* encourage a 'humanistic' or 'personal response' to films, and at times focus on the techniques by which certain effects are produced. They risk falling into the trap, therefore, of 'geography as personal response', identified by Henley in relation to geographical language (see p. 105). While these are worthwhile activities, we would argue that a critical media literacy requires that students are helped to understand the ideological work that films do – that is, teachers and students need to focus on the messages about people, places and environments that films offer. This can be illustrated with reference to one popular film, *The Full Monty* (see Box 6.3).

BOX 6.3 *THE FULL MONTY*

The Full Monty is a film that is loaded with geographical meaning. The film is set in the aftermath of the deindustrialisation of Sheffield, and starts with footage of dated promotional film that depicts Sheffield as 'steel city', a city on the move, with trendy nightclubs, and located at the centre of Britain's industrial north, with 90,000 men employed in steelworks. Almost immediately, the film cuts to present-day Sheffield, with a steelyard that is derelict, rusted and abandoned, except for two redundant steelworkers 'liberating' (stealing) a girder.

The film explores issues of gender politics in a post-industrial context, and the common feature of all the male characters is that they are experiencing a 'crisis of identity' following their redundancy. This crisis of masculinity is manifested in a variety of ways: the redundancy of fathers, the infantilisation of unemployed men, and sexual impotency. The central characters have lost their work and as such their foundational identities. This is symbolised in the film by the advance of women into 'men's space'. Thus the working men's club is appropriated by women for the Chippendales event, a point stressed by the fact that women even use the men's toilets.

There are significant opportunities for geography teaching here. Most notably, there are themes about the gendered nature of work, the separation of the private and public spheres, and the gendered use of space that could usefully be explored. The organisation of many places around

---

such a set of gendered relations could be discussed. The film is also a commentary on changing economic activities. The types of work shown in *The Full Monty* reflect wider patterns of employment in Britain, where nearly half the workforce is female, mostly in casualised and low-paid forms of white-collar work. In the film, places of active employment are supermarkets, where women serve and men act as security guards, and female dominated factory work, which men (predictably) avoid at all costs. The film tends to focus on gender relations, with the effect that questions of class are downplayed. The geography teacher might want to raise questions about the 'invisible' forces that are shaping such places as Sheffield. The film makes use of the metaphors of 'stripping' in relation to the stripped nature of the landscapes of industrialisation, and in the fact that the craft skills of the men are no longer needed (as one of the characters says 'like skateboards'), and the men are stripped of their identities. In order to regain their identities, they learn to 'strip', in the process becoming commodities (again, the gendered role reversal is notable, in that this time the male strippers are the ones who are watched, subject to display, rather than the traditional female stripper). Indeed, this notion, that in order to regain their identities men must repackage themselves as 'commodities', comes close to the role envisaged for workers in post-Fordist capitalism; workers must be flexible, adaptable, enterprising and skilled at packaging themselves for the demands of the market.

It is important to ask how geography teachers might develop a cultural pedagogy to make use of a film such as *The Full Monty*. Such an approach is always discursive in that it revolves around discussions about the meanings of the text, drawing out its meanings and making them speak to the reader. In developing this approach to teaching it is less important to provide 'correct' interpretations about a text than to achieve a critical position on it. There is no inherent meaning in the text itself, but films are read socially.

Final comments

In this section we have begun to suggest some ways in which geography teachers can find ways to develop a critical media literacy. Kincheloe and Steinberg (1997) discuss the need for educators to come to terms with the 'cultural curriculum of hyperreality':

We can develop as many wonderful multicultural school curriculums as we like, but as important and influential as they may be, such lessons often don't address the cultural curriculum being taught by TV, movies, popular music, video games and the Internet. Popular cultural consumption shaped by TV and movie corporations and other entertainment industries positions power-wielding commercial institutions as the teachers of the new millennium.

(p. 92)

The contours of this consumer culture are described by Naomi Klein (2000) in her book *No Logo*, a book that could usefully be mined by teachers seeking to learn more about consumer capitalism and its relationship to young people. In *Consuming Children* Kenway and Bullen (2001) describe the links between education, entertainment and advertising. They argue that education has been corporatised, as big business sees schools as sites where the minds of young people can be captured and harnessed. They argue that the formal knowledge of the curriculum finds it hard to compete with the images and dreams offered by business, and suggest that there is a need for teachers in all subjects to find ways to help young people develop a critical perspective on consumer-media culture. Finding ways to engage with the informal cultures of young people is a challenging task, not least because there is a danger that teachers' attempts to teach about media culture are seen as a critique of the pleasures of everyday life. However, the potential benefits of '*re-enchanting*' the geography curriculum are great.

CONCLUSION: BEING CRITICAL – AN APOLOGY?

We have used the word 'critical' many times in this chapter. Whenever we write it, we are tempted to say 'Ouch'. On the one hand, we are all encouraged to be (and encourage our students to be) critical thinkers. On the other hand, advocating critical geography teaching risks being accused of political indoctrination. We have persisted with the term because, for us, to be critical is to examine the terms of the discourses we use. We have shown, through the use of examples, the need for geography teachers to examine geographical texts in order to understand the processes of inclusion and omission that characterise them. For example, in our discussion of textbook representations of the British coal industry, we highlighted that these representations cannot be viewed as neutral, but offer highly selective treatments of the topics. Unless we are aware of these processes, there is a danger that geography lessons will fail to offer pupils a range of perspectives.

In recent times the term 'critical' has had a bad press. It has been associated with so-called 'political correctness' and it has been suggested that teachers who claim to be critical are in fact seeking to move pupils from their unconscious and incorrect views to conscious and correct views. Critical pedagogy is thus a form of political imposition. There are, of course, dangers in this. However, it seems that the only alternative is to give up being critical altogether, and simply agree that there is a body of geographical knowledge that needs to be passed on to all children. Surely the better solution is for geography teachers, who have been trained in the construction of geographical knowledge, to make choices about content based on their understanding of the structure of the discipline.

David Buckingham (2003) makes some interesting comments about the limitations of being critical. His studies of media education classrooms suggest that being critical can involve pupils becoming aware of alternative discourses and using the language of deconstruction in order to demonstrate their superiority over others. Thus these pupils would watch television programmes armed with critical tools and demonstrate their 'knowingness'. This became a form of 'cultural capital'. We, too, have noticed this tendency. For example, beginning students have come to our courses having completed studies of the geographies of nightclubs or the geography of shopping. While this is all well and good, there is nevertheless a danger if they are not aware of the politics of knowledge construction at work. These are the risks associated with any type of knowledge – the danger that knowledge will be used for socially divisive purposes. We are under no illusions about this; in the past, present and most likely the future, geographical knowledge has been created to serve particular interests and reinforce divisions between people. This is what we mean when we say that geographical knowledge is socially constructed or produced. That does not mean we should give up on the idea of encouraging all students to be critical interpreters of the world, of trying to see geographical knowledge as socially constituted and therefore capable of being re-written or re-thought. This suggests that we need geography teachers who have a thorough grasp of how geographical knowledge is created and have a deep understanding of the purposes of geographical education. In other words, they are able to answer convincingly the question of what constitutes 'progress' in geography education. It is to this question that we turn in the final chapter of this part of the book.

131

FOR FURTHER THINKING

1 Teaching geography well is concerned with far more than supplying for students an engaging 'pedagogic adventure'. Is it possible to think about 'teaching and learning' without thinking about the curriculum at the same time?

2 What in your view is the main value of developing literacy skills (and understanding) in geography?

3 The National Curriculum requires geography to be learned using 'enquiry' methods. We would prefer to say critical enquiry. What is it about the nature of geographical knowledge that demands critical engagement?

Chapter 7

Evaluating geography education

INTRODUCTION

One of the ubiquitous pieces of advice offered to geography teachers is that they must evaluate their teaching. Teacher education courses place a strong emphasis on encouraging beginning teachers to evaluate their lessons in order to improve their day-to-day work. Course assignments encourage them to evaluate the quality of pupils' learning achieved through units of work, partly because there is a presumed relationship between the quality of learning and the quality of teaching. This is all well and good, and it introduces beginning teachers to what are perhaps the most difficult questions they face:

- What constitutes progress in learning geography?
- How does geographical understanding develop – and is this development possible to measure or judge in a realistic and dependable way?
- How can assessments of learning feedback and improve teaching?

However, we would suggest that just as important is the ability to stand back and ask good questions about the overall quality of the work undertaken in school geography. This requires a different set of lenses, or, as we would prefer, a different language or way of thinking about our work as teachers. We think it unfortunate that this language sometimes gets lost from discussions of geography education when they focus too strongly on attainment and measures of 'value added'. In making such a claim we do not intend to upset anybody. However, we want to suggest in this chapter that part of the problem is the way discussions of what constitutes progress in geography education have become rather one-dimensional, to the extent that, as a community, our thinking has become a bit 'flabby'. The first part of this chapter makes that case. In the rest of the chapter, we offer our own provisional map of how we might evaluate geographical education. As with all the arguments in this book, we are not claiming to have all the answers, and we certainly do not want to have the last word. But we do want to make sure that certain ideas are shared with the wider community of practice (see Chapter 10) – of which you are a part.

MAKING PROGRESS?

In the first paragraph of Chapter 2, we declared our desire to develop a 'progressive' approach to teaching geography. That word may have triggered alarm bells in some readers. It is time for us to think out loud about what we mean. John Rennie Short (1998) makes a distinction between *progress of geography* and *progress in geography*.

Progress of geography refers to the ability of geography to maintain and strengthen its position in the education sector. The argument goes something like this. Geography is important, and students need to experience geography in all its variety and depth. As a result, its value will be recognised and this will consolidate society's demand for geographical knowledge and geography. The measure of the progress of geography will be the extent to which it is afforded high status in schools and universities. One of the by-products of this definition of progress is that geographers make great claims about the subject's ability to play its part in virtually all aspects of the curriculum. There are many examples of this to be found in educational debates at the present time. For example, geography has staked a claim in education for sustainable development, has made much of its potential to develop knowledge, understanding and skills in citizenship, and geographers' contribution to developments in 'Thinking Skills' are visible in the Key Stage 3 Strategy. Perhaps the most notable example in recent years is how geographers in schools have embraced information and communications technology.

While it is understandable that geography teachers will seek to play a central role in developments in schools, we want to sound a note of caution. Such initiatives risk being implemented without the required degree of informed discussion about how they relate to the nature of geography as a subject. For example, in relation to ICT, questions need to be asked about the assumptions that underpin particular forms of software, and about the ways in which the 'geographical imagination' is shaped by the introduction of ICT. One of the great changes brought about by ICT is the almost instant availability (at a low cost) of all sorts of maps. This has potential implications for the work of geography teachers. However, their use needs to be informed by an understanding of the political and social questions that surround the use of maps. Without such a consideration, we risk teaching in ways that are bereft of theory and devoid of moral purpose. Another example is the drive to introduce literacy across the curriculum. As we saw in the previous chapter, The Department for Education and Skills recently published a document, *Literacy in Geography* (DfES 2002), which has been issued to all geography departments in England. Again, while the development of literacy within geography is laudable, questions need to be asked about how literacy is conceptualised in the document and, just as important, how geography as a subject constructs literacy (geography, after all, literally means 'earth-writing'). Similarly, it is quite possible for geography departments to introduce ideas and activities from publications such as *Thinking through Geography* (Leat 1998), without re-evaluating the nature of the geographical content about which students are asked to think! The point we are making here is that it is quite possible for geographers to get swept along by whole school development policies and initiatives and constantly find they are responding to other people's agendas.

What is lost in the race for the progress of geography is any prolonged and sensitive discussion of what constitutes *progress in geography*. Short (1998) defines progress in geography as 'the ability of geographers to make their world more understandable' (p. 62). This begs important questions that face any social project. What do we mean by more knowledge and understanding? Who is to decide what is progress? Answering these questions entails a very different way of thinking as a community of geography educators. It is less about how to implement pedagogical strategies, and more about what and why as the necessary prelude to any teaching activity. In this book, we are arguing that it is this type of thinking that will allow geography teachers to initiate and sustain conversations that will make the world more understandable.

The shift away from thinking about 'progress of geography' towards 'progress in geography' is a risky one. However, it enables (even impels) us to contemplate some really difficult and important questions. First, it

135

forces us to confront the possibility that 'more geography' is *necessarily* a 'good thing'. Focusing on 'progress of geography' encourages us to think that if geography is advancing in schools, then that is a positive development. However, this tends to assume that we all agree on what geography is, what purposes it serves, and whose interests it represents. As we hope we have shown in this book, this is not necessarily the case, and we would argue that we need to think very carefully about the purposes of geography education (this is the argument we made in Chapter 4).

Second, and related, thinking about what constitutes progress in geography raises the question of whether schooling is always synonymous with education. For example, it might be argued that a document such as *Literacy in Geography*, which has been designed and written by a team of experts, and which contains a particular view about the purposes of literacy, actually reduces the scope of geography teachers to make informed professional decisions about language and literacy that might be based on their own experiences in their subject communities of practice. Geography's involvement in such strategies to 'raise standards' may actually reduce the quality of education.

Third, a focus on what constitutes 'progress in geography' raises the possibility (and here we *are* being heretical) that societies get the kind of education they deserve. If students are deserting the subject in favour of subjects such as politics, sociology, media studies, business studies and psychology, then it may be because those subjects seem to offer some purchase on how young people experience the world. Rather than bemoan the lack of a ministerial ear, or the fickle choices made by young people, a focus on what we mean by 'progress in geography' could prompt us to seriously engage with the substance of geography as a discipline in the contemporary world.

We are clearly seeking to arouse some passion in this debate, but we hope we are making some telling points. In order to develop our argument, it is useful to return to a moment in the past when geographers believed they were making progress in making the world more understandable. It is well expressed in Peter Ambrose's book *Analytical Human Geography* (1969) which presented, for school teachers, some of the seminal articles of the 'new' geography, and which suggested that the material 'constitutes a clear statement that human geography has taken a step in a new direction' (p. 283). Ambrose proposed the term 'locationalist' to describe this work, and noted that:

A concern with the patterns made by phenomena on the earth has for long been central to the geographer's interest. But only recently, it seems, has the spatial pattern made by some phenomena been recognised as the normal point of entry for research work. Only recently has such systematic attention been given to the problem of measuring and interpreting distributions . . . It may soon, perhaps, be appropriate to define human geography as *the science of the location and spatial distribution of man and his works.*

(1969: 284, original emphases)

Ambrose was particularly taken by the prospect of using certain spatial concepts as the basis for the organisation of geographical study. The four he picked out for special attention were gradient, network, least cost location and cumulative causation. These concepts shared two common features: the universality of their application and their progressively increasing complexity:

each word or phrase sums up some universally operating aspect of the total process of man's interaction with his social and physical environment. People everywhere are concerned to save money by wise choice of crops or wise location of factories. People everywhere form part of various networks. Similarly, people everywhere spread ideas and have a natural inclination to live and work with similar, rather than with different, people.

(1969: 291)

In terms of progression, Ambrose thought:

Each of the concepts mentioned shares the characteristic that it can be made intelligible at the level of complexity required to suit the reader. Thus examples of the working of each concept could be found for those in the first year of secondary education. The same concepts, much elaborated, are likely to appear in doctoral theses. The processes of refinement development . . . that occur between these two stages seem to be much more educationally valid than the long process of accretion of fact which is a more accurate characteristic of much geographical study at the moment.

(1969: 291)

Here then, we have a vision of progress based on a more 'logical' and integrated structure for geographical study. However, it might be argued that, in Short's terms, it was still primarily a vision of progress *for* geography rather than *in* geography. Smith and Ogden (1977) argued that changes in academic disciplines do not occur in isolation, but reflect the society in which they take place:

> Stepping back from the battleground, we can now see that the quantitative revolution closely reflected the contemporary reverence with technological gymnastics, reverence for cybernetics, and the sense that human ingenuity in an era of general prosperity would automatically generate solutions to our problems. It was the geography of the decade of space exploration – the era of what Eliot Hurst has aptly described as 'the geographer as mechanic'.
>
> (1977: 50)

In the same publication, Roger Lee (1977) suggested that the new geography should be understood as representing a methodological revolution that, although it led to change at the frontier of higher education, led to the 'passing down of "instructions" down the educational hierarchy and so to the consequent distortion rather than the replacement of orthodox geography' (p. 4). Lee also noted that at the same time as the methodical revolution was finding its way down the educational 'hierarchy', there was, taking place in geography, a 'truly radical epistemological revolution' that involved a 'fundamental critique of existing economic structures'. For it was quickly realised that the methodical revolution did not provide the basis for a re-constituted geography education. The models did not fit the reality; the statistical exercises left pupils and teachers cold; the issues and problems thrown up by the 'real world' constantly broke in to the ordered world presented to pupils in school geography textbooks. Lee, from his historical materialist perspective, argued that this was inevitable: 'Such an understanding came (could come only) from the blackboard jungle, not from the ivory tower' (p. 5).

The implications of this realisation are potentially profound: 'It challenges, in a most fundamental way the notion an educational "hierarchy" and the structure which assumes that impulses for change run from top to bottom and not the other way round' (p. 5).

It is this vision of change coming from the 'blackboard jungle' rather than the 'ivory tower' that informs Derek Gregory and Rex Walford's discussion in the introduction to *Horizons in Human Geography* (1989). The book was conceived as a follow-up to two earlier books by Chorley and Haggett and was 'directed primarily at teachers'. They note their belief that 'the study of geography in schools and in higher education is a common enterprise', that 'there is a linking thread which ties together the different curiosities about the world of the primary-school child and the post-graduate researcher' (p. 3). They argue that the book follows in the footsteps of 'Models' and 'Frontiers' and is intended to 'make current developments more accessible so that teachers could consider them carefully and critically'. The approach suggested in the book amounts to an argument for a theoretically informed and historically sensitive regional geography and an argument for a new 'geographical literacy' and 'geographical awareness'. This will rely on 'traditional' geographical skills, but also a revival of 'practical' or hermeneutic skills involving the clarification of meaning, interpretation, translation and understanding. These, the authors argue, are essential for the development of a 'genuinely critical geography'.

In line with the argument that such 'relevance' comes from the desire of geographers to speak about and to the world they live in, this geography must be participatory, and it must emerge from the 'blackboard jungle': 'But more important is our conviction that, in the contemporary reconstitution of human geography, teachers in schools are likely to be much more closely involved in its direction than they were in previous "revolutions"' (Gregory and Walford 1989: 6). It is interesting to read those words now, from the vantage point of 2005, since it hardly needs saying that school teachers have not played a major part in the reconstitution of human geography, and the gap between academic and school geography has grown so wide as to become a chasm.

Here then, we have a clear example of an argument about what 'progress' means for geographers. This debate is about fundamental educational aims and purposes. It makes a direct link to the work of the American educationalist, John Dewey (1916; 1966), about what the subject of geography is for. However, at the risk of repeating ourselves, this is a debate that has been strangely absent in public discussions of geography teaching. While geography teachers are well versed in the discourses of 'thinking skills', 'literacy strategies', and 'levelled assessments', the language of educational aims and purposes is seemingly lacking (see Lambert 2003).

139

We will leave it there, and let readers decide for themselves what constitutes progress in geography education. This is something that has motivated the writing of this book, and so we feel we should take this opportunity to sketch our own map of what we mean by progress in geography. In line with the argument that runs through the whole of this book, we think this is best done by geographers using their knowledge and understanding of geography as a subject. In the rest of this chapter, we provide some examples of the type of issues we would like geography educators to engage with in the future.

EVALUATING PROGRESS IN GEOGRAPHY

In writing this section of the book, we are mindful of our own conception of 'progress in geography', which, adapting Derek Gregory's phrase, is 'doubly human':

> human in the sense that it recognizes that its concepts are specifically human constructions, . . . and human in the sense that it restores human beings to their own worlds and enables them to take part in the collective transformation of their own human geographies.
>
> (1978: 172)

Although we realise that this formulation underplays physical geography, it seems to us to express what geography teaching can be, at its best. In the first case, it demands that we develop geography lessons that are self-reflective and critical of their own assumptions. If we recognise that concepts are constructions – conventions agreed upon by a community of scholars – then we have to be attentive to how they were constructed, and continually seek to re-evaluate and re-think them in the light of new evidence, and in the light of different ways of viewing the world.

For example, a concept often found in geography teaching is 'least-cost location'. Teachers will immediately recognise the concept as one used in economic geography and more specifically, linked to the models of industrial location devised by Alfred Weber. Weber began his work at a time when German idealism was in the ascendant. Idealism argued that people were free to invent their worlds through the force of ideals. Weber sought to challenge these ideas by stressing the intervention of economic reality. He asked whether it was 'sensible for us to argue about cultural and social motives when perchance we are simply fettered by the iron chains of hard economic forces'. His search for the 'pure laws of industrial location' was an attempt to show that people were constrained by these iron chains. However, Weber was also influenced by the work of his elder brother Max, especially his idea that any science of society was always historically specific. This led Alfred Weber to qualify the abstract form of location theory and accept that patterns of contemporary industrial development did not result from the operations of 'pure' laws alone and that resulted 'to a large extent from very definite central aspects of modern capitalism which might disappear with it' (cited in Gregory 1978: 39).

These qualifications were lost when geographers 'rediscovered' Weber in the 1960s, with the result that generations of students have been introduced to the arcane world of Varignon frames, locational triangles and isodapanes. Similar problems can be seen in the more recent development of concepts in geography such as globalisation or sustainable development. Often, these concepts are defined and delimited for consumption by students, with the result that much of the history of these terms and the complex arguments about them are lost. Derek Gregory urges geography teachers to develop a critically reflective approach where commonsense concepts and theories are held up to question. The problem, of course, is that such teaching is not easy. It requires us to make sense of complex arguments and debates and make decisions about whether and how to engage students in this community of scholars. But just because such teaching is difficult does not mean that we should not try.

The second 'human' Gregory mentioned concerns the social purposes of geographical knowledge. He is suggesting that such knowledge should be judged as more or less useful according to whether it returns people to a world made clear, where ideology is unveiled, and where the structures that shape the making of the world are also made clear. It implies that geographical knowledge should be 'empowering' and lead to people feeling more in control of their lives. As Kincheloe and Steinberg (1998: 5–6) put it: 'Emancipated students ... question their self-image, inherited dogmas, and comfortable ways of thinking.'

What this might mean in practice is well expressed in the following statement by a 17-year-old student:

> The notion of writing prize-winning essays on tropical rainforests without taking some kind of action would be seen as strange. Schools would be part of the local and international community and would take part in solving some of its problems. This would re-attach effort

141

to real tangible results and would have a positive effect on motivation to learn. It would mean pupils and teachers were not just working for some esoteric result.

(Quoted in Burke and Grosvenor 2003: 63)

As Short argues: 'As geographers we have a special responsibility to make sense of the ambiguities and polarities involved in the relationship between people and environment, space and place, the social and the spatial, the structural and the personal' (Short 1998).

EVALUATION IN PRACTICE

We will confine ourselves to two aspects we see as central to geography education – a commitment to the 'human' in human geography, and a commitment to an understanding of the relationship between people and environment.

Evaluating human geography

A number of geographers have written about their concern with the 'dehumanising' of human geography – for example, Chris Philo (2000) has written about the 'desocialising' of geography and calls for geographers to:

continue paying urgent attention to the mundane workings of families and communities; it is to register the battles to get by on a daily basis, to earn a crust, to keep the house warm, to cope with the neighbours, to walk down the street without being afraid; it is to take a stab at sharing the happiness and sadness of being people with or without friends, groups to hang out in, things to do, to share, to enjoy, to complain about; it is to pay attention to the child crying in the road, the old man shuffling to the pub, the young mother and her pram negotiating the kerbstones; and so on and so on.

(2000: 37)

If we were to apply Philo's concern for the social geographies of everyday life to an educational context, geography teachers would evaluate their practice according to how far it helps students to gain an understanding of the lives and issues facing the full range of people in the world (see also Kitchin 1999 and Box 7.1).

BOX 7.1 POPULATION STUDIES: AGEING

Geographers are increasingly sensitive to the range of human experiences. The work of feminist geographers urged geographers not to ignore half the world's people, and social geographers such as Susan Smith and Peter Jackson alerted geographers to the issue of race and racism. The circle of concern has widened to encompass a broad range of groups, including children and young people, people with disabilities and mental illness, and the elderly.

Geographers have studied ageing in a variety of ways. These include:

- the distribution of the elderly and how this has changed over time;
- the decision-making involved in retirement migration;
- housing issues for the elderly;
- the impact of transport policy on the elderly;
- the distribution of health care facilities; and
- the implications of an ageing population for land use planning.

Much of this work is based on positivist and behavioural models. It is easy to see how this type of approach could be used in schools, especially in GCSE and AS course work. One of the problems with this type of work is that it assumes that categories such as 'old age' and the 'elderly' are universal, and even where interviews are conducted, it reveals little about the meanings associated with ageing. It focuses on the personal experiences of ageing and risks downplaying the structural aspects of ageing, or the ways in which older people's lives are constructed as part of a wider society.

An alternative way of thinking about ageing then is to look for the deeper, invisible forces that structure people's experience of ageing. For example, the exclusion of older people from paid work, the experience of poverty in old age, the tendency for old people to spend time in institutions are not 'natural', but are outcomes of the way society is organised. Using this approach in schools would involve helping students to understand ageing in historical and societal terms. This might involve historical studies based on oral or literary testimony, studies of literature that deals with themes of ageing, or how older people are represented in the media.

In economic geography, examples might focus on the pensions industry and the role of the state in providing welfare. This type of structural

143

account of the geographies of ageing might risk giving the impression that older people's lives are determined by their location in a capitalist society, and downplay the considerable diversity of experiences of ageing. Indeed, recent strands of social theory point to the ways in which age-based identities (like other identities) are flexible and capable of change. Clearly, there are physical limits to this, but it is possible to imagine a geographical study of ageing that was sensitive to the ways in which elderly people negotiate, resist, transgress and make use of different spaces (based on Morgan 2003).

The example of the geographies of ageing serves to illustrate some of the complexities involved in planning and teaching rigorous geography lessons that can be defended on scholarly and ethical grounds. The decision to teach about the geographical experiences of older people in itself represents a selection, a purposeful choice to widen pupils' understanding of the world. It might be defended on the grounds that it allows pupils to recognise that people experience the world differently. The fact that elderly people are largely absent from mainstream geographical discourse could be used as a means of helping students understand something of the politics of knowledge production. Box 7.1 points out that there are different ways of approaching the geographies of ageing. Some of these approaches accept the category of 'old age' uncritically, while others suggest that it is a socially constructed category; some approaches stress the structural contexts of ageing, while others focus on the possibilities of human agency. Importantly, some approaches accept the parameters of society as it exists, while others seek to alert students to the idea that society might be organised differently.

Geography teachers are faced with important choices. One thing seems clear, however. Surely it is incumbent on teachers to use their understanding of the subject to alert students to the fact that geographical knowledge is a human production and thereby offers (sometimes) implicit messages about the nature of society. Helping students to deconstruct geographical knowledge for themselves is a crucial task. The idea of the 'banking' method of teaching, whereby supposedly objective chunks of knowledge are 'deposited' in pupils' minds is untenable. Here the role of the teacher is crucial, since geography teachers with a critical understanding of the subject matter and the contexts in which it is produced are in a position to help students learn about processes of knowledge production. They are more likely to ask the right questions at the right time to challenge and deepen understanding. They are able to construct frameworks that facilitate cognitive and affective development in pupils.

Evaluating environmental geography

Our second example illustrates some further issues surrounding the status of geographical knowledge through the example of the tropical rainforest biome (see Box 7.2). This is a topic commonly studied in school geography, where pupils are introduced to the idea that rainforest ecosystems are under threat from human development. But what understandings do we want pupils to learn from studying the tropical rainforest (more than the careless propaganda that they should be 'saved')?

BOX 7.2 UNDERSTANDING THE TROPICAL RAINFOREST – TEACHING LIES?

Recent developments in the study of environmental change have cast doubts on the ecology of 'tropical rainforests'. Ecology as a science has been characterised by discussions about the extent to which environments are characterised by change and uniformity, instability and equilibrium, competition and co-operation, integration and individuality. These terms represent either end of the spectrum, but in the struggle of ideas it was the *concept of equilibrium* that won through, with the result that there is an emphasis on notions of 'climax', 'optima', 'balance', 'harmony', 'stability', and 'ecosystems'.

The development of ecology was closely linked with ideas of conservation. For example, ecologists such as Arthur Tansley (1935), who coined the term ecosystem, were influential in the development of nature conservation in Britain. They made the distinction between 'manipulated' and 'natural' ecosystems. This promoted the idea that there was a distinction between nature and people. Nature was presumed to exist in its 'pristine' state and any human disturbance to such 'ecosystems' was interpreted as interfering with the delicate balance or equilibrium.

These ideas about homeostasis and equilibrium were challenged from the 1970s onwards as a result of the non-linearity seen in disturbance ecology. Those working in the field found that what they were observing did not match the models. For instance, take this description, from a leading biogeographer:

> I am uneasy with the repeated assertions that nature's norm is balance, that this balance is fragile, and that current human activities invite the collapse of entire, complex ecosystems. In contrast, what I have seen during decades of fieldwork is neither pervasive order nor chaos, but comfortable disorder.
>
> (Drury 1998, cited in Head 2000)

Moore *et al.* (1996) spell out the implications of this change in the way ecosystems are viewed for tropical rainforests. They suggest that a simplistic view of tropical rainforests is that they are equilibrium systems in balance with the climate of the humid tropics and that they have existed, largely undisturbed, under such a climate for millions of years. Large-scale human disturbance is seen as disrupting the age-old equilibrium, thus reducing sustainability and causing ecological mayhem. They challenge this view:

> We now know that this view is totally fallacious, and that humid tropical climates, just like those of the high latitudes, have altered dramatically over geological time, and that the tropical rainforests themselves are dynamic systems, with gaps, building and mature phases, and an ever-changing flux of species, each responding individualistically to environmental change.
>
> (Moore *et al.* 1996: 200)

One implication of this argument is that the very concepts of 'sustainability' and 'equilibrium' are intrinsically flawed, and that the reality is one of disequilibrium systems, which gain their essential resistance and persistence through a constant individualistic response to change. This is not really surprising, since these concepts derive from the 'outdated' vegetation climax concepts developed in northern Europe and North America during the early part of the twentieth century, where anything which was not 'forest' tended to be perceived as a 'sub-climax' below the 'optimum'; it was believed that such 'sub-climaxes' would return to forest when the relevant disturbance factor (such as fire or grazing) was removed.

Philip Stott (1998) points out that, as a subdiscipline, biogeography is characterised by the hegemony of forest ecology, the hegemony of equilibrium theory and the hegemony of northern Europe and North America. This is perfectly illustrated by the fascination for tropical rainforests. Thus, it has become accepted that rainforests are the 'biological wonder of the world', that rainforest clearance is a bad thing, and that we will all suffer if the rainforests are destroyed. In an article in *History Today* (2001) Stott argues that 'tropical rainforests' are an 'invention', the result of a particular way of seeing and interpreting the landscape. He makes the point that 'tropical rainforests have many "values"', which vary from North to South, country to country, and people to people. For some, tropical rainforests are a sign of 'underdevelopment' and a lack of progress; to others they are vital for the very ecology and survival of the whole earth. The question is: whose values dominate decision-making concerning rainforests in our changing world?

Moore *et al.* (1996) offer the example of the following question set by the University of London's Examinations Board. Candidates were presented with five practices that are threatening the existence of tropical forests, including 'Firewood' and 'Charcoal burning' (candidates were required to choose one 'misuse' and explain why it is a cause for concern). In discussing the question, Moore *et al.* comment:

> Such a set of values could only have been conflated in the North. The majority of people in the world depend on firewood and charcoal for all their energy requirements, indeed for their very livelihood. Moreover, this firewood and charcoal are often produced by systems which have been maintained for many generations.
>
> (Moore *et al.* 1996: 210)

They suggest that the 'values' exhibited in this question are those of a comfortable Northern suburbia, long divorced from the forests it seeks to save: 'The examination question shows no understanding whatsoever of the values of most of the world; it is frankly a nonsense, and was largely unanswerable' (Moore *et al.* 1996: 210–11).

They argue that the Northern middle classes see the preservation of 'rainforest' as a key item on their global 'stability' agenda. Having agreed this agenda, they have started a process of scientific 'myth-making' to bolster their case. These myths are the 'little green lies' of the current paradigm. The fundamental aim behind them is to make us all believe that we really do *need* rainforests, not just want them or like them. Moore *et al.* offer some alternative 'facts':

- Tropical rainforests are not the most complex ecosystems on earth. There are many competitors for this title, depending on how you define 'complexity'.

147

- Tropical rainforests are not millions of years old. The fossil record clearly indicates that the majority of present-day 'rainforests' are less than 18,000 years old, having been subject to drought, fire and cold during the peak of the last ice age.
- The plant diversity beneath the canopy is actually quite low.
- The rainforests are not the lungs of the world. In fact, because of their decomposition processes, most rainforests tend to use up as much or even more oxygen than they give out.
- Rainforests are portrayed as vital in preventing soil erosion. While this may be true in some cases, in others it is not, and grassland ecosystems might be more effective in preventing soil erosion.

Moore *et al.* suggest that this 'cavalcade of "little green lies"' has three main purposes, all relating to the essential political ecology of rainforests:

- The desire of the North to maintain a controlling interest over the resources of the South.
- The worry that changes in the South, both ecological and economic, might damage the political stability of the North.
- The 'desperate drive' of scientists to obtain continued funding for research into the questions that the current paradigm places on the agenda.

Global environmental change represents one of the dominant modern 'green' paradigms, creating both the current scientific agenda and demanding certain solutions. However, all science operates within a political context, and there is a need to deconstruct this context. This is the theme of political ecology which asks important questions such as: Who actually placed global environmental change on the agenda? Why did they do so? Is the agenda agreed and shared by all, rich and poor, North and South, scientist and lay person?

The purpose of the example in Box 7.2 is not to adjudicate on the reality of tropical deforestation. However, it is to suggest that this debate has important implications for school geography teachers, who are each day charged with the task of 'teaching something'. Some searching questions about evaluating what we teach are set out below:

- How do you react to the arguments presented in the rainforest example?
- If we accept the idea that we can never achieve 'secure knowledge' of a topic like this, how should we, as geography teachers, respond?
- What are the implications of the argument that the knowledge sanctioned by the exam board is 'nonsense'?

There are a variety of responses to the arguments in Box 7.2 and the searching questions. Our argument is that, as geography educators, we need to be able to grapple with their implications without ignoring the complexities. If these are arguments made by geographers in the academic discipline, part of our skill must be to think through the educational implications of these debates. This involves thinking about the pedagogical strategies that they imply, and about the political and social construction of geographical knowledge. It involves asking questions about whose knowledge is being prioritised in the classroom, and it involves thinking through ideas about development and how children's cognitive skills can be encouraged to grow.

THE PURPOSE OF EVALUATION – WHY TEACH GEOGRAPHY?

These discussions have led us to the important question of ethics in the teaching of geography. As we have been stressing throughout the whole of Part II, the design of lessons is wrapped up with the creation of ethical spaces for students to dwell in. The examples we have discussed in this chapter reflect choices on behalf of geographers about what constitutes 'progressive' geography. This raises the issue of the place of controversial issues in the classroom and how to deal with these. As Campbell (2003) has written: 'Given that teaching is inherently and unavoidably infused with aspects of social and moral inquiry, the inevitability of controversial issues emerging as routine elements of classroom discourse should not be a surprise to anyone' (p. 79).

Campbell argues that teachers should not shy away from controversial issues, but advises teachers against offering their personal views on a topic since their voices carry with them the power and legitimacy of their professional position: 'My advice to the ethical teacher is to refrain from saying or deliberately implying "this is what I support or believe" on issues of a truly controversial nature' (p. 81).

She offers warnings about teachers selecting resources and materials that favour their particular points of view, since this 'starts to look like indoctrination in its deceit and intent' (p. 81). She offers some examples of what she sees as biased teaching, notably an article written by a teacher in Toronto entitled 'Why America is hated' published three months after the events of 11 September 2001 and offered as a useful classroom resource for history and geography teachers (Wente 2001).

Many readers of this book may well have experienced the same worries about possible bias and indoctrination. However, one of the problems with Campbell's position is that in the quest to avoid upsetting people and maintaining public standards of teachers as honourable, moral and trusted, certain perspectives are omitted and excluded from classrooms. This may simply be a similar example of why certain places, such as Russia or the Middle East, are rarely studied in geography lessons since they are seen as being 'too political'. The worry we have about Campbell's argument is that it seems to suggest that academic subjects are seamless entities that break down into 'chunks' of relatively unproblematic knowledge that the teacher decides when and how to pass down to students. As we have been at pains to argue in this book, this cannot be assumed. Once we get the idea that it matters whose geography we are teaching, moral and ethical issues come to be matters of pressing concern in the everyday work of putting together geography lessons. Chapter 8, in Part III, carries this discussion forward in the context of the professional development of teachers. As a *beginning* teacher you may feel overpowered by the prospect of engaging with the issues raised in this chapter, faced as you are with the practicalities of making geography classrooms work. But we take a long view on this. We are happy to accept the mere acknowledgement of these issues, for the moment, and a readiness to take responsibility for a 'curriculum thinking' approach to school geography – which includes the need for thoughtful and informed evaluation of what is taught.

CONCLUSION: THE ROLE OF ASSESSMENT?

We began this chapter with a reference to three difficult questions. We have only answered the first in any detail. When it comes to 'measuring' progress we have been silent. We have given you the reasons for this, but we do need to acknowledge that assessment in education – the process by which attainment is judged – is very important and prominent in schools.

Indeed, it can often provide evidence on which evaluations are based – evaluations that is, that are concerned with the easily measurable.

There are many sources of guidance on the technical processes of assessment (see, for example, Lambert and Balderstone 2000 for a discussion on geography assessment). Most modern discussions of assessment refer to a fundamental distinction between the assessment *of* learning and the assessment *for* learning, a distinction not wholly dissimilar to that between progress of geography and progress in geography referred to earlier in this chapter. The distinction is important and profound, the former being concerned with the application of various technical apparatus (tests, decision-making exercises, essays, etc.) to assess how much learning has taken place. It is a quantitative matter and less concerned with the quality of learning. The processes are best learned in the company of skilled practitioners for there is nothing less than an operation of 'case law' in this aspect of teaching – that is, new teachers gain from learning the ropes by 'tuning in' to experience and judgements built up over years. But we do not need to emphasise the dangers inherent in this process if you have read the contents of this chapter.

The second form of assessment, assessment *for* learning, has in its sights the learner and is far more concerned with quality. Indeed these approaches may not use quantification (grades or scores) at all (see Black *et al.* 2003). The aim under this form of assessment is to engage both teachers and learners in understanding the learning – and improving it. Again, readers of this chapter will realise that even here there are far more significant issues at play: the fundamental question still remains, namely what is worth learning?

And in this context it is necessary to be honest and clear about yet another problem that faces geography teachers – another problem that can be ignored in the short term, but which ultimately comes back to haunt the specialist teacher. While it is possible to discuss 'progression' in geography in the round and in fairly commonsense terms (see, for example, Bennetts 1996), when push comes to shove it is exceedingly difficult to say what constitutes progress in geographical understanding or geographical thinking. This is why the National Curriculum level descriptions are so vague. This is why teachers find it so very difficult to provide feedback to pupils that is subject specific (rather than generic – including comments focused only on presentational aspects of the work). It may also be why the original National Curriculum for England overemphasised content (facts) or the accumulation of knowledge.

We are unable to offer a watertight resolution for this conundrum. But it does serve to emphasise the significance of the individual teacher's views on what is worth teaching and what the overall purpose may be – a theme taken up in Part III. And of course, we need to remember that the purpose of teaching and learning geography certainly is not settled: it is contested, which is the nature of the subject. There is clearly a need for research on pupils' geographical understandings – the kind of research that can be conducted small scale, in schools, looking carefully at what the pupils can do. You may be interested in doing such research later in your career.

Our hunch is that geographical understanding involves the combination of a small range of valued *concepts* which seem to recur among geographers – place, scale, interconnectedness, etc. (see, for example, Box 9.4, p. 185) – and *processes* such as selecting evidence, communication and argumentation. But the geographical concepts need to be in the driving seat. Left to generalists, assessment in geography is reduced to levels of description and explanation; what is a *geographical* explanation? Even more important, what constitutes in your opinion *worthwhile* geographical explanation?

FOR FURTHER THINKING

1   We live in a period of obsessive accountability whereby the system demands measures of progress and value added. No one can argue against the desirability of pupils making progress and geography lessons 'adding value' to the pupil's educational experience. But there are crucial differences between the assessment and the evaluation of progress. Can you say what some of these are?

2   What in practice can a geography teacher do in order to deal with the following connected issues:

   a   The 'impossibility' of the teacher achieving a secure knowledge of many aspects of geography.
   b   The need to prepare pupils for enquiries that are complex and where 'answers' are not clear cut and are often uncertain.
   c   Having to prepare pupils for examinations and tests that reward clarity and certainty.

Part III

The teacher

If Part I focused your attention on the subject geography, and Part II re-focused you on to the geography classroom and its principal inhabitants, the students, this part turns your gaze back on to yourself.

In Chapter 8 we start with what could be understood as an appeal to the idealistic motives that fire and sustain many teachers. We ask 'What kind of teacher do you want to be?' The idealistic notion we plant is that teachers have to be first and foremost learners. They tend to be good learners, that is, good listeners with open minds and with a constant interest in finding out about and getting to know their students. But we also explore some ethical aspects of teaching – of teaching geography in particular. We introduce the idea that it is possible to teach in a morally careless way, which, through the application of technical skill and deep understanding, can be avoided.

In Chapter 9 we develop the extended delineation of 'professionalism' (introduced in the previous chapter) in relation to the official standards for the award of newly qualified status. We point out that while these are very useful – and in some ways very ambitious – they are relatively 'silent' on the single most important aspect of a secondary teacher's professional identity, namely her or his subject specialism. At its worst, such a tendency to disregard 'the what' of teaching (that is, *what* is worthwhile and relevant to teach), reduces teachers to skilful technocrats. The chapter discusses why this is an inadequate basis for teaching.

Finally, in Chapter 10 we open up an important debate on the meaning of professional development. In a healthy autonomous profession, continued professional learning is essential to nurture. For subject specialist geography teachers this can be equated directly with the need for continued curriculum renewal. Put another way, effective and meaningful professional development happens through curriculum development. Renewal of the curriculum is the product of effective professional development. This chapter also spends a little time explaining the role of the Geographical Association (GA) which itself grew out of a commitment not only to geography but to the teaching of geography. The GA provides an outlet for teachers' creative energy and the means to communicate the products of this effort. It can therefore support teachers of geography (who may not always see themselves as geographers). But most of all, the GA can use the authority of its membership to help represent teachers of geography with policy-makers.

Chapter 8

What kind of geography teacher?

Those who can, teach.
(Teacher Training Agency, TTA advertising slogan)

INTRODUCTION

Taken as a whole, one of the purposes of this book is to help you make sense of your professional identity as a geography teacher. It is important to grapple with this because 'professional identity' is not so much given, as won. The standards for the award of Qualified Teacher Status (QTS) (www.tta.gov.uk/training/qtsstandards/)can provide the basis on which to establish what we call 'practitioner capacity'. But we want to appeal to the subject specialist in you. It is the desire to create 'productive pedagogies' – i.e. designing geography lessons that stimulate relevant, worthwhile and enjoyable learning – that fuels the *growth* in this capacity. Certainly, this is not a 'child-centred' view, but neither is it a 'subject-centred' view. It is arguably teacher-centred, however, in that it is interested in melding from these equally limited 'positions' a *learning*-oriented motive, steered by the teacher's interest in the pupils' well-being and happiness, and the value or relevance of what is being learned.

A good teacher (see Box 8.1) requires high-level training, technical skill and competence, and something more besides: a *generous disposition* perhaps (it is a job that requires you to 'give' of yourself, physically, emotionally and intellectually, to an unusual degree); or a commitment to *establishing relationships*, often with young people who are not easily likeable but who nevertheless deserve your 'unconditional positive regard'. At this point, careful readers will be asking what we mean by the 'good' teacher. It is clear that conceptions of the 'good' teacher (and

---

BOX 8.1 AN *ETHICAL* GEOGRAPHY TEACHER?

One of the main arguments of this book is that any discussion of what it means to be a geography teacher in the early twenty-first century must take into account the role of values, ethics and morality. This must be seen as a significant historical shift. The major development in geographical knowledge of the last quarter century had been the realisation that knowledge is not neutral or value free (see Kobayashi and Proctor 2003). This leads us into considerations of ethics. Do notions of 'good' and 'moral' have self-evident meaning for geography teachers? Unfortunately, there is little written to guide geography teachers in this area. Essentially, the moral dimension concerns questions of right and wrong. Moral education is concerned with the ways in which individuals and groups make judgements of right and wrong. This is not concerned with teaching *what is* right or wrong, but *how to make* worthwhile distinctions.

---

by extension the 'good' geography teacher) vary from time to time and from place to place. Indeed, Alex Moore (2004) identifies three distinctive dominant discourses of the good teacher in operation in schools and, having critiqued these, he offers two more. Clearly, the question of what it means to be a good geography teacher is subject to debate and contestation, and this book is itself an attempt to broaden the terms of the discussion. If we were to identify for ourselves one key feature of good geography teaching (as argued in this book), it would be the ability to take a distanced and critical view of how geographical knowledge is constructed, and to explore the implications of this for teaching.

In the context of professional development, or, as we would prefer, professional *learning*, we therefore replace high 'standards' with the notion of high *ambition*. Good teachers are fired by the sense of moral purpose to what they are doing: the teaching – *and the learning* – are not seen as ends in themselves but as the means to change people in some significant and beneficial way. Thus, a good geography teacher can say convincingly how geography lessons provide experiences that contribute to a pupil's educational entitlement.

It is, of course, very important for a teacher to be able to distinguish for themselves (and others) the difference between education and indoctrination in this respect, for both aim to 'change people in some significant way'. For the moment, we might simply say that whereas the latter is

BOX 8.2   MORALLY 'CARELESS' GEOGRAPHY TEACHING?

Perhaps the main purpose of teaching geography is to enable young people to respond more intelligently to the big, booming, confusing world in which they live. Or, as a US geography educator puts it, to consider the question 'What, where, why there and why care' (Gritzner 2002: 38).

So, in what ways may geography be taught 'carelessly'? We think the following list is worth consideration:

■ As if examinations were the only thing that mattered in an overbearing 'answer culture'. This is where the teacher attempts to 'deliver' a set list of contents. Pupils attempt to acquire the list for the purposes of examinations. Shallow learning is emphasised.

■ As if there were 'no right or wrong answers'. This is where a teacher, in his or her desire to muddy the water by trying to show that there are competing perspectives and different points of view, carelessly gives the message that *any* answer will do. Perhaps he or she meant to say that there are 'no clear-cut answers'.

■ As if the mission were to change society or create a 'better world'. There is a great danger in teaching with an overt mission that it becomes something other than education. Teaching for any 'good cause' (see Marsden 1989, 1997) runs the risk of indoctrinating rather than educating students, by which we mean leading students to conclusions rather than providing them with the means to evaluate a range of possibilities.

■ As if the pedagogic adventure were all that mattered. Here the need to 'engage' pupils (or perhaps, keep them busy) takes precedence over judgements about the value of what is being learned.

More positively, what characterises 'morally careful' school geography lessons?

■ Strategies to address the most *difficult questions*. This would typically tackle conflicts, forced population movements, growing inequality and environmental sustainability. This means taking a look at what isn't taught in school geography, or what Britzman

(1989) calls the *null* curriculum. For instance, is it simply a coincidence that school geography syllabuses rarely cover the Middle East?

■ Emphasis on frameworks and models that guide *critique and argument*. In this way geography is a vital induction to students as to 'how the claims of social science work'. What we know about the world does not just appear or get discovered, but is created in a 'culture of argument'.

■ Providing opportunities to practise making *informed decisions and expressing viewpoints*, thus contributing to the 'foundation of moral judgement' (Sack 1997, cited in Smith 1999: 119). In geography, a particular opportunity arises through the study of place – not as a 'container' with fixed boundaries (which contains various 'features' to be described), but as a site with porous boundaries. Places are like *meeting points* of great interaction where it is often possible simultaneously to show the individual and unique (at the local scale) *and* the universal and general (at the global scale). Walk down any High Street and note the global connections – in what the shops are selling, clearly, but also in the faces you see.

likely to be concerned with telling (i.e. telling pupils *what* to think), the former is usually more open-ended and discursive (i.e. emphasising *how* pupils should think). While the indoctrination can involve sophisticated techniques, it is essentially a far simpler process than education: planning conversational or discursive, open-ended lessons is technically very challenging. Maintaining the stamina and commitment over years in order to develop and refine such teaching techniques requires high ambition and moral courage – part of what Robin Richardson (1983) meant by 'daring to be a teacher'. In a nutshell, what we say in this chapter is that good training is essential for good teaching – but in the long term it is in itself insufficient to sustain the continued learning that characterises the best teachers. The best teachers are in the first place good learners, and their learning is guided by a strong sense of moral purpose.

We have identified the centrality of an ability to deal with questions of values and ethics in our notion of professional practice. However, one of our concerns with this type of 'encouragement' is that it tends to suggest that individuals alone are responsible for their own development as teachers, at the risk of underplaying the barriers to such development. For example, it will be quite difficult to adopt the reflective and critical stance to geographical knowledge advocated in the previous sections of this book in a geography department where such discussions are at best marginalised and at worse actively discouraged. For this reason, Chapter 10 also focuses on the wider notion of 'communities of practice'. Like the Standards for the award of QTS, your Career Entry Development Profile[5] and the opportunities to undertake any 'inset' or continuing professional development (CPD) activity, this book addresses you mainly as an *individual*. The temptation must be for you to see yourself as a single entity within a massive infrastructure of departments, schools, local education authorities, government agencies and publishers, not to mention the digital world of information that bombards us all. There is also inevitable pressure from the word 'go' for you to think in terms of developing a career; indeed, CPD is often understood to be relevant mainly in these terms – career advancement – and this seems to place the individual in competition with others. *You* are responsible, apparently, for the path you take, and the rate of progress you make, on the 'career ladder'.

And yet we know that the most effective learning takes place in the company of others; it is a social process at least as much as it is an individual, mental process. Good departments and good schools are brilliant at realising this. Informal and formal structures are in place to support, nurture and challenge. However, it is commonplace for secondary teachers to feel relatively isolated, not so much in general matters, but in terms of their subject specialism. In extreme cases, you may find yourself as the *only* full-time qualified geography teacher in school. In other schools, where there could be a lively geography department of, say, five qualified staff, departmental matters are dominated by organisational and administrative 'paperwork', leaving virtually no time to think about, let alone discuss, questions of moral purpose and entitlement which may guide the teacher on how to develop the scheme of work, the fieldwork offer or the choice of examination syllabus. Even in departments where time is taken for such debate, it is very difficult indeed to feed it with ideas and developments from beyond the school gates.

There is, therefore, a very strong case for secondary geography teachers to operate within a wider 'community of practice'. However, where does such a thing exist? You soon lose contact with your initial training

5 The Career Entry Development Profile is issued to trainees at the end of their period of initial teacher training. It records their experiences to date and informs the programme of the support that will be offered to them during their induction year.

provider (and fellow trainees), and university departments of geography are not easily geared towards school needs. Furthermore, support from local education authorities (LEAs) is very patchy and in some places is virtually non-existent (humanities, environment and geography in particular are rarely, if ever, seen as training priorities). It is therefore up to individual teachers or departmental groups to 'buy into' a wider support community via their subject association. Fortunately, geography is richly blessed in this respect and Chapter 10 examines the opportunities for you in some detail.

But before we embark on the quest, there are some further preliminaries to consider, not least the meaning of 'professionalism' as it applies to teaching.

WHAT IT MEANS TO BE PROFESSIONAL

What it means to be professional is problematic in a variety of ways. To many it denotes largely positive characteristics, such as drawing respect and trust from the public, working within an accepted and honourable code, and requiring high standards of training and education. On the other hand, as in the case of the 'professional foul' in football, it can imply cynical self-interest, not above bending or even breaking the rules in order to wring benefit from commercial transactions in particular. Nevertheless, the idea of 'being professional' has often been deployed by government to carry the day when in conflict with teachers, especially during disputes over pay. When used like this it has meant to imply behaving in a 'responsible' manner, for individuals not to disrupt the education service through a sense of community well-being, although in the past some teachers (in our view misguidedly) resisted the notion of being 'professional', exactly to free themselves of this moral hold. On the whole, professional virtues carry the day and most teachers are comfortable about being described as professional. Indeed, it is hard to imagine schools functioning as the essentially calm and civilising places they usually are without staff working together with students, parents and others in a 'professional' manner: being considerate, for example, ensuring shared responsibilities are undertaken conscientiously, and working with honesty, integrity and prudence.

However, because 'professionalism' encapsulates the procedures and strategies that occupations have sometimes consciously used in order to promote their own interests above those of the common or greater good, the professions found themselves under attack during the last quarter of the twentieth century, as the Thatcher governments in particular found the established, producer oriented professions to be powerful inhibitors of radical change towards a more consumer oriented economy. For teachers, radical change has meant localised financial management of schools and the sidelining of the LEAs, plus more testing and the publication of results in the form of league tables in order to pitch schools into comparison with each other (for the benefit of the 'consumer' – i.e. parents making school choice decisions on behalf of their children). Paradoxically, such measures have been accompanied by a centralisation of other aspects of education, notably in the form of National Curriculum 'orders' and a tightening up of national criteria governing examination syllabuses (or subject 'specifications' as they became known for a while). The combined effect of these changes has been to take power away from teachers – or at least their capacity to take decisions about what to teach and how to teach it.

The steady reduction of teachers' power has been described as an attack on their 'professional autonomy'. It is the degree to which an occupational group can exercise control over its activities – its autonomy – that many commentators regard as one of the defining characteristics of 'professionalism' (e.g. Hoyle and John 1995), to the extent to which a perceived attack on autonomy is often considered to be an attack on professionalism itself. This is largely because it implies a loss of trust. Thus, we have heard a lot in recent years about teaching being 'reduced' to a highly skilled, but essentially technocratic, occupation (see Box 8.3). This is an issue we take seriously as it has impacted on geography teaching with particular force.

The legacy in geography education of a national curriculum which, in its original form, was designed explicitly to 'put the content back in geography' (following the overriding influence of a certain deficit view of the subject fuelled by anecdote and Gallup polls which demonstrated people's ignorance of geographic facts – see Lambert 2004) has been significant. Readers who want to pursue the substance of this claim more fully can do no better than refer to Eleanor Rawling's *Changing the Subject* (2001), published by the Geographical Association. The geography National Curriculum became dominated by a single textbook author who claims to have introduced the double-page spread to geography (Waugh 2000), and whose books claimed to be able to 'deliver' the curriculum (a beguiling promise, specially for departments staffed by non-specialists). Local curriculum developments, in tune with students' interests and informed by developments in the wider discipline (see Chapters 2–4 in this book), simply dried up in the shadow of the official definition of the contents of

---

BOX 8.3   WORDS THAT *DON'T* COME EASY

The public language of education that we are invited to engage with, and the discourse which frames our aspirations and practices, is now dominated by the persistent prodding of performance, the bullying imperatives of bullet-point thinking and the unremitting emphasis on 'delivery'. Not only does this marginalise much that should be central, it also gives rise to (a) particular concern:

. . .

I worry about the hectoring dreariness of it all. The government's way of expressing its aspirations and articulating its requirements is deeply and damagingly dull. Too much is managerialist, too often enunciated in ways which are overbearing in their insistence. Why is it that we have such little confidence in the capacity of the more subtle, ethically-nuanced language of education to express what is important to us teachers and learners? Why do we feel impelled to borrow the disfiguring language of 'performativity' which has neither the capacity nor the inclination to articulate what matters most to us in our daily work and our enduring intentions? Teachers are leaving in droves, not just because the job is so demanding and all consuming in largely unproductive ways, but also because the archetypal language of 'delivery' is symptomatic of an approach to teaching and learning that is intellectually dishonest (you cannot deliver learning) and personally offensive (education is primarily a personal and not a technical process).

(Fielding 2001a; see also Fielding 2001b)

---

school geography which, even when it was set down in the early 1990s, was already strangely dated. In this context it is amazing that teachers managed to maintain the interest of students to the level they did during this period. That they did so is a tribute to their professionalism, and a refusal just to 'deliver' a dead curriculum (see Box 8.4).

Despite this, in many schools during the first ten years or so of the National Curriculum, geography lost popularity and the power to convince students (or their parents?) that taking geography beyond KS3 was a worthwhile option. That this has resulted partly from a loss of autonomy (in the sense that the geography curriculum was placed under

BOX 8.4 KEEPING INTEREST ALIVE!

An influential initiative that has ensured continuing curriculum renewal in geography is David Leat's inspirational *Thinking Through Geography* (Leat 1998). It was heavily influenced by various projects such as Cognitive Acceleration through Science Education (CASE) (Adey and Shayer 1994).

As the title suggests the 'TTG' strategies developed by teachers took geography as a medium for education, a means rather than an end in itself. This follows quite a long tradition – see Frances Slater's *Learning Through Geography* (1982). It is perhaps a rather belated sign that the value of geography in itself needs to be reasserted that the more current work by Margaret Roberts significantly changes the emphasis with her book title: *Learning Through Enquiry* (2003).

However, in reality these different approaches interlock and borrow from each other. We will always be able to debate the precise balance between content (geography) and process (enquiry), but what is essential is to keep alive the creative professional impulse to try new things. This keeps the classroom alive. In his discussion of his work with teacher groups David Leat (Bright and Leat 2000: 259) writes:

> We discussed the idea of the 'expert' needing to become the 'novice', and were able to identify with this notion.
> 'Normal lessons are safer . . . [with TTG] you feel more out of control, you don't know what's coming next.'
> 'You feel slightly more out of control.'

This reminds us of a PGCE student who in her second period of teaching practice remarked, 'Classrooms are slowly becoming less familiar to me.' This we take to be a positive sign of a person struggling to understand complexity. It takes some courage.

political, rather than teachers' control) is only part of the explanation, however. There is another kind of professional autonomy that is quite apart from notions of freedom from political control. This is to be found in the moral and intellectual strength that hopefully resides in individuals (and which allows them to *behave* autonomously even, heaven forbid, in conditions of oppression). This could be described as 'personal' autonomy or perhaps *responsibility*. This refers to the professional process (some may even say *duty*) by which the teachers work to ensure the pupils' needs are met in accordance with the teacher's own *judgement* as to what those needs are and how best to serve them. The highlighted words here all occupy a moral terrain and the fulfilment of these professional responsibilities rest fairly and squarely on trust. When that trust has been damaged then there is an immediate loss of confidence on all sides that the teacher's judgements can indeed be trusted.

We argue that the decade or so following the introduction of the National Curriculum in geography featured an erosion of trust and a subsequent loss of confidence among some practitioners that independent judgements could be made about what to teach and how to teach it. Schools had in many cases become 'high stress–low risk' establishments in which uncertain teachers were encouraged to play safe in order to secure positive Ofsted evaluations. The results of this scenario have been as disappointing as they have been predictable. Ofsted has consistently, since the mid-1990s, reported concerns over teaching quality in KS3 geography (similar concerns are also reported for geography in the primary school curriculum, where it is consistently seen as one of the weakest taught subjects). It is possible to deflect some of this concern by pointing to the shortage of geography specialist teachers, but it would be tantamount to a state of denial to disregard the significance of these Ofsted judgements. 'Poor teaching quality' masks a host of possible issues – including unchallenging and repetitive work, fragmented and disjointed lessons and lesson sequences, lack of topicality and the use of old data, lack of depth (leading to superficiality or even stereotypical representation of people and places) and an absence of authentic enquiry (and an over-reliance on 'telling' and copying). Glance again at Box 8.2, for we are again calling for teaching that avoids such carelessness. Such carelessness arises from a mix of subject content *and* process issues, concerning geography curriculum *and* pedagogy (although it is unlikely that a single department simultaneously exhibits *all* the deficiencies listed above).

We are calling for geography teachers to re-establish – from a position of confidence that the subject is relevant, worthwhile and enjoyable – a sense of professional responsibility to develop the curriculum in accordance to what they feel is motivating and worthwhile to learn (and here we can cross-refer you to p. 82 where, for example, in the case study of development we stated 'Geography teachers who have gone through the process of engaging with (deep) questions (about the subject) are more likely to be able to plan learning experiences based on a rigorous and scholarly approach to the topic'). Thus, like Rawling (2001), we believe the time is now right for a new period of school-based, local curriculum development to begin. The policy agencies including Ofsted, QCA and indeed the DfES (Department for Education and Skills) itself cannot any longer be seen as inhibitors; although the KS3 strategies appear formulaic and bureaucratic, they are not to be confused with *instructions* in a way that limits teachers' ingenuity and imagination. They are *enablers* and form a framework in which skilled subject specialists can once again decide what is worth teaching and how to approach this.

Recently trained new teachers should expect to be in the forefront of grasping new opportunities to excite and inspire young people with, and through, geography. This may take place locally, supported from within the school. But because CPD is often focused heavily by the needs of bureaucrats and central policy initiatives the support from outside school is often quite limited. In Chapter 10 we shall examine in more detail the role of subject associations such as the Geographical Association (GA) in generating and supporting the kind of CPD that can 'further the learning and teaching of geography' (this is the mission statement of the GA).

The highly significant difference between the place of teachers' professional responsibility today from that which pertained before the Education Reform Act of 1988 (from which flowed the National Curriculum and its assessment arrangements), is the context of *professional accountability* that now exists. A government, of course, has every right to set out expectations on behalf of the 'consumers' of education – which in some ways means the whole of society, or at least all taxpayers. As we have seen, governments in the past have chosen to do this by taking more control over what is taught. They have also chosen to introduce more testing, and targets in relation the outcomes of these tests, to ensure that teachers can demonstrate their compliance and conformity in relation to the expectations placed upon them. While geography teachers are relatively cushioned from the full force of this – KS3 results are not assessed by means of SATs but solely by teacher assessment – there is nevertheless a powerful tension between professional autonomy and responsibility on the one hand and the need to demonstrate awareness and understanding of the expectations of the 'client group' on the other. What we want to emphasise, however, is that neither has the ability to cancel out the other. Put more bluntly, setting out to ensure that your GCSE group achieves the best possible grades is not a recipe for boring, repetitive and unimaginative teaching and learning! Excellent, cutting edge teaching, the kind that occasionally takes risks and which does not always come off, is absolutely consistent with the achievement of good grades with your students.

Perhaps the professional responsibility, then, is to be able to say, convincingly, what the characteristics of good teaching and learning in geography are. More specifically, this suggests that teachers acquire the professional capacity to say:

- what educational aims are being served by this or that lesson design;
- the purpose of that or this teaching strategy; and
- how the whole experience knits together to form a coherent whole, so that students 'see the point' of learning geography (Lambert 2004).

We therefore agree with Michael Fielding (see Box 8.3) who concluded his article in the *Times Educational Supplement* with the observation that despite the obvious fact that teaching is supremely a practical activity, the most important teacher tasks are intellectual. Perhaps the key professional responsibility invested in teachers is to ensure that they do not drown in practical 'busy-work' featuring marking and memos. Intellectual work is hard and needs time, but is also relatively 'invisible' and easier to set aside for another time. So let us be honest. For example, what are the functions of marking (see Chapter 7)? Can some of these be fulfilled in (appropriately structured) lesson time, possibly freeing the odd Sunday evening for creative design work instead?

In summary, there are, following Hoyle and John, three aspects of 'professionality', namely:

- Teachers' knowledge. Following Shulman (1987) this includes specialist subject knowledge (your geography), pedagogic content knowledge (the approaches, metaphors and techniques that help make specialist knowledge accessible to young learners) and knowledge of how children learn (which may not only help you organise learning for your students but may also help you analyse what sense they make of what you give them).
- Understanding of the significance of autonomy for effective practice – the acknowledgement and acceptance that teaching is

quintessentially an intellectual task requiring a creative input well before the teacher sets foot in the classroom. The teacher plays a prominent role in deciding what to teach and how to teach it.

- Willingness to accept a level of responsibility for helping shape the moral purpose of the educational transaction, within the context of the accountability structures in place and the need to build trust with all partners and co-participants.

We feel that this list summarises *our* discussion well and serves as a useful check for those who would treat teaching as primarily a technical function. The next section also pursues this point.

IS 'COMPETENCE' ENOUGH?

There is nothing as sad as an incompetent teacher. To be incompetent in teaching is to put on show weaknesses and – let us be honest – failings or inadequacies to an audience of critics, possibly up to eight times every day. There is no hiding place. It is hard to imagine anyone wanting to endure such public humiliation for long. We are not, of course, talking about the incompetent lessons we have taught (and regretted). We are certainly not talking about the occasional lapse when 'things went pear shaped'. Teaching is far too complicated an undertaking for anyone to be able to guarantee success all the time. What we are referring to is the 'spectre' of incompetence, the reason why any reasonably minded man or woman becoming a teacher would want to expend all efforts to avoid incompetence.

Furthermore, it matters. Although rarely a case of life or death, consistently incompetent lessons do damage. At worst (in lessons that are to all intents and purposes out of control), they 'teach' unacceptable behaviour in the sense that rudeness, bad manners and disrespect can be tolerated. More insidiously damaging, in lessons that have the surface appearance of calm and order, consistently incompetent teaching can fail to 'connect' the lesson to the learners, turning it into a neutral occasion simply to be endured. We can all find, and possibly know from first-hand experience, examples of such incompetence. Better to find the opposite, shining examples of sheer competence. Take the fictional example (in Box 8.4) of a person who traumatically lost his hearing in his teenage years, describing his teacher, Harry, who taught him to lip-read and much more.

BOX 8.4 HARRY

Harry's approach was, I now realise, holistic. Not only did I have to be able to use my eyes to hear, I had to be able to speak clearly, not be allowed to be lazy so my words slurred and jumbled. I had to learn to read people's faces as well as their lips, be able to read their whole bodies. I had to be able to write clearly, know how things were spelled so I could crack the shell of their sound on my teeth. He taught me to modulate my voice, taught me not to shout (I had been yelling for months) but rather to pitch my voice like a ball at the right height for the listener to catch. He had to make sure that I was learning all these things equally so that I was armed as well as able. Harry was a gentle man, a gentle teacher. . . . (H)e had learned to read my face and knew when I was struggling, when I was bored, when I'd slipped away and was thinking of other things. But he was relentless: . . . (H)e made me *mind*, so that I would ask people to repeat things, ask them to turn their faces to me, rather than mentally shrugging and turning away from conversation.

(Hardy 2002: 106, original emphasis)

The passage in Box 8.4 is a rich paragraph. It is often said that relentlessness is a requirement of all teachers, including geography teachers. It is certainly the case that competent teachers get to know their students, just as Harry was able to 'read' his pupil's moods. They use metaphor and analogy like Harry did with 'like a ball'. But what is eye-catching about the passage is the significance of Harry's real achievement, to make his pupil care. Look around your school: who are the teachers who make their pupils *mind*? Are you one of them (yet)?

How does a teacher make his or her students *mind* about geography? A competent teacher would want to find ways to counter the 'mental shrugging' that teenagers are so adept at (usually accompanied by the obligatory 'whatever'). This is perhaps a question best left to the individual to work through, but it is worth emphasising that there are few, if any, short cuts. *Saying* you care, say, about global poverty or climate change, perhaps with illustrations of how 'important' geography is, mixed with a little 'or else' pressure, cuts no ice with many students. The proof of the pudding has to be in the eating – that you mind about geography will be demonstrable through your enthusiasm and your expert and current knowledge, through your clear expectation of what is good enough from every pupil you teach, and your ability to offer concise, constructive, critical comment on *their* geography.

But as Hodson (1998) says in relation to science education, engaging successfully with students, constructing knowledge together, involves teachers being able to shift their conceptions of confidence:

> When students make their own decisions, ask questions and challenge teachers, and when lesson planning cannot be conducted with precision and certainty of outcome, some teachers may feel that their authority is being challenged, or even undermined. Developing alternative perceptions of what it means to be 'in control' of student learning is an essential part of effecting a shift of emphasis towards science teaching as enculturation.
>
> (Hodson 1998: 170)

In short, making your *students* mind about geography, a great achievement by any standard, is possible if *you* also mind about geography – how it is represented, and the quality of the experience in terms of its learning outcomes as measured against that familiar triumvirate of criteria: was the learning worthwhile, relevant and enjoyable?

Competence is not often described in these terms (as we see in the next chapter). It may be that we are aiming too high, but we think not. Competent teachers need to be ambitious or else they too may slip into 'mentally shrugging' and turning away from the beautiful struggle that can characterise teaching geography – whether it is getting sixth formers to understand atmospheric lapse rates or year 9s to comprehend the difference between weathering and erosion.

We can all agree that we cannot tolerate incompetence in the classroom. We may however be less sure about its defining features, for competence in our terms may not be won easily. There is a long continuum from clear cut incompetence to what we called 'sheer competence'.

Is competence enough? Certainly, so long as it inhabits the professional territory we have described in the previous section, and has the relentless ambition to *mind*.

CONCLUSION: AN ILLUSTRATIVE CASE

To conclude this chapter we can 'drop in' on an on-line discussion forum for a practitioner based Masters degree, the Master of Teaching (the

169

MTcg from the Institute of Education, University of London). One participant's email contribution is given in Box 8.5. It is interesting because it exhibits several features of 'professional' practice that you can identify from the discussion in this chapter. The email is from a teacher of some five years' experience and the topic for discussion was 'Teachers need to be research literate. Are there persuasive arguments to convince most teachers that this statement is true?' All names have been changed.

BOX 8.5   EXCERPT FROM TIM'S EMAIL

I believe that teachers are initiating change all the time through being reflective and receptive, whereas change that is 'inflicted' (Alan's term) upon us is unwelcome as it is often irrelevant and usually less of a priority to us in our current situation. Alan's final comment about our discussions being a 'journey' highlights the luxury of being able to consider and reflect on not only our own views but those of the wider group. This course is providing us with the opportunity . . . to do this and I agree it is proving a very positive experience. . . .

I agree with Gertrude's comment that the reading of research empowers teachers. We become more knowledgeable and are in a position to make informed decisions about our practice. However, I occasionally feel over-whelmed by new initiatives finding it impossible to implement everything I believe to be 'good practice'. Following on from Gertrude's thoughts on her literacy co-ordinator role, I wonder if it is a question of becoming more outspoken, in other words, less accepting of what we are told. As professionals we should feel able to question change and not be content with having it 'inflicted' upon us. Does this confidence come from the research literature?

Michael's concluding comment about 'how useful research would be' made me consider the importance of contemplating and discussing the 'whys' of new initiatives rather than, as is usually the case, the 'hows'. We are always told 'how' to implement policies but rarely 'why'. Without this 'why' knowledge it is difficult to be flexible and develop our practice effectively. Does this knowledge become more accessible to those who are research literate? I think yes.

(Daly *et al.* 2004)

Being research literate means teachers being able to read education research critically and apply it to the known context – as well as being able to conduct small-scale enquiries themselves. We also apply the idea to geography too, in the sense that when emerging as a geography teacher, it is desirable to maintain a sense of *being* a geographer. There is more about this in Chapter 9. For now it is simply noteworthy that this experienced teacher (who clearly has not tired of learning) values 'research literacy' because it enhances his professionalism. It does this because it enables him to build his professional knowledge. This gives him greater authority in his quest to maintain his professional autonomy.

What is also of note is that this teacher, who seems to be thinking aloud, edges towards identifying his professional responsibility – to worry about the 'whys'. Finally, it is also clear from this piece that both he and his peers value greatly the professional conversation that enables the intellectual process to take place. Return to Chapter 5 and remind yourself of the anxiety that the teachers featured there had about being able to maintain a scholarly discourse about their teaching (see pp. 95–6).

FOR FURTHER THINKING

1 What kind of teacher do you want to be?

    a What is your purpose – your teaching ethic?

    b What is your take on 'professionalism'? Are you comfortable with that description?

2 In what ways do you *mind* about geography?

3 How can you make your students mind about geography?

Chapter 9

Learning professional values and practice: teachers with high standards

My geography teacher wasn't handsome, he wasn't loud and he wasn't a show off. But he was an inspiration to me because he allowed me to grow. No, he made me grow! I have absolutely no doubt that what we learned in geography lessons has lasted a lifetime.

(Anon.)

INTRODUCTION

We began the previous chapter with the claim that teachers need actively to create a professional identity and that they cannot rely on this as a 'given'. To illustrate what we mean by this, we can refer once again to the notion of 'standards', in this case, *professional* standards. There are several ways to interpret the idea of standards. For example, are standards imposed by a central authority, an agency of the government such as the Teacher Training Agency (TTA)? Or are they established by a body representing the profession itself, such as the General Teaching Council for England (GTCE) perhaps? Can standards be articulated in words and laid down in a legal document – the rules of engagement, so to speak – or are they impossible to capture in their entirety, being constantly negotiated and re-negotiated within the professional community and communicated by example and through accepted practice?

In fact, we believe these are false choices and that professional standards consist of all of these aspects – and more besides. The government and its agencies, the professional bodies and individuals who work within the profession (and those it *serves*, including students as well as their parents, and other 'interests' such as employers) all have a say. It is unlikely that these voices all sing the same notes and from time to time the overall effect may be quite discordant. In other words, there may be disagreements and conflicting messages from different constituencies of interest.

What we conclude from this is that all teachers, whether they like it or not, are agents in the never-ending process of *establishing* professional standards. You need to know where you stand (or if that is too much to ask at this point, what you do *not* stand for!) or else you will be at risk of being blown about by any passing band-wagon or initiative. In more formal terms, you may end up feeling you lack 'autonomy'. This is a dangerous situation to be in, for those who feel 'on the receiving end' all the time are those who tend to adopt negative coping mechanisms – looking for reasons why something 'can't be done' as opposed to a more satisfying 'can do' attitude and approach. It is well to remember that good teachers need to be energy creators, not consumers.

To put this more bluntly:

- Just what kind of geography teacher do you want to be? You cannot leave it to others to decide.
- How do you want your students to *experience* learning geography? You are the single most important element influencing their perception – you can shape their perception.
- How do you want geography to be perceived by other teachers/parents/senior managers? Is it your passion that helps shape this or are you content with how the official documents represent geography?

These questions recur (usually implicitly) throughout this whole section. We want to arm you with the means to become influential agents in the specialist field of geography teaching. Of central importance to this goal are the twin ideas that:

- *Good geography education* really matters. We want to confirm and support the belief (which we hope you share) that learning geography is a purposeful and creative act. It can help students think and respond more intelligently to the challenging task of making sense of the world.
- *Good geography*, however articulated (for example, see Box 9.1), usually implies values that are entirely consistent with education

values that talk of purpose and creativity: a thirst for discovery, making meaning from complexity, respect for others, making judgements about impact, a concern for the future . . . somehow these things should be experienced by all young people.

BOX 9.1 THE POWER AND RELEVANCE OF GEOGRAPHY

The physical world: the land, water and air. Can involve the spiritual dimension ('awe and wonder') in addition to physical, chemical and biological processes.

The human environment: work, homes, consumption, leisure. Can involve the moral dimension and centre on the relationship between people and nature.

Interaction: movement (the spatial) and interdependence. Takes in the economic and the political as well as the social, cultural and environmental.

Place: the 'vocabulary' (the 'facts') and the 'grammar' (how the 'facts' link) of geography. Can involve ecological perspectives, integration and synthesis.

Scale: the construct, lens or dimension through which the subject matter is 'seen', helping pupils understand locality in relation to regional, national and international contexts and global perspectives.

Pupils' lives: images, change, experience and meaning, identity. Can take an explicit 'futures' orientation.

The remainder of this chapter considers such questions from the perspective of your continued professional development – or *learning* as we prefer. 'Development' will almost certainly happen, whether you intend it to do so or not. The reason we prefer learning to development is that it implies more intentionality on the part of both the individual striving to become a certain kind of teacher and those who have responsibility for guiding them.

LEARNING TO TEACH GEOGRAPHY

From the beginning, the 'training input' from a tutor and/or mentor is important to anyone starting to teach. For example:

- Lectures and seminars can clarify the theoretical and/or policy context of, say, the KS3 curriculum or the examination syllabus. It is always useful to know what the parameters are and what influences the 'given' circumstances.

- Workshops can model practical approaches, strategies and techniques applicable to teaching particular aspects or topics.

- Observing lessons live, or on video, can provide insight into how to organise and manage the creation and maintenance of various learning environments.

- Lesson debriefings can steer thinking about your own approach to lessons, identifying strengths as well as weaknesses, for the former are sometimes harder for the self to see.

But although we believe that certain things can be taught – you can be taught specifics such as how to use remote sensing images in the classroom, for example – the training input alone cannot 'deliver' high standards to you, just as you should not position yourself simply to 'consume' the training and expect it to turn you into a teacher. The *experiences* you are provided with, such as those listed above, remain relatively neutral and maybe even marginal to your *practice*, until, that is, they are combined with *ideas* and concepts that you have already acquired and which do form the basis for your understanding of teaching, thus guiding your practical actions. In line with the argument in this book, we would suggest that this requires a clear stance in relation to subject knowledge.

Subject knowledge is a key component of the government Standard known as 'Knowledge and Understanding' (see Box 9.2). To become a teacher you need to be able to show competence – specified as *'secure' knowledge and understanding* – in geography. This means you can claim a geography qualification at degree level; but it also means knowledge of the specific programmes of study, syllabus specifications and pathways and an understanding of the levels of expectation you may have of pupils. The latter implies a knowledge and understanding of 'progression' in geographical understanding, about which there is perhaps surprisingly little research (see Bennetts, forthcoming).

On the face of it, these standards may seem perfectly reasonable, perhaps as a minimum expectation of the level of preparedness that the general public may expect from teachers. But does a geography degree, and a commitment to 'mug up' on the syllabus requirements, express adequately what an education system really wants from its teachers?

BOX 9.2   S2: KNOWLEDGE AND UNDERSTANDING

Those awarded Qualified Teacher Status must demonstrate all of the following:

S2.1   They have a secure knowledge and understanding of the subject(s) they are trained to teach. For those qualifying to teach secondary pupils this knowledge and understanding should be at a standard equivalent to degree level. In relation to specific phases, this includes:

[Foundation and Key Stages 1 and 2 are omitted]

c   For Key Stage 3, they know and understand the relevant National Curriculum Programme(s) of Study, and for those qualifying to teach one or more of the core subjects, the relevant frameworks, methods and expectations set out in the National Strategy for Key Stage 3. All those qualifying to teach a subject at Key Stage 3 know and understand the cross-curricular expectations of the National Curriculum and are familiar with the guidance set out in the National Strategy for Key Stage 3.

d   For Key Stage 4 and post-16, they are aware of the pathways for progression through the 14–19 phase in school, college and work-based settings. They are familiar with the Key Skills as specified by QCA and the National Qualifications Framework, and they know the progression within and from their own subject and the range of qualifications to which their subject contributes. They understand how courses are combined in students' curricula.

S2.2   They know and understand the values, aims and purposes and the general teaching requirements set out in the *National Curriculum Handbook*. As relevant to the age range they are trained to teach, they are familiar with the Programme of Study for citizenship and the National Curriculum Framework for personal, social and health education.

S2.3   They are aware of expectations, typical curricula and teaching arrangements in the Key Stages or phases before and after the ones they are trained to teach.

S2.4   They understand how pupils' learning can be affected by their physical, intellectual, linguistic, social, cultural and emotional development.

S2.5   They know how to use ICT effectively, both to teach their subject and to support their wider professional role.

S2.6   They understand their responsibilities under the *SEN Code of Practice*, and know how to seek advice from specialists on less common types of special educational needs.

S2.7   They know a range of strategies to promote good behaviour and establish a purposeful learning environment.

S2.8   They have passed the Qualified Teacher Status skills tests in numeracy, literacy and ICT.

Source: Teacher Training Agency

To put this another way, is it too much to ask geography teachers *to be* geographers in some way? The degree qualification needs to signal something more than an educational level or, like an equity card or passport, simply the bureaucratic requirement.

But there seems to be little in the official standard to encourage a view that teachers are to be expected to be actively engaged in the making of the subject they teach. Indeed, there is a sense that the use of the term 'secure' is profoundly unhelpful in this sense – for as is well accepted, one of the features of higher learning is uncertainty. The more you know, the more you realise what you don't know, and given the enormous complexity of the social, cultural, economic, political and physical environmental processes that combine to shape the world in which we live, there is perhaps no other subject where this is more true than geography. This, then, is another reason why we have argued with a passion that teaching is primarily an intellectual endeavour.

Some beginning teachers near the end of the initial training year were asked to reflect on aspects of learning to teach geography.[6] With regard to '*subject knowledge*' in particular, these new teachers were aware of

6 Thanks to the Cambridge University PGCE geography cohort of 2002–3.

their limitations, their responsibility to develop their subject expertise and how this was best achieved. This provides a good example of the iterative relationship between experience and ideas in teacher formation. With an understandably heavy emphasis on *experience* during the *initial* training year, it seems to us that there is a risk that other sources of *ideas* are vital to identify for the *continuing* growth of teacher competence: or else, how can geography remain leading edge, forward looking and capable of providing students with new possibilities of understanding? To put this frankly, if all teachers need to know about is the syllabus, what fuels the dynamic development of that syllabus that is the source of excitement and enjoyment in learning?

Several new teachers admitted serious and continuing anxieties, partly to do with difficulties crossing the widening gap between the academic communities of geography in higher education and schools and partly to do with the immense territory covered by geography and the poor chance therefore of any new graduate of geography 'covering' the discipline at degree level:

My subject knowledge has become quite detached from the 'basics' of school geography.

I found teaching topics I was not familiar with extremely challenging.

Does this matter? These teachers were entirely clear that it does:

You have to really understand the subject, or else how can you teach it?

Being confident in subject knowledge reflects in teaching . . . but I need to be confident in teaching even if not (yet) confident in subject knowledge.

Feeling confident about a topic allows you flexibility in how you choose to approach it.

Others made candid remarks about how subject knowledge gaps and weaknesses can be addressed:

Watching others teach topics can be helpful.

I am aware that I need to read around much more.

Not reading! (But lots of watching and trying out.)

Learning by doing is the only way for me.

Sometimes I would realise that the lesson could be arranged or even taught differently. The second time around was easier partly because I felt more competent.

Y11 revision sessions were effective for me!

This list we feel is indicative of where the new teachers feel their priorities lie. Although aware of 'gaps', their main need was for practical solutions to become fluent in what the students need to know. It is interesting that there is a difference of opinion over reading (by which, we assume, is meant all forms of material whether in textbooks, websites or other sources). Research shows that good student textbooks are highly valued by new teachers – not so much to enable the teacher to keep 'one step ahead of the class' but to help them acquire quickly the overall content area. We think this should not be underrated as a source (and would encourage new teachers to start building a 'library' of different student texts for this purpose), for a geography graduate should be able to bring to the student text concepts and wider information to deepen and extend the material (to provide a basis for the 'confidence' that teachers said good knowledge brings).

What is clear, reading between the lines of the comments above and those that follow, is that 'doing geography' for these new teachers is not (usually) understood as a justifiable end in itself. Hence, when 'needs must' and a teacher is faced with the challenge of teaching a topic that is mainly new to them, they know that they need to become au fait with it. They have sources (texts) to consult, people to observe and ask, and the growing sense of 'student need', which (ironically) helps them gain extra purchase on the topic. As one new teacher observed, 'You think you know what K=3 means in Central Place Theory . . . until you try to explain it to a sixth former.' Incidentally, this realisation is a powerful one from a pedagogic point of view too, for it reminds us of the power of talk and learning through social engagement and interaction. Thus, comments such as these are commonplace:

You don't learn anything thoroughly until you have to teach it.

You realise you don't really know anything until you teach it!

My subject knowledge has been learnt through planning and teaching lessons.

And yet, we believe there is also a place for the subject discipline itself to take a leading position from time to time, not in an abstract sense but *embodied* by the subject specialist teacher. In other words, the teacher develops a special interest or area of expertise – and a sequence of lessons – because they have the impulse to share their enthusiasm and a belief that it satisfies those time-honoured criteria of relevance, worthwhileness and enjoyment for the learner. The official subject knowledge standards do not provide encouragement to new teachers to do this, and in so doing limit (perhaps inadvertently) the professional role of the teacher. We shall say a little more about the importance of curriculum development and how it intersects with teacher development in the next chapter.

LEARNING TO BE A TEACHER

The preceding paragraphs have been concerned mainly with subject knowledge. With regard to *other knowledges* expected of teachers we will be briefer, although this not to underestimate the importance of aspects of behaviour management, for example, and the need to recognise knowledge concerning specific learning needs, particularly when this can inform you about how to address special educational needs (SEN). In response to a question on how classroom management strategies and techniques were learned, one new teacher remarked, 'I learned about classroom management from my own teaching and from observing other teachers, but I cannot articulate quite what I have learned.' We regard this as an honest statement (rather than a cop-out) and feel that it reinforces the notion of agency discussed earlier in this chapter. It is not advisable to wait *to be told* how to manage the behaviour of teenagers, for some of the most accomplished practitioners in this sense will not be able to tell you exactly how they do it. Furthermore, even if they can, what works for them may not easily be transferable to you – who may be younger, of the opposite sex, of a quieter disposition . . . The way you teach may also be different, for you may place a high value on paired work and small groups and place yourself in the spotlight less frequently than your colleague.

As in the previous discussion, this is not to say that you cannot benefit from specific training in 'assertiveness', say, or 'decisive discipline'. We can all agree that unless your class is under your control things will probably happen to reduce the level of learning possible: students shouting out; some students being afraid to speak; you running out of time (the lesson ends without a summing up); homework not explained fully . . . you can continue the list! Various techniques can be practised repeatedly and new teachers have said how important this is:

I have learned the importance of consistency – and that it is easier said than done!

I now know what 'firm but fair' means for me – and also not to shout, using people's names, pausing for compliance, using positive language . . .

Always follow through: this means not giving (many) threats.

Give choices (do the work now, or in break time), and take control straight away (seating plan; getting there before they do).

Be aware that children may be different on different days.

Pick some individuals off for a one to one (so they do not have an audience).

Keep trying things!

However, we emphasise that, ultimately, systems of rewards and sanctions, important though they are in setting the limits to unruly youngsters, are for nothing, unless:

- You make them your own, in the sense that they work for you. You may remember, or have observed, teachers for whom (in some classes, rarely in all that they teach!) sanctions simply do not work. Students soon learn which teachers move rapidly to ejection when goaded, which sometimes is an attractive proposition. Remember, it is the *relationship* you are trying to get right, not the weight of punishment! Many students remark admiringly that such and such a teacher is able to 'have a laugh' – to students this is of equal importance to 'being strict' (knowing the limits).
- The lesson is worth being in. This may sound brutal, but in today's 'client culture', because the teacher says so, often in a

context of deferred gratification ('suffer now, prizes later'), no longer makes a persuasive case for student compliance. Some students may appear to be almost unbelievably rude and unwilling, which is frustrating. But rather than search for who is to blame for a difficult situation, the professional response must include the possibility that 'What's the point of being here' may be the unspoken question that explains unruly behaviour. This leads us back to the importance of subject knowledge. 'How is it *possible* to make *geography* boring?' a former colleague used to say, 'But plenty of folk seem to succeed!'

With regard to the content of lessons (as opposed to discipline strategies), our new teachers remarked (for example):

It is really important to maintain good pace to the lesson.

Good starters (stimulating motivation via an authentic 'need to know'), chunking and well rehearsed 'plenaries' have all really helped.

These are important *technical* aspects of teaching. But it is difficult to imagine how these practical necessities can work – that is, making the lesson vital and interesting – without a really strong understanding of what the lesson is for – in what ways it is relevant and worthwhile – and how a participant is meant to derive enjoyment from the experience. If you can understand the point we are making here you have grasped what is a very important, but often a very slippery, distinction for beginning teachers. This is the difference between aims (or purposes) and objectives (specific outcomes). Simply to specify objectives in teaching tends to limit what can be achieved. Ambitious aims on the other hand can drive the teaching and learning relationship by providing a sense of purpose.

It is this kind of rationale and distinction that possibly fuelled the Secretary of State's personal commitment to subject specialism as expressed by him in 2003:

Our very best teachers are those who have a real passion and enthusiasm for the subject they teach. They are also deeply committed to the learning of their students and use their enthusiasm for their subject to motivate them, to bring their subject alive and make learning an exciting, vivid and enjoyable experience.

It is teachers' passion for their subject that provides the basis for effective teaching and learning. These teachers use their subject expertise to engage students in meaningful learning experiences that embrace content, process and social climate. They create for and with their children opportunities to explore and build important areas of knowledge, and develop powerful tools for learning, within a supportive, collaborative and challenging classroom environment.

It is clear therefore that teachers who retain and nurture the passion for their subject are more likely to fire the interest and enthusiasm of learners and to promote work with appropriate challenge. The Government believes this approach will help improve teaching and learning, raise standards – particularly at Key Stage 3 – and provide the basis for the professional development of teachers and support staff.

(Charles Clarke in the preface to *Subject Specialisms*,
DfES 2003a, paras 1–3)

WIDER PROFESSIONAL STANDARDS

Although we are a little critical about what the official standards do *not* say or encourage, especially with regard to the role of specialist subject knowledge in teaching, it must be said that the more generic 'professional values' section is more ambitious. We have reproduced the preamble in full in Box 9.3, and it is in some ways an intimidating read. The tone struck here could be summed up, as we saw in relation to the fictional teacher profiled on p. 168, as *relentlessness* in the goal to lift students' eyes to their capacities and potentials. Readers will not be surprised, however, that we do take issue on the grounds that the paragraph fails, even within the context of 'general teaching', to recognise the role of subjects.

The actual standards are reproduced in Box 9.4 on p. 185. They successfully articulate the nature of the relationships that teachers need to establish. All we say in the context of the present discussion is that the words on the page make little sense on their own. That is to say, they can gain no real purchase or meaning without a particular context. The context that geography teachers operate in is their subject specialism: geography serves both as a vehicle to 'carry' such values and practices and as a provider of what we have shown is the moral purpose that underpins effective teaching and learning: relevant, worthwhile and enjoyable subject matter.

BOX 9.3 THE STANDARDS FOR THE AWARD OF QTS: INTRODUCTION

Teaching is one of the most influential professions in society. In their day-to-day work, teachers can and do make huge differences to children's lives: directly, through the curriculum they teach, and indirectly, through their behaviour, attitudes, values, relationships with and interest in pupils.

Good teachers are always optimistic about what their pupils can achieve, whatever their background or circumstances. They know from experience how pupils respond to success by succeeding further. They understand that all their pupils are capable of significant progress and that their potential for learning is unlimited. But teaching involves more than care, mutual respect and well-placed optimism. It demands knowledge and practical skills, the ability to make informed judgements, and to balance pressures and challenges, practice and creativity, interest and effort, as well as an understanding of how children learn and develop. It recognises the important part other people play in pupils' learning: in the classroom, the home and the local community. Just as teachers must have high expectations of their pupils, so pupils, parents and carers are entitled to have high expectations of teachers. Teaching is a creative, intellectually demanding and rewarding job, so the standards for joining the profession must be high too. Skilled practitioners can make teaching look easy but they have learned their skills and improved them through training, practice, evaluation and by learning from other colleagues.

Qualified Teacher Status (QTS) is the first stage in a continuum of professional development that will continue through the induction period and throughout a teacher's career. Initial training lays the foundation for subsequent professional and career development. During the induction period, newly qualified teachers can build on the strengths identified in their initial teacher training (ITT), and work on the areas which they and those working with them have highlighted as priorities for future professional development. This should help them to play an active role in their early professional development and performance management, and that of their colleagues.

(TTA)

BOX 9.4   PROFESSIONAL VALUES AND PRACTICE

Those awarded Qualified Teacher Status must understand and uphold the professional code of the General Teaching Council for England by demonstrating all of the following:

S1.1   They have high expectations of all pupils; respect their social, cultural, linguistic, religious and ethnic backgrounds; and are committed to raising their educational achievement.

S1.2   They treat pupils consistently, with respect and consideration, and are concerned for their development as learners.

S1.3   They demonstrate and promote the positive values, attitudes and behaviour that they expect from their pupils.

S1.4   They can communicate sensitively and effectively with parents and carers, recognising their roles in pupils' learning, and their rights, responsibilities and interests in this.

S1.5   They can contribute to, and share responsibly in, the corporate life of schools.*

S1.6   They understand the contribution that support staff and other professionals make to teaching and learning.

S1.7   They are able to improve their own teaching, by evaluating it, learning from the effective practice of others and from evidence. They are motivated and able to take increasing responsibility for their own professional development.

S1.8   They are aware of, and work within, the statutory frameworks relating to teachers' responsibilities.

* In this document, the term 'schools' includes further education and sixth form colleges and early years settings where trainee teachers can demonstrate that they meet the Standards for Qualified Teacher Status.

Source: Teacher Training Agency

CONCLUSION

We asked the geography PGCE students to reflect on the most significant thing they had learned concerning the 'wider professional responsibilities' of teachers. One could say no more than: 'There is so much more to teaching than . . . teaching!' Well, yes. This rather illustrates the elastic definition that encompasses the job, one of the reasons why teachers are often heard wishing they 'had a life' (outside teaching). This is very important to realise of course. Just as the air steward tells you to save yourself before attending to children, *self-sacrifice* among the teaching profession serves nobody's interest particularly well. The respondent was not arguing for never-ending work, however, simply that teachers should do so much more than provide lessons. Another beginning teacher expressed this entirely differently: 'My defining moment was realising that pupils have lives too.' This really goes to the heart of the concern for healthy relationships that lie at the heart of teaching. Another new teacher wrote:

> Shadowing one SEN pupil for a day helped me understand what it is like to be a pupil with learning difficulties; not entirely, but in some way I could understand how difficult a school day can be. It is important to incorporate (allow for) this in your lesson planning so that they can access and achieve and for it to be meaningful to their own lives.

So demanding are the 'wider aspects' of teaching – emotionally, physically and intellectually – and so important are these matters that sometimes they seem to become all encompassing. There are tensions that can surface with respect to how individual teachers see themselves. Classically, this tension is expressed by that often-heard self-conscious assertion: 'I teach children not geography.' The first time you hear this it will have an attractive cleverness about it: of course, *any* caring teacher is essentially child centred. We, also, hold the person to be the most important thing about education, and we have stated that teachers are often fired by the responsibility and excitement tied up with the notion of changing people, or at least exerting influence on them, helping them think more intelligently, introducing them to new ways of seeing . . .

However, there are two matters to be careful about here (taking us back to the previous chapter). First, let us be clear: you cannot simply 'teach children'. You have to have something to teach them (or else they will get bored very quickly). Second, the matter of what to teach them has to be driven by some understanding of moral purpose – changing people is a fine intention, so long as the change is educational. Setting out to change people to become something you want them to be is probably indoctrination.

Thus, even when we enter the wider realms of teachers' responsibilities, the role of the subject is still of great importance.

FOR FURTHER THINKING

1   Can you live with the 'power and relevance of geography' as provided on p. 174? Think about the pros and cons of such a definition being adopted generally by all teachers of geography.

2   Why do you think official documents appear reluctant to accept teacher autonomy over what is worthwhile and relevant to teach?

3   We are also reluctant to accept full teacher autonomy to decide what to teach – it seems right that society takes some responsibility for this. But we are passionate – and want you to be too – over the role of subject specialist teachers. Exactly what is this role?

Chapter 10

Professional development and developing geography

Teaching is not a research based profession. I have no doubt that if it were, teaching would be more effective and more satisfying.

(Hargreaves 1996)

WHAT IS 'PROFESSIONAL DEVELOPMENT'?

It is self-evident to anyone entering the teaching profession that the barely one year postgraduate training is insufficient fully to prepare a person for the professional duties and responsibilities of the job. Those selected for a 'fast track' into teaching are arguably even less well prepared. And of course, those who have been in teaching for many years will freely admit that they too do not always feel on top of the job and are still learning. Thus, the need for 'professional development' opportunities is obvious. This chapter of the book identifies what forms professional development can take and suggests ways to think about professional development to help you make the most of opportunities, as and when they arise. They should arise frequently, for: 'Every teacher now has the opportunity, under the performance management arrangements, to discuss their learning and development needs annually with their line manager and to set one or more development objectives' (DfES 2002).

The 'opportunity' referred to here is very significant. It requires great skill to articulate your development objectives partly because there is often a tension between what your department or school wants from your 'development' and what you value. The short discussion that follows provides a broad context in which to think about these matters, particularly from the point of view of your professional identity as a teacher of geography.

Is professional development about career development?

This book is aimed at those beginning to teach and those in their years of early professional development. Newly qualified readers will be expecting professional support during their induction year and we hope that senior colleagues will have tried to tune this to individual needs partly through the use of the 'career entry profile'. More experienced new teachers will undoubtedly be encouraged to think about their career development – or their career path – and the government's 'Learning and Teaching Strategy', published in 2001, strongly endorses the link between professional development and career enhancement.

To have a teaching force populated by individuals who are ambitious in terms of their own career path is no bad thing. Any vibrant profession needs movers and shakers in the form of people who want to 'get on' and wield influence – for example, as a headteacher. But it would be a sorry state of affairs if this were the only way in which 'professional development' was articulated. Indeed, we need to exercise a little caution in our assumptions about 'career'. Just as important as the realisation that not every teacher can become a headteacher are the equally mundane understandings that not all teachers have the capacities that heads need to possess – and that not all teachers want to become heads in the first place! What we say is that teachers who are not motivated by an essentially linear career path which seems to rely heavily on individual motivation to 'climb the ladder' are still in need of professional development opportunities, but not necessarily of the kind that 'the system' requires and in which it invests so heavily, such as headship qualifications.

Is professional development about leadership?

There are in any case career options for teachers that are not concerned with management responsibilities, such as Advanced Skills Teachers (ASTs). Furthermore, roles often designated as *middle* management, most notably the head of (geography) department role (HOD), are often exceedingly rewarding and offer more than enough 'career enhancement' for many teachers. Perhaps the prime reason for this is that even though the managerial aspects of the HOD are significant, it is the subject leadership responsibility that in a sense defines the role. The creative possibilities to ensure that the departmental team has a shared moral purpose are important to realise, for example, to ensure that:

189

- all pupils enjoy their geography;
- geography has a presence in whatever curriculum framework is adopted post-14;
- the geography curriculum is current, relevant and worthwhile.

All teachers of geography can – indeed must – contribute to this process. Moreover, it is probably most effective when it happens locally, in school, so that the creative work is fashioned by the particular needs of the local context. Various CPD programmes devised externally and from central agencies often fail in this respect. Indeed, they are often so concerned with reaching teachers generally they sometimes fail even to engage seriously with the subject at all.

The need to belong to a creative community of practice

What this final discussion centres on therefore is the association between professional development and the creative development of geography in education – the subject matter, teaching and learning approaches and the assessment of understanding. In the end, this is a matter of *career fulfilment*, for unless practitioners are engaged with the tricky questions of what it means to learn geography, or for pupils to think geographically and to demonstrate geographical understanding, then we fear geography in schools may get left behind, perceived as a low-level service subject dealing in general knowledge.

This kind of professional development can be stimulated from outside – for example, from the wider 'community of practice' that is represented by groupings such as the Geographical Association (see p. 194) – but it is clear that because professional development of this kind is concerned primarily with *what pupils are learning and how they are learning it*, it needs focusing on *your classroom*. 'Solutions' to the curriculum and pedagogic challenges that abound are rarely simple and hardly ever of a 'one size fits all' character, but can be worked out by practitioners on the ground in the company of others (often real and sometimes virtual). Professional development under this kind of rubric can be entirely localised, and to be sure, it may not be prudent to await the course or inset (in-service training) pack to be brought to your door.

What about 'CPD'?

Professional development, therefore, occurs in both formal and less formal settings, tapping energy sources from outside agencies, colleagues and individual teachers who want to improve. For subject specialist teachers it often takes a cue, and becomes indistinguishable, from the development of curriculum, pedagogy and assessment in the subject. Thus, professional development is concerned with a far wider field than that associated with 'CPD' (continuing professional development), by which is usually meant the formal and usually funded inset days and courses.

Attitudes towards CPD vary enormously. One survey (DfES 2003b) shows that although teachers tend to value CPD, older teachers are often cynical about in-service training opportunities that appear simply to promote government priorities rather than allow them to focus on their own professional needs. On the other hand, the same survey showed that NQTs in secondary schools are more likely to do courses and attend conferences out of 'personal interest' – particularly those that enable them to develop teaching skills and subject knowledge. It seems that, when it comes to CPD, the challenge is how to maintain personal interest and motivation. For us, the way to do this is to 'take ownership' in the sense that if you assume CPD is something *done to you*, or you wait for CPD to *provide you* with something useful, then you can become dissatisfied or frustrated.

Professional learning

It is now widely advocated that one of the most useful attributes a teacher can bring to pupils is to be able to model the characteristics of a genuine learner. This is perhaps easiest to imagine in the context of coming to something new together – as in field work, for example. But it applies to all settings. Such a teacher is confident enough to be uncertain, and therefore to be seen in the process of learning. Such a teacher is not only skilful at getting pupils to think and talk about their learning, but can analyse his or her own professional learning. 'CPD' becomes just another (usually very positive) opportunity to contribute to the process of professional learning – by provoking a new thought, or by looking at the familiar in a new way. The value of the CPD may therefore rest on what *you bring to* the experience as much as the experience itself.

In much the same vein as this, David Hargreaves has analysed the desirable characteristics of schools in the so-called knowledge society in which we live (Hargreaves 1999). He advocates the 'knowledge creating school', using Manuel Castells' (1996) concept of the networked society as his cue, identifying the personal qualities that matter in the transformed workplace – how to be autonomous, self-organising, networking, entrepreneurial and innovative. Tellingly, he writes:

An effect of recent educational reforms has been to discourage teachers from engaging in the process of professional knowledge creation by which, in rapidly changing social conditions in schools and society, the profession generates new knowledge to become more effective. Some believe we already possess enough knowledge to make the education service more effective, and the task is to make sure that all teachers and schools, not just the outstanding ones, have access to, and deploy, this knowledge. On this view, the problem is one of the dissemination of existing 'best practice' and/or research evidence. Certainly if the most effective schools and classrooms were replicated throughout the system, educational standards would indeed rise. But the dissemination of *existing* good practice is an inadequate basis for making a success of schools in the knowledge economy: we need to generate better knowledge and practices. In high technology firms the importance of knowledge creation, not just its dissemination, is acknowledged, for to be content with current knowledge and practice is to be left behind. My thesis is that the same now applies to schools.

(Hargreaves 1999: 123)

What Hargreaves omits to mention in this quotation is the rapidly changing *subject knowledge* that teachers also need to engage with. Readers of this book will realise that we do not think school subjects should crudely try to follow and apply developments in the wider discipline. But the changing discipline certainly helps inform geography teachers grappling with their 'confident uncertainty' about how to arrange a relevant, enjoyable and worthwhile learning experience through geography lessons. To echo Hargreaves, therefore, an important product of the knowledge creation industry represented by good schools is *the curriculum*, and it is teachers who are the knowledge producers in this regard. To contribute to this process teacher teams need to be able to identify, communicate and assess each other's strengths and specialist knowledge and understanding.

Hargreaves himself states that the embryo of such a process exists in many schools (and we would say geography departments) where teachers quite naturally engage in what is called *tinkering* – the almost constant process of adjusting, refining, applying 'good ideas', keeping up to date – indeed, you may have found that it is often quite difficult to use someone else's lesson materials without doing some tinkering. This could be the beginnings of curriculum development, based on mutual professional learning. Thus, 'knowledge creation' does not require a blank sheet and is not often a root and branch revolutionary change, but it does require a stage more than individualised tinkering: the process needs to be explicit and communicated. It cannot be made to happen easily by teachers working alone and in isolation.

Aiming for 'scholarship of teaching'?

Teaching is a very practical activity, but at its heart is an intellectual process. The one without the other is useless. We have been at pains to emphasise the latter because, especially early in a teaching career, one is judged (and often judges oneself) by practical success: Can I make the pupils listen to me and to each other? Can I get them to do their homework? Can I teach a decent lesson on contours?

'Tinkering' is essentially practical, but will never really contribute to the 'knowledge creating school' or a wider 'community of practice' (of geography educationists) unless it gets beyond what is usually understood by 'reflective practice'. We certainly support and encourage reflective practitioners, but also want to point out the limitations to this orthodoxy of professional practice. The main problem is that it is usually, in our experience, essentially self-referential, and not often subject to critical evaluation from others or from the literature. As we have argued throughout this book, this is especially the case in relation to the *content* of geography lessons.

The idea of the 'scholarship of teaching' has been introduced mainly from the US, at first in the context of higher education (Boyer 1990), but applied more and more to school teaching. It requires teaching to be less instinctive, less habitual and routine and more thoughtful, informed and adventurous (being prepared to risk failure and setback). It is a useful notion which links directly to the idea quoted at the beginning of this chapter, namely that if teaching became more research oriented, it would not only become more effective but also more satisfying. Again, it is hard to imagine one without the other.

What the scholarship of teaching requires is a kind of 'going meta' in which you and your colleagues:

- get better and better at asking questions about *what* students are learning, and *how* this is being organised and arranged; and
- become committed to deepening and broadening the learning, so that geography becomes a fantastically motivating mental 'climbing frame' for young minds making sense of the modern world.

In conclusion

Professional development probably happens whether you will it to or not. What we have in mind is *purposeful* professional development which is steered as much by what you need to make geography teaching exciting and enjoyable as it is by matters outside your immediate control such as the schools development plan, the demands of Ofsted and so on. Developing your capacity to use the enormous potential that resides in geography as a resource for learning about the world is perhaps the key to your professional development – contributing to your effectiveness in 'switching on' the pupils and to your own sense of professional satisfaction and worth.

There is little doubt in our minds that such a conception of teaching not only deserves the epithet 'scholarship', but requires it.

THE ROLE OF SUBJECT ASSOCIATIONS

In recent years the education service in England has been transformed from being essentially locally designed and delivered to becoming highly centralised. The government and its agencies control the curriculum framework and teacher training, but in 1997 began to 'roll out' and disseminate 'good practice' through strategies and initiatives from the Standards and Effectiveness Unit. Government policy restricted teacher freedom (perhaps unintentionally), for example, by the introduction of league tables that seriously erode teachers' propensity to take any risks at all. As a result, agencies (LEA advisers, for example, and even local examination bodies) that have supported teachers' professional development – especially for developing the curriculum – have withered away.

In this environment the subject associations became called the 'sleeping giants' of the education world. The reason for this is that while there were organisations and agencies that have been established to provide CPD for teachers – notably, the TTA, the National College for School Leadership (NCSL) and the GTCE – there were none that had a remit, nor the expertise, to support subject specialists. More recently, as we have seen, there has been a growing realisation even from central government that teaching and learning could become very dull indeed without encouraging the subject enthusiasm of teachers: to re-quote Charles Clarke in 2003:

> Our very best teachers are those who have a real passion and enthusiasm for the subject they teach. They are also deeply committed to the learning of their students and use their enthusiasm for their subject to motivate them, to bring their subject alive and make learning an exciting, vivid and enjoyable experience.
>
> (Clarke in DfES 2003a)

Subject associations therefore have assumed an important role in providing direct support for teachers, but also links, networks and other possibilities for teachers of geography in search of professional nourishment. In what follows we provide a brief case study of the Geographical Association which, often in partnership with the Royal Geographical Society with the Institute of British Geographers (RGS-IBG), has sought to provide an independent but effective and positive influence on the world of school geography and those who teach it.

This has always been the purpose of the GA, ever since its origins in 1893 when it was set up specifically so that modern, practical teaching techniques could be shared and taken seriously. In those days it was the use of 'lantern slides' that attracted attention. Throughout the last century to the present the GA maintained an interest in teaching technologies, but never losing sight of the passion for communicating the power and potential of geography in education. Other constant themes have included geography and international understanding, geography and fieldwork, and geography and environmental understanding. More recently, the GA has grown to a membership that reaches into most secondary schools and maybe a third of all primary schools. It needs to be more, but already this provides a good basis for a national and international community of practitioners that encourages, supports and motivates through:

- termly journals, with practical teaching ideas and background debates;
- *GA News*, containing updates and information;
- a lively, interactive website, with advice, forums and essential links;
- practitioner focused books and resources to support teaching;
- leading-edge student materials;
- national and regional conferences, for information, updates and networking;
- funded project work to develop the curriculum, pedagogy and assessment in geography (known as *Geovisions*);
- sponsored student activities and competitions to raise geography's profile (known as *Worldwise*).

The Appendix gives a detailed summary (agreed in late 2003) of how the GA and the RGS-IBG see their strengths in supporting the advancement of geography and geography education. Within the context described in this 'manifesto' for promoting excellence in geography and geography education as a whole, the GA has derived its own particular vision (see Box 10.1).

BOX 10.1 THE GA'S VISION

The GA will continue to have a *growing membership*.

New teachers of geography will normally join the Association and most will retain their membership, often throughout their careers.

Members gain access to a range of *benefits* including substantial discounts to an impressive list of professional publications and learning resources, available in print and on the web.

Through a lively and active website, newsletter and journals, members will feel a sense of belonging to a *community of practice* in which subject specific *professional learning* is the driving force.

Journals will each continue to evolve clear professional and/or research identities, reflecting the main fields occupied by the GA. Broadly, this field can be characterised as '*geography in education*', including research, teaching and learning across all age ranges and the formal and less formal sectors of education.

A substantial number (c. 10%) will strive to become GA 'teacher consultants', in recognition of their proven ability and track record to innovate and show leadership in the field. All members will be encouraged to make manifest their passion for geography through curriculum development via 'Geovisions' projects.

Members will see the GA as a worthwhile 'site' in which to *invest energy and expertise*, as well as a relevant source of *professional support*.

By seeking to maximise participation and encouraging an active membership, the GA will gain increased *authority* on which to base its networking and *lobbying* with government and its agencies. High profile national events, under the banner 'Worldwise', will provide a key opportunity for participation with students.

The *Annual Meeting*, attended by activists, will reflect on and review recent achievements and developments. It will feed forward to the *strategic targets* for the year, and involve a high-level policy input (eg from DfES, QCA).

The *Annual Conference and Exhibition* (April) will attend to the needs of the wider community, providing opportunities for networking, updating, stimulation and renewal. It will also provide leading edge *professional development* packages for teachers, in the context of the *lively discipline* of geography.

Volunteers' energy will be well focused through their involvement in a key *scrutiny* role and by providing *policy advice* via a sharper committee structure.

Quasi-autonomous local *Branches* will be able to play a part in the national network and existing links will be strengthened. Branches will be crucial in developing Worldwise. Many Humanities Specialist Schools will form local Branches.

Increasingly, the GA will find ways to release teachers' creative energy, literally through the *buying* of time under the auspices of *funded projects, providing* 'local solutions' *to curriculum and pedagogic challenges in geography education.*

Local solutions will be communicated nationally and internationally via the website, journals and conference, contributing to a lively, grounded debate on *curriculum, pedagogy and assessment*, under the banner of Geovisions.

In time, funded *projects* will provide a third income stream roughly equivalent to those of *membership* and *publications*.

197

> The GA will be forming *strategic partnerships* with a range of organisations of both a commercial and educational character (e.g. the RGS-IBG). As well as strengthening geography's place in the curriculum, this will ensure that geography's contribution to wider concerns is fully recognised, particularly in relation to the exploration of *sustainability*, *citizenship* and issues associated with *globalisation*.
>
> www.geography.org.uk

In summary, the clear intention of the GA is to create and maintain a wider specialist *community of practice* for teachers of geography. It focuses particularly on those in the 'compulsory years' of education (Years 1–11), but of course realises that a true community is impossible to maintain without links to the post-compulsory curriculum, higher education (HE), lifelong learning and indeed the 'real world' of employment and leisure. The GA maintains its independence by relying heavily on its membership, which provides the Association with its authority to speak for geography and its role in education. It is helpful to teachers of geography, engaged in the kind of purposeful professional development discussed earlier in this chapter, simply to know that such a wider community exists. Often, when family and job commitments allow, individuals and departments become active volunteers – managing web-based forums, sitting on advisory groups and committees or running sessions at conferences. Occasionally the GA provides paid opportunities – writing materials or becoming part of a funded project team.

There is no doubt that the GA played an essential role in establishing geography as a lively school subject during the last century, culminating in its place in the National Curriculum. It will carry on playing its part to maintain geography's relevance in the school curriculum, not as a divine right but through guiding the development of the subject and its capacity to adapt to the needs of modern curricula and the interest of young people (Lambert 2004). For this it is reliant on the energy and imagination of its practitioner members to provide 'local solutions' to the various challenges as they arise and its ability to communicate these across the community. The GA does not have a single vision of geography and aims to be inclusive. In the end, the GA is against teachers of geography battling in isolation.

FOR FURTHER THINKING

1 What do you understand by a 'research based profession? How does the idea of a research based profession intersect with 'CPD'?

2 In what ways is your own professional development tied up with the development of the geography curriculum? As a teacher, are you a curriculum developer? Where do you place yourself on this continuum?

3 In what ways do you feel to be part of a 'community of practice'? Does the idea appeal to you or does it make you feel nervous?

Chapter 11

Conclusion

This is a conclusion, but only for this book. Not least, this is because we are inclined to think of the book as a starting point for discussions about geography education and the teaching of geography in secondary schools. We hope readers will see it that way too, and find ways to debate and develop the ideas in this book.

It is perhaps worth trying to place this book in context. Our argument in this book is that geography teachers have a long history of engaging with debates about the contribution of the subject to a broad education. This is inevitable, since geography studies the world and therefore reflects it in some way. Of course, there have always been arguments about how exactly geographers should do this, and these are documented in the first section of the book. This should be seen as part of a long tradition of geography educators reflecting on the purposes of geography teaching. At the same time, the book is also written in response to more immediate events. The last two decades have seen the centralisation of curriculum debates, with the result that many of the discussions about the content of the school curriculum have been muted. It is almost as if the 'curriculum problem' posed by Norman Graves (how to select what to teach) had been 'solved' (Graves 1975). Teachers know what they are expected to teach, and what concerns them is how to 'deliver' the agreed content of the curriculum. The consequence of this turn is that the school geography curriculum soon becomes 'stuck' because it is increasingly difficult to stimulate any sustained and serious engagement about what should be its contents. This is an argument we have sought to convince readers of this book that they need to engage in. We have provided examples to show how questions of geographical knowledge are never settled, being always subject to revision and change.

A further consequence of the 'death of curriculum debate' is that school geography has become increasingly distanced from developments in geography as taught and studied in universities. We hope we have made it clear that we do not hold a simplistic view that school geography should ape intellectual fashions. Instead, we argue that it is the proper role of teachers to engage with developments in geography as a discipline, and assess and evaluate their educational implications. This has just not happened in recent years, with the result that any claims to convince the wider public that 'geography matters' tend to be rhetorical and are not fully thought through. For example, it is ironic that although geography educators have been arguing that the subject can make a special contribution to issues of environmental concern, much of the discussion of these issues has ignored the important work about the relationship between society and nature produced by geographers in universities. The result, we suggest, is a form of intellectual inertia. This ultimately makes teaching the subject uninteresting. In such circumstances the pupils can be forgiven for striking an attitude to lessons that draws on their capacity to endure rather than enjoy.

All this perhaps sounds rather negative. But that is the nature of critique – at least to begin with, before something new is created. Writing a book that claims to take a critical look at geography education inevitably means that the gaps in our thinking are stressed. But this is where you come in. We hope we have also provided a convincing vision of the power and relevance of geography and its educational potential for all young people, and at the same time a picture of our unswerving belief in the role of teachers in reaching this potential.

If geography's reputation as a leading school subject has been damaged in recent years (it has, for according to repeated Ofsted reports there is 'cause for concern' about the quality of teaching in KS3 geography, for example, and there has been some decline in take up for GCSE and beyond), then it is because teachers have been taken out of the creative business of curriculum making. There are many reasons why this has happened and it probably has not been the result of any single deliberate policy. Things are now changing, however, not least since the government's apparent policy shift to support 'subject specialism' (see pp. 182–3) in schools.

There is now a fine opportunity for anyone coming into a career in geography teaching to really make a difference and we hope this book has provided some encouragement and a framework for you to take up this challenge, both with colleagues and with your students.

Strengths of the Royal Geographical Society (with the Institute of British Geographers) and the Geographical Association

The Geographical Association (GA) and the Royal Geographical Society with the Institute of British Geographers (RGS-IBG) are the two subject bodies that directly support geography and geography education. The different and complementary strengths of the two organisations are set out below.

ROYAL GEOGRAPHICAL SOCIETY AND THE INSTITUTE OF BRITISH GEOGRAPHERS

The RGS-IBG strengths derive from its objective to 'advance geography and geographical learning' as the learned society and the professional body. Its strengths describe a community of knowledge and of engagement and interaction across the education, research, professional and lifelong learning sectors. The RGS-IBG is concerned mainly with secondary and higher education. The strengths are:

1 Well-developed links and strong engagement with geography as a developing research discipline and its community of practitioners across the UK through the Society's network of geography departments in higher education institutions, its 23 speciality research groups, conferences and Fellowship. The Society thus has ready access to new knowledge.

2 Well-developed links and strong engagement with geography teaching in higher education and its community of practitioners through the Society's departmental network, Higher Education Study Group, individual Fellows, and its partnership in the Learning and Teaching Support Network (LTSN) for higher education.

3 Well-established links and engagement with the secondary education community through the Society's teacher members, school membership, and collaborative funded work, including that with the DfES, QCA, TTA and Becta (British Educational Communications and Technology Agency).

4 A proven experience of delivery and management of secondary education support activities by the permanently staffed education and events departments and the specialist fieldwork and expedition advisory centre. This includes innovative and exciting web-based teaching resources, CPD training, advisory services, briefings and publications.

5 A national and international membership and outreach and strong partnerships and networks with other subject and learned societies, and the NGO (non-governmental organisation), business, government and professional communities.

6 Respected and sought out for guidance, and for facilitation and co-ordination roles, by statutory bodies and government, including issues in education of standards, benchmarking, curriculum development, professional development, funding and training.

7 Active involvement with, and professional accreditation (Chartered Geographer) of, geographers working in the wider professional communities throughout the UK using their geographical knowledge and skills. This includes a strand for teachers who have developed and led their subject in secondary education over and above 'standard' classroom teaching.

8 Substantial geographical information resources that the Society holds, disseminates, and increasingly adds value to by means of interpretation, interactive use and engaging new audiences in geography. The resources are in its three leading scholarly journals, its historic and contemporary collections of over 2 million items, and its Fellows' knowledge.

9 A world-class location in the heart of one of the largest cultural and learning quarters in London, with an education centre, conference facilities and, from 2004, a public display space on Exhibition Road.

10 Inclusion in the Society's activities through the Society's eight regional branches in England and Wales, and more widely with its popular website; and a strong track record in supporting lifelong learning and the wider public understanding of geography by means of lectures, field visits and publishing.

THE GEOGRAPHICAL ASSOCIATION

The Geographical Association's strengths derive from its mission – 'to further the learning and teaching of geography'. The GA is concerned mainly, but not solely, with primary and secondary education and interacts increasingly with education and practitioner research. The particular strengths of the GA are:

1 Well-developed and large teacher membership drawn from primary, middle and secondary schools, and smaller numbers from colleges and higher education institutions, providing authority to a 'community of practice' covering the UK and increasingly with international influence.

2 Substantial and significant publications to support the professional development of teachers: for example, three professional journals that span all phases of education, *Handbooks* (for primary and secondary), professional support series (such as *Theory into Practice*) and scholarly works that develop theoretical perspectives (such as *Learning Through Enquiry* and *Changing the Subject*).

3 Successful and influential publication of leading-edge teaching and student learning resources, for example, from *Barnaby Bear* (primary) to *Changing Geography* (post 16).

4 Well-established and popular Annual Conference and Exhibition that forms the hub around which the events and activities of 'Worldwise' and 'Geovisions' develop and evolve. This features geographers from all phases of education including top academics and has a growing international impact.

5 Successful track record of influence and creativity with regard to the curriculum development of school geography. This in part flows from strong links with teacher education in higher education institutions and in schools, and the proven ability to work collaboratively in joint projects.

6 Drawing from its wide membership base, the capacity to wield influence in pedagogic debates and developments, including the provision of professional development units at its own conferences and supporting commercial providers of CPD, for example, with publications and speakers.

7 Respected source of advice and guidance on school geography matters such as time allocations, specifications and fieldwork issues. Also sought after advice on citizenship, education for sustainable development and other whole curriculum matters. Increasingly, such advice will be available directly and indirectly via the developing interactive website.

8 Rapidly developing professional project culture emphasising curriculum and pedagogic development at primary and secondary levels, promoting 'local solutions'. Recent funders include, for example: DfID (Department for International Development), DfES, TTA, QCA, Becta, Wellcome Foundation and Excellence in Cities.

9 Branch and regional activities provide local opportunities and perspectives on the study and teaching of geography within the national organisation and networks and typically include sixth-form lecture programmes, 'Worldwise' activities and informal CPD.

10 Fully staffed professional office in the north of England, which, as well as administering the organisation, is able to initiate and lead developments on publications, conferences and project development in relation to school geography.

Main contact: ga@geography.org.uk
www.geography.org.uk

References

Adey, P. and Shayer, M. (1994) *Really Raising Standards: Cognitive Intervention and Academic Achievement*, London: Routledge.

Ambrose, P. (ed.) (1969) *Analytical Human Geography*, London: Longman.

Apple, M. (1988) *Teachers and Texts: A Political Economy of Class and Gender Relations in Education*, London: Routledge & Kegan Paul.

Apple, M. (1990) *Ideology and Curriculum*, London: Routledge (2nd edition).

Armstrong, M. (1973) 'The role of the teacher' in P. Buckman (ed.) *Education Without Schools*, London: Souvenir Press, pp. 49–60.

Bale, J. (1983) 'Welfare approaches to geography' in J. Huckle (ed.) *Geographical Education: Reflection and Action*, Oxford: Oxford University Press, pp. 64–73.

Bale, J. (1987) *Geography in the Primary School*, London: Routledge & Kegan Paul.

Bale, J. (1996) 'The Challenge of Postmodernism', in M. Williams (ed.) *Understanding Geographical and Environmental Education: the Role of Research*, London: Cassell, pp. 287–96.

Ball, S. (1994) *Education Reform: a Critical and Post-structural Approach*, London: Routledge.

Barnes, T. (1996) *Logics of Dislocation*, New York: Guilford Press.

Barnes, T. (2003) 'Introduction: "Never mind the economy. Here's culture"' in K. Anderson, M. Domosh, S. Pile and N. Thrift (eds) *Handbook of Cultural Geography*, London: Sage, pp. 89–97.

Barnes, T. and Duncan, J. (eds) (1992) *Writing Worlds*, London: Routledge.

Barnes, T. and Gregory, D. (eds) (1997) *Reading Human Geography: the Poetics and Politics of Inquiry*, London: Arnold.

Bennetts, T. (1996) 'Progression and differentiation' in P. Bailey and P. Fox (eds) *Geography Teachers' Handbook*, Sheffield: Geographical Association.

Bennetts. T. (forthcoming) 'Progression in Geographical Understanding', *International Research in Geographical and Environmental Education*.

Bjerknes, J. and Solberg, H. (1922) 'The life cycle of cyclones and the polar front theory of atmospheric circulation', *Geofys. Publ.*: 3(1).

Black, J. (2000) *Maps and Politics*, London: Reaktion Books.

Black, P., Harrison, C., Lee, C., Marshall, B. and Wiliam, D., (2003) *Assessment for Learning: Putting it into Practice*, Milton Keynes: Open University Press.

Boardman, D. (1983) *Graphicacy and Geography Teaching*, London: Croom Helm.

Boardman, D. and McPartland, M. (1993a) 'Building on the foundations: 1893–1945', *Teaching Geography*, 18(1): 3–6.

Boardman, D. and McPartland, M. (1993b) 'From regions to models: 1944–69', *Teaching Geography*, 18(2): 65–69.

Boardman, D. and McPartland, M. (1993c) 'Innovations and change: 1970–82', *Teaching Geography*, 18(3): 117–20.

Boardman, D. and McPartland, M. (1993d) 'Towards centralisation: 1983–93', *Teaching Geography*, 18(4): 159–62.

Boyer, E. (1990) *Scholarship reconsidered: Priorities of the Professoriate*, Princeton NJ: Carnegie Foundation for the Advancement of Teaching.

Bradford, M. and Kent, A. (1977) *Human Geography: Theories and their Application*, Oxford: Oxford University Press.

Bright, N. and Leat, D. (2000) 'Towards a new professionalism' in A. Kent, (ed.) *Reflective Practice in Geography Teaching*, London: Paul Chapman Publishing.

British Film Institute (1999) *Making Movies Matter*, London: BFI.

British Fim Institute (2000) *Moving Images in the Classroom*, London: BFI.

Britzman, D. (1989) 'Who has the floor? Curriculum, teaching and the English Student Teacher's Struggle for Voice', *Curriculum Inquiry*, 19(2): 143–62.

Buckingham, D. (2003) *Media Education*, Cambridge: Polity Press.

Bullock, A. *et al.* (1975) *A Language for Life*, London: HMSO.

Burgess, E. W. (1925) 'The growth of the city' in R. Park, E. W. Burgess and R. D. Mckenzie (eds) *The City*, Chicago: Chicago University Press, pp. 117–29.

Burgess, J. and Gold, J. (1985) *Geography, the Media and Popular Culture*, London: Croom Helm.

Burke, C. and Grosvenor, I. (2003) *The School I'd Like: Children and Young People's Reflections on an Education for the 21st Century*, London: RoutledgeFalmer.

Butler, R. and Parr, H. (eds) (1999) *Mind and Body Spaces: Geographies of Illness, Impairment and Disability*, London: Routledge.

Campbell, E. (2003) *The Ethical Teacher*, London: Open University Press.

Carlson, D. (2002) *Leaving Safe Harbors: Towards a New Progressivism in American Education and Public Life*, New York: RoutledgeFalmer.

Carrington, B. (1998) '"Football's coming home" but whose home? and do we want it?: nation, football and the politics of exclusion' in A. Brown (ed.) *Fanatics! Power, identity and fandom in football*, London: Routledge, pp. 101–23.

Castells, M. (1996) *The Rise of the Network Society*, Malden, MA, and Oxford: Basil Blackwell.

Castree, N. (2001) 'Socializing nature: theory, practice and politics' in N. Castree and B. Braun (eds) *Social Nature: Theory, Practice and Politics*, Oxford: Blackwell, pp. 1–21.

Chisholm, M. and Manners, G. (eds) (1971) *Spatial Policy Problems of the British Economy*, Cambridge: Cambridge University Press.

Chorley, R. and Haggett, P. (1967) *Models in Geography*, London: Methuen.

Chorley, R., Beckinsale, R. and Dunn, A. (1973) *The History of the Study of Landforms, Volume II*, London: Methuen.

Clements, R. E. (1928) *Plant Succession and Indicators*, New York: H. W. Wilson.

Cloke, P. (ed.) (1992) *Policy and Change in Thatcher's Britain*, Oxford: Permagon.

Cloke, P., Philo, C. and Sadler, D. (1991) *Approaching Human Geography*, London: Paul Chapman.

Cloke, P., Cook, I., Crang, P. *et al.* (2004) *Practising Human Geography*, London: Arnold.

Connell, J. and Gibson, C. (2003) *Sound Tracks: Popular Music, Identity and Place*, London: Routledge.

Contemporary Issues in Geography and Education, 1(1), (Autumn): 1–3.

Cooke, R. and Warren, A. (1973) *Geomorphology in Deserts*, London: Batsford.

Corbridge, S. (1986) *Capitalist Word Development: a Critique of Radical Development Geography*, London: Macmillan.

Corney, G. (ed.) (1985) *Geography, Schools and Industry*, Sheffield: Geographical Association.

Crush, J. (ed.) (1995) *Power of Development*, London: Routledge.

Curry, M. (1998) *Digital Places: Living with Geographic Information Technologies*, London: Routledge.

Daly, C., Pachler, N. and Lambert, D. (2004) 'Teacher learning: towards a professional academy' in *Teaching in Higher Education*, 9: 99–111.

Dear, M. (1988) 'The postmodern challenge: reconstructing human geography', *Transactions of the Institute of British Geographers*, NS 13(3): 262–74.

Dear, M. (2000) *The Postmodern Urban Condition*, Oxford: Blackwell.

DES (Department of Education and Science) (1972) *New Thinking in School Geography*, Education Pamphlet No. 59, London: HMSO.

Dewey, J. (1916, 1966) *Democracy and Education*, London: Collier-Macmillan.

DfEE/QCA (1999) *Geography: The National Curriculum for England*, London: DfEE/QCA.

DfES (2002) *Literacy in Geography*, London: DfES.

DfES (2003a) *Subject Specialisms: A Consultation Document*, London: Department for Education and Skills.

DfES (2003b) *Teachers' Perceptions of Continuing Professional Development*, Department for Education and Skills, Research Brief 429, www.dfes.gov.uk/research.

Dickenson, J., Clarke, G., Gould, W. *et al.* (1983) *A Geography of the Third World*, London: Methuen.

Dobson, J., Sander, J. and Woodfield, J. (2001) *Living Geography: Book 1*, Cheltenham: Nelson Thornes.

Domosh, M. and Seager, J. (2001) *Putting Women in Place: Feminist Geographers Make Sense of the World*, New York: Guilford Press.

Everson, J. and FitzGerald, B. (1969) *Settlement Patterns*, London: Longman.

Fielding, M. (2001a) 'Words that don't come easy', *Times Educational Supplement*, 6 July, p. 25.

Fielding, M. (ed.) (2001b) *Taking Education Really Seriously: Four Years of Hard Labour*, London: RoutledgeFalmer.

Fien, J. (1983) 'Humanisitc geography' in J. Huckle (ed.) *Geographical Education: Reflection and Action*, Oxford: Oxford University Press, pp. 43–55.

Fien, J. and Gerber, R. (eds) (1988) *Teaching Geography for a Better World*, London: Longman.

Frank, A. G. (1967) *Capitalism and Underdevelopment in Latin America*, London: Monthly Review Press.

Freire, P. (1972) *Pedagogy of the Oppressed*, Harmondsworth: Penguin.

Friel, B. (1984) *Brian Friel: Plays 1*, London: Faber & Faber.

Furlong, J., Barton, L., Miles, S. *et al.* (2000) *Teacher Training in Transition: Reforming Professionalism*, Buckingham: Open University Press.

Gilbert, R. (1984) *The Impotent Image: Reflections of Ideology in the Secondary School Curriculum*, London: Falmer Press.

Gilbert, R. (1989) 'Language and ideology in geographical teaching' in F. Slater (ed.) *Language and Learning in the Teaching of Geography*, London: Routledge, pp. 151–61.

Gill, D. (1982) 'The contribution of secondary school geography to multicultural education: a critical review of some materials', *Multiracial Education*, 10(3): 13–26.

Gleeson, B. (1999) *Geographies of Disability*, London: Routledge.

Goodson, I. (1983) *Social Subjects and Curriculum Change*, London: Croom Helm.

Graves, N. (1975) *Geography in Education*, London: Heinemann.

Graves, N. (1979) *Curriculum Planning in Geography*, London: Heinemann.

Gregory, D. (1978) *Ideology, Science and Human Geography*, London: Hutchinson.

Gregory, D. (1981a) 'Human agency and human geography', *Transactions of the Institute of British Geographers*, 6: 1–18.

Gregory, D. (1981b) 'Towards human geography' in R. Walford (ed.) *Signposts for Teaching Geography*, London: Longman, pp. 133–47.

Gregory, D. (1994) *Geographical Imaginations*, Oxford: Blackwell.

Gregory, D. and Walford, R. (eds) (1989) *New Horizons in Human Geography*, Basingstoke: Macmillan.

Gregory, D., Martin, R. and Smith, G. (1994) *Human Geography: Society, Space, and Social Science*, Basingstoke: Macmillan.

Gregory, K. (1984) *The Nature of Physical Geography*, London: Edward Arnold.

Gregory, K. (2000) *The Changing Nature of Physical Geography*, London: Arnold.

Gritzner, C. (2002) 'What is where, why there and why care?', *Journal of Geography*, 101(1): 40.

Haggett, P. (1965) *Locational Analysis in Human Geography*, London: Edward Arnold.

Haggett, P. (1996) 'Geography into the next century: personal reflections' in E. Rawling and R. Daugherty (eds) *Geography into the Twenty-First Century*, Chichester: Wiley, pp. 11–18.

Hall, D. (1976) *Geography and the Geography Teacher*, London: Allen & Unwin.

Hall, D. (1990) 'The national curriculum and the two cultures: towards a humanistic perspective', *Geography*, 75(4): 313–24.

Hamnett, C. (2001) 'The emperor's new theoretical clothes, or geography without origami' in G. Philo and D. Miller (eds) *Market Killing: What the Free Market Does and What Social Scientists Can Do About It*, Harlow: Longman, pp. 158–69.

Hardy, J. (2002) *Altered Land*, London: Simon & Schuster.

Hargreaves, D. (1996) *Teaching as a Research Based Profession: Possibilities and Prospects*, The Teacher Training Agency Annual Lecture, London: Teacher Training Agency.

Hargreaves, D. (1999) 'The knowledge-creating school', *British Journal of Educational Studies*, 47(2): 122–44.

Harvey, D. (1969) *Explanation in Geography*, London: Edward Arnold.

Harvey, D. (1973) *Social Justice and the City*, London: Edward Arnold.

Harvey, D. (1989) *The Condition of Postmodernity*, Oxford: Blackwell.

Harvey, D. (1996) *Justice, Nature and the Geographies of Difference*, Oxford: Blackwell.

Harvey, D. (2000a) *Spaces of Hope*, Edinburgh: Edinburgh University Press.

Harvey, D. (2000b) 'Reinventing geography: An interview with the editors of the New Left Review', *New Left Review*, Second Series, 4 (July–August): 75–97.

Harvey, D. (2001) *Spaces of Capital: Towards a Critical Geography*, Edinburgh: Edinburgh University Press.

Hassell, D. (2002) 'Issues in ICT and Geography' in M. Smith (ed.) *Teaching Geography in Secondary Schools*, London: RoutledgeFalmer, pp. 148–59.

Head, L. (2000) *Cultural Landscapes and Environmental Change*, London: Arnold.

Healey, M. and Roberts, M. (1996) 'Human and regional geography in schools and higher education' in E. Rawling and R. Daugherty (eds) *Geography into the Twenty-First Century*, Chichester: Wiley, pp. 229–306.

Heffernan, M. (2003) 'Histories of Geography' in S. Holloway, S. Rice and G. Valentine (eds) *Key Concepts in Geography*, London: Sage, pp. 3–22.

Henley, R. (1989) 'The ideology of geographical language' in F. Slater (ed.) *Language and Learning in the Teaching of Geography*, London: Routledge, pp. 162–71.

Herbert, D. (1982) *The Geography of Urban Crime*, London: Longman.

Hirst, P. (1974) *Knowledge and the Curriculum*, London: Routledge, Kegan & Paul.

Hodson, D. (1998) *Teaching and Learning Science: Towards a Personalized Approach*, Buckingham: Open University Press.

Holloway, L. and Hubbard, P. (2001) *People and Place: the Extraordinary Geographies of Everyday Life*, London: Prentice Hall.

Holloway, S., Rice, S. and Valentine, G. (eds) (2003) *Key Concepts in Geography*, London: Sage.

Hoyle, E. and John, P. (1995) *Professional Knowledge and Professional Practice*, London: Cassell.

Hubbard, P., Kitchin, R., Bartley, B and Fuller, D. (2002) *Thinking Geographically: Space, Theory and Contemporary Human Geography*, London: Continuum.

Huckle, J. (ed.) (1983) *Geographical Education: Reflection and Action*, Oxford: Oxford University Press.

Huckle, J. (1985) 'Geography and schooling' in R. Johnston (ed.) *The Future of Geography*, London: Methuen, pp. 291–306.

Huckle, J. (1987) 'What sort of geography for what sort of school curriculum?', *Area*, 19(30): 261–65.

Huckle, J. (1988) 'Social and political literacy' in D. Watson (ed.) *Learning Geography with Computers,* Coventry: Microelectronics Support Unit, pp. 58–60.

Hudson, R. and Williams, A. (1995) *Divided Britain*, Chichester: Wiley (2nd edition).

Hutton, J. (1795) *Theory of the Earth*, Edinburgh: William Creech.

Inglis, F. (1985) *The Management of Ignorance: a Political Theory of the Curriculum*, Oxford: Basil Blackwell.

Jacks, G. and Whyte, R. (1939) *The Rape of the Earth*, London: Faber & Faber.

Jackson, P. (1989) *Maps of Meaning*, London: Unwin Hyman.

Jackson, P. (1996) 'Only connect: approaches to human geography' in E. Rawling and R. Daugherty (eds) *Geography into the Twenty-First Century*, Chichester: Wiley, pp. 77–94.

Jackson, P. and Smith. S. (1984) *Exploring Social Geography*, London: Allen & Unwin.

Jacques, M. and Hall, S. (eds) (1989) *New Times*, London: Lawrence & Wishart.

Jenkins, S. (2003) 'A cross marks the spot', *Times*, 9 May.

Johnston, R. (1986) *On Human Geography*, Oxford: Blackwell.

Johnston, R. (1997) *Geography and Geographers: Anglo-American Human Geography since 1945*, London; Edward Arnold (5th edition).

Johnston, R. (2003) 'Geography and the social science tradition' in S. Holloway, S. Rice and G. Valentine (eds) *Key Concepts in Geography*, London: Sage, pp. 51–71.

Johnston, R. and Sidaway, J. (2004) *Geography and Geographers; Anglo-American Human Geography since 1945*, London: Arnold (6th edition).

Johnston, R., Pattie, C., and Allsopp, J. (1988) *A Nation Dividing?: The Electoral Map of Great Britain 1979–1987*, London: Longman.

Jones, K. (2001) 'Reculturing the school: The New Labour project in context', *The School Field*, 12(5/6): 43–57.

Joseph, K. (1985) 'Geography in the school curriculum', *Geography*, 70: 290–97.

Kent, W. A. (2000) 'Geography: changes and challenges' in W. A. Kent (ed.) *School Subject Teaching: the History and Future of the Curriculum*, London: Kogan Page, pp. 111–31.

Kenway, J. and Bullen, E. (2001) *Consuming Children: Education, Entertainment, Advertising*, Buckingham: Open University Press.

Kincheloe, J. and Steinberg, S. (1997) *Changing Multiculturalism*, Buckingham: Open University Press.

Kincheloe, J. and Steinberg, S. (eds) (1998a) *Unauthorized Methods: Strategies for Critical Teaching*, London: Routledge.

Kincheloe, J. and Steinberg, S. (1998b) 'Students as researchers: critical visions, emancipatory insights' in S. Steinberg and J. Kincheloe (eds) *Students as Researchers: Creating Classrooms that Matter*, London: Falmer Press, pp. 2–19.

Kitchin, R. (1999) 'Creating an awareness of others: highlighting the role of space and place', *Geography*, 84(1): 45–54.

Klein, N. (2000) *No Logo*, London: Flamingo.

Kobayashi, A. and Mackenzie, S. (eds) (1989) *Remaking Human Geography*, London: Unwin Hyman.

Kobayashi, A. and Proctor, J. (2003) 'Values, Ethics, and Justice' in G. Gaile and C. Wilmott (eds) *Geography in America at the Dawn of the Twenty-First Century*, New York: Oxford University Press, pp. 721–29.

Kuhn, T. (1962) *The Structure of Scientific Revolutions*, Chicago: University of Chicago Press.

Lambert, D. (2004) 'Geography' in J. White (ed.) *Rethinking the School Curriculum*, London: RoutledgeFalmer: *Values, Aims, Purposes*, pp. 75–86.

Lambert, D. (forthcoming) 'What's the point?' in D. Balderstone (ed.) *Teaching and Learning Geography: the Secondary Teachers' Handbook*, Sheffield: The Geographical Association.

Lambert, D. and Balderstone, D. (2000) *Learning to Teach Geography in the Secondary School*, London: RoutledgeFalmer.

Lambert, D. and Machon, P. (eds) (2001) *Citizenship through Secondary Geography*, London: RoutledgeFalmer.

Leat, D. (ed.) (1998) *Thinking Through Geography*, Cambridge: Chris Kington Publications.

Lee, A. (1996) *Gender, Literacy, Curriculum: Re-writing School Geography*, London: Taylor & Francis.

Lee, E. (1980) 'Pop and the teacher: some uses and problems' in G. Vulliamy and E. Lee (eds) *Pop Music in School*, Cambridge: Cambridge University Press, pp. 158–74

Lee, R. (1977) 'The ivory tower, the blackboard jungle and the corporate state: a provocation on teaching progress in geography' in R. Lee (ed.) *Change and Tradition: Geography's New Frontiers*, London: Queen Mary's College, University of London, pp. 3–9.

Lee, R. (2000) 'Values' in R. Johnston, D. Gregory, G. Pratt and M. Watts (eds) *Dictionary of Human Geography*, Oxford: Blackwell (4th edition).

Lewis, J. and Townsend, A. (eds) (1989) *The North–South Divide*, London: Paul Chapman.

Leyshon, A. (1995) 'Missing words: whatever happened to the geography of poverty?', *Environment and Planning A*, 27: 1021–28.

Leyshon, A., Matless, D. and Revill, G. (eds) (1998) *The Place of Music*, New York: Guilford Press.

Livingstone, D. (1992) *The Geographical Tradition*, Oxford: Blackwell.

Lyell, C. (1830) *Principles of Geology*, London: John Murray.

McDowell, L. (2002) 'Understanding diversity: the problem of/for "Theory"' in R. Johnston, P. Taylor and M. Watts (eds) *Geographies of Global Change: Remapping the World*, Oxford: Blackwell, pp. 296–309.

McEwen, N. (1986) 'Phenomenology and the curriculum: the case of secondary-school geography' in P. Taylor (ed.) *Recent Developments in Curriculum Studies*, Windsor: NFER-Nelson, pp. 156–67.

Machon, P. (1987) 'Teaching controversial issues: some observations and suggestions' in P. Bailey and T. Binns (eds) *A Case for Geography*, Sheffield: Geographical Association, pp. 38–41.

McLaren, P. (1988) 'Culture or canon? Critical pedagogy and the politics of literacy', *Harvard Educational Review*, 58(1): 211–34.

Maguire, D. (1989) *Computers in Geography*, London: Longman.

Mannion, A. (1997) *Global Environmental Change,* Harlow: Longman.

Marsden, W. E. (1989) 'All in a good cause: geography, history and the politicisation of the curriculum in nineteenth and twentieth century England', *Journal of Curriculum Studies,* 21(6): 509–26.

Marsden, W. E. (1997) 'On taking the geography out of geography education; some historical pointers', *Geography* 82(3): 241–52.

Marsden, W. E. (2001) 'Citizenship Education: permeation or perversion?' in D. Lambert, and P. Machon (eds) *Citizenship through Secondary Geography*, London: RoutledgeFalmer, pp. 11–30.

Masterman, L. (1985) *Teaching the Media*, London: Comedia.

Meinig, D. (1979) 'The beholding eye: ten versions of the same scene' in D. Meinig (ed.) *The Interpretation of Ordinary Landscapes: Geographical Essays*, New York: Oxford University Press, 33–48.

Mercer, D. (1984) 'Unmasking technocratic geography' in M. Billinge, D. Gregory and R. Martin (eds) *Recollections of a Revolution: Geography as Spatial Science*, London: Macmillan, pp. 153–99.

Middleton, N. (1999) *The Global Casino*: *An Introduction to Global Issues,* London: Arnold (2nd edition).

Mohan, J. (1989) 'Introduction' in J. Mohan (ed.) *The Political Geography of Contemporary Britain*, London: Macmillan, pp. xi–xvi.

Mohan, J. (1999) *A United Kingdom? Economic, Social and Political Geographies*, London: Arnold.

Moore, A. (2000) *Teaching and Learning: Pedagogy, Curriculum and Culture*, London: RoutledgeFalmer.

Moore, A. (2004) *The Good Teacher: Dominant Discourse in Teaching and Teacher Education*, London: RoutledgeFalmer.

Moore, P., Chaloner, B. and Stott, P. (1996) *Global Environmental Change*, Oxford: Blackwell.

Morgan, J. (2003) 'Teaching social geographies: representing society and space', *Geography*, 88(2): 124–34.

Naish, M., Rawling, E. and Hart, C. (1987) *The Contribution of a Curriculum Project to 16–19 Education*, London: Longman/SCDC.

National Research Council. Rediscovering Geography Committee (1997) *Rediscovering Geography: New Relevance for Science and Society*, Washington, DC: National Academy Press.

Newman, O. (1972) *Defensible Space: People and Design in the Violent City*, London: The Architectural Press.

Nichols, A. (2001) *More Thinking Through Geography*, Cambridge: Chris Kington.

Pain, R. (2001) 'Crime, space and inequality' in R. Pain, M. Barke, D. Fuller, J. Gough, R. MacFarlane and G. Mowl, *Introducing Social Geographies*, London: Arnold, 231–53.

Peet, R. (1975) 'The geography of crime: a political critique', *The Professional Geographer*, 27: 277–80.

Peet, R. and Thrift, N. (eds) (1989) *New Models in Geography*, London: Unwin Hyman.

Pepper, D. (1985) 'Why teach physical geography?', *Contemporary Issues in Geography and Education*, 2(2): 62–71.

Pethick, J. (1984) *Introduction to Coastal Geomorphology*, London: Arnold.

Philo, C. (2000) 'More words, more worlds: reflections on the "cultural turn" and human geography' in I. Cook, S. Naylor and J. Ryan (eds) *Cultural Turns/Geographical Turns*, London: Prentice Hall, pp. 26–53.

Ploszajska, T. (2000) 'Historiographies of geography and empire' in B. Graham and C. Nash (eds) *Modern Historical Geographies,* London: Prentice Hall, pp. 121–45.

Porter, P. and Sheppard, E. (1990) *A World of Difference: Society, Nature, Development*, New York: Guilford Press.

Proctor, J. (2001) 'Solid rock and shifting sands: the moral paradox of saving a socially constructed nature' in N. Castree and B. Braun (eds) *Social Nature: Theory, Practice and Politics*, Oxford: Blackwell, pp. 225–39.

Rawling, E. (1997) 'Geography and vocationalism – opportunity or threat?', *Geography*, 82(2): 173–78.

Rawling, E. (2001) *Changing the Subject: the Impact of National Policy on School Geography 1980–2000*, Sheffield: Geographical Association.

Relph, E. (1976) *Place and Placelessness*, London: Pion.

Richardson, R. (1983) 'Daring to be a teacher' in J. Huckle (ed.) *Geographical Education: Reflection and Action*, Oxford: Oxford University Press, pp. 122–31.

Roberts, M. (1994) 'Interpretations of the Geography National Curriculum: a common curriculum for all?', *Journal of Curriculum Studies*, 27.

Roberts, M. (2003) *Learning Through Enquiry*, Sheffield: Geographical Association.

Roberts, N. (ed.) (1994) *The Changing Global Environment*, Oxford: Blackwell.

Rose, J. (2001) *The Intellectual Life of the British Working-Classes*, Yale: Yale University Press.

Ross, A. (2000) *Curriculum: Construction and Critique*, London: Falmer Press.

Rostow, W. (1960) *The Stages of Economic Growth: A non-communist manifesto*, London: Cambridge University Press.

Sachs, W. (1992) *The Development Dictionary: a Guide to Knowledge as Power*, London: Zed Books.

Sack, R. (1997) *Homo Geographicus: A Framework for Action, Awareness and Moral Concern*, Baltimore and London: The John Hopkins University Press.

Sarup, M. (1978) *Marxism and Education*, London: Routledge, Kegan & Paul.

Seager, J. (1990) *The State of the Earth: an Atlas of Environmental Concern*, London: Unwin Hyman.

Seager, J. and Olson, A. (1986) *Women in the World Atlas*, London: Pluto Press.

Shaw, C. and McKay, H. (1942) *Juvenile Delinquency and Urban Areas*, Chicago: University of Chicago Press.

Short, J. (1998) 'Progressive human geography' in J. Short *New Worlds, New Geographies*, New York: Syracuse University Press, pp. 91–102.

Shuker, R. (2001) *Understanding Popular Music*, London: Routledge (2nd edition).

Shulman, L. (1987) 'Knowledge and Teaching: Foundations of the New Reform', *Harvard Educational Review*, 57, 1–22.

Shurmer-Smith, P. (2002) *Doing Cultural Geography*, London: Sage.

Sibley, D. (1995) *Geographies of Exclusion*, London: Routledge.

Simmons, I. (2001) *An Environmental History of Great Britain: 10,000 Years to the Present*, Edinburgh: Edinburgh University Press.

Sims, P. (2003) 'Previous actors and current influences: trends and fashions in physical geography' in S. Trudgill and A. Roy (eds) *Contemporary Meanings in Physical Geography: From What to Why?*, London: Arnold, pp. 3–23.

Skelton, T. and Valentine, G. (eds) (1998) *Cool Places: Geographies of Youth Cultures*, London: Routledge.

Slater, F. (1982) *Learning Through Geography*, London: Heinemann.

Slater, F. (ed.) (1989) *Language and Learning in the Teaching of Geography*, London: Routledge.

Small, R. (1970) *The Study of Landforms*, Cambridge: Cambridge University Press.

Smith, D. (1975) *Human Geography: a Welfare Approach*, London: Edward Arnold.

Smith , D. M. (1999) 'Conclusion: towards a context-sensitive ethics', in J. D. Proctor and D. M. Smith, *Geography and Ethics: Journeys in a Moral Terrain*, London and New York: Routledge, 275–90.

Smith, D. (2000) *Moral Geographies: Ethics in a World of Difference*, Edinburgh: Edinburgh University Press.

Smith, D. and Ogden, P. (1977) 'Reformation and revolution in human geography' in R. Lee (ed.) *Change and Tradition: Geography's New Frontiers*, London: Queen Mary's College, University of London, pp. 47–58.

Sparks, B. (1972) *Geomorphology*, London: Longman (2nd edition).

Steans, J. (2003) 'Gender inequalities and feminist politics in a global perspective' in E. Kofman and G. Youngs (eds) *Globalization: Theory and Practice*, London: Continuum (3rd edition), pp. 123–38.

Stott, P. (1998) 'Biogeography and ecology in crisis: the urgent need for a new metalanguage', *Journal of Biogeography*, 25: 1–2.

Stott, P. (2001) 'Jungles of the mind: the invention of the "Tropical Rain Forest"', *History Today*, 51(5): 38–44.

Sugden, D. and John, B. (1976) *Glaciers and Landscape*, London: Arnold.

Tansley, A. (1935) 'The use and abuse of vegitational concepts and terms', *Ecology xvi*, 16 July.

Taylor, P. (1985) *Political Geography: World-economy, Nation-state and Community*, London: Longman.

Thomas, W. (ed.) (1956) *Man's Role in Changing the Face of the Earth*, Chicago: University of Chicago Press.

Thrift, N. (1983) 'On the determination of social action in space and time', *Environment and Planning D: Society and Space*, 1(1): 23–57.

TTA (2004) *Qualifying to Teach*, www.tta.gov.uk/php/read/php?sectionid=108&articleid=458 (accessed February 2005).

Tuan, Y-F. (1976) *Topophilia*, London: Prentice Hall.

Urban, M. and Rhoads, B. (2003) 'Conceptions of nature; implications for an integrated geography' in S. Trudgill and A. Roy (eds) *Contemporary Meanings in Physical Geography; From What to Why?*, London: Arnold, pp. 211–31.

Walford, R. (2000) *Geography in British Schools 1850–2000*, London: Woburn Press.

Waugh, D. (2000) 'Writing geography textbooks' in C. Fisher and T. Binns (eds) *Teaching and Learning Geography*, London: RoutledgeFalmer. pp. 93-107.

Weber, A. (1929) *Alfred Weber's Theory of the Location of Industry*, Chicago: University of Chicago Press.

Wente, M. (2001) 'Why America is hated: all that and more from your teachers union', *The Globe and Mail*, 6 December.

Whatmore, S. (1999) 'Culture-nature' in P. Cloke, P. Crang and M. Goodwin (eds) *Introducing Human Geographies*, London: Arnold, pp. 4–11.

Whatmore, S. (2003) *Hybrid Geographies*, London: Sage.

White, J. (2002) *The Child's Mind*, London: RoutledgeFalmer.

White, J. (ed.) (2004) *Rethinking the School Curriculum*, London: RoutledgeFalmer.

Whitty, G. (2002) *Making Sense of Education Policy: Studies in the Sociology and Politics of Education*, London: Paul Chapman.

217

Whyte, I. (2002) *Landscape and History*, London: Reaktion Books.

Williams, R. (1958) *Culture and Society*, London: Chatto & Windus.

Williams, R. (1961) *The Long Revolution*, Harmondsworth: Pelican.

Williams, R. (1973) *The Country and the City*, London: Chatto & Windus.

Williams, R. (1976) *Keywords*, London: Fontana.

Witherick, M., Ross, S. and Small, J. (2001) *A Modern Dictionary of Geography*, London: Arnold.

Wright, D. (1983) 'Viewpoint: the road to Malham Tarn', *Teaching Geography*, 8(3): 139–41.

Yapa, L. (2000) 'Rediscovering geography: on speaking truth to power', *Annals of the Association of American Geographers*, 89(1): 151–5.

Zipf, G. (1949) *Human Behaviour and the Principle of Least Effort*, New York: Hafner.

Index

Page references to boxes and figures are in *italic*

'adjectival studies' 32
Advanced Skills Teachers (ASTs) 189
ageing, study of *143–4*
'Air Quality', map on 113
A Language for Life (Bullock Report) 101
Alonso, W. 10
Altered Land (J. Hardy) *168*
Ambrose, Peter 136–7
Analytical Human Geography (P. Ambrose) 136–7
Apple, Michael 73, 87, 93, 120
areal studies, defined 88
Armstrong, M. 86–7
assessment, role of 150–2; of learning/for learning distinction 151
Association for Curriculum Development 35
Association of American Geographers 12
ASTs (Advanced Skills Teachers) 189
asylum seekers, study in 92–5; citizenship, meaning of 94–5
atlases 83, 111
autonomy, professional 163, 166–7; threats to 161, 162, 173

Balderstone, D. 115, 123, 125, 151
Bale, J. 108
Ball, S. 37, 38
'banking model' (geography teaching) 98, 99, 144
Barnes, Trevor 5, 7, 11, 22, 51, 55–6
'basic skills' 34, 39
behaviourism 74, 90
Bhangra music 126
Billy Elliott (film) 124
biogeography 19
biological sciences *45*
Bjerknes, J. 19
Black, Jeremy 112, 113, 114
Boardman, D. 108
Bradford, M. 104
Brazilian Indians, and mapping issues 113
British Educational Communications and Technology Agency (Becta) 204
British Film Institute 127–8
Buckingham, David 131
Bullen, E. 130
Bullock Report (*A Language for Life*) 101
Burgess, E. W. 10, 44, *45*

Burgess, J. 122, 123
Burke, C. 142

Callaghan, James (Prime Minister)
   33
Campbell, E. 149–50
capitalism 79
career development 189
Career Entry Development Profile
   159
Carlson, Denis 67
Carrington, Ben 125
Castells, Manuel 192
Castree, N. 61
Changing Global Environment
   (N. Roberts) 21
*Changing Nature of Physical
   Geography* (K. Gregory) 20–1
Changing the Subject (E. Rawling)
   161
Cheddar Gorge, tourist leaflet usage
   84, 85
child-centredness 30, 33, 155
Chorley, Richard 9, 19, 27, 139
Christaller, Walter 9, 44
citizenship education 39; meaning of
   citizenship 94–5; National
   Curriculum requirements 88;
   Programme of Study *176*
Clarke, Charles 183, 195
Clements, R. E. 19
climatology 19
Cloke, P. 14, 53–4
coal industry, text on 106–7
Cognitive Acceleration through
   Science Education (CASE) *163*
community of practice 190, 193
concentric zone model
   (E. W. Burgess) *45*; *see also*
   Burgess, E.
Condition of Postmodernity
   (D. Harvey) 11
Connell, J. 124
constructivism 55–6
Consuming Children (J. Kenway
   and E. Bullen) 130

*Contemporary Issues in Geography
   and Education* (Association for
   Curriculum Development) 35–6
continuous professional
   development (CPD) 159, 165,
   190, 191, 195
Cooke, R. 20
Corbridge, S. 79–80
Corney, G. 34
crime and local community (unit of
   study) 87–92, 95; definition of
   crime 91; environmental
   measures 89; 'geography of
   crime' 88; local policies 90;
   'neighbourhood watch' schemes
   91; offences 89; resource
   allocation 89
critical cultural theory (1990s) 8
critical literacy 106
critical social theories (1980s) 8,
   61–2
critical thinking 97, 100, 130–1
Crush, J. 56–7
cultural geography 16, 17; physical
   21
cultural literacy 106, 107
cultural turn 16, 17, 122
culture, and curriculum 24
cumulative causation, spatial
   concepts 137
curriculum: 'absolutist' 98;
   'assertive' curricular practices 32;
   changes in, Schools Council
   objective 29; 'core' 66–7; culture,
   and 24; design of *see* curriculum
   design; development 29–30,
   76–82; as human creation 25;
   National *see* National
   Curriculum; planning of *see*
   curriculum planning; 'received'
   98; as representational text 81–2;
   social and environmental issues
   31; teaching approach, and 48;
   'Thinking Skills' 100, 134
curriculum design 73–96; asylum
   seekers, study of 92–5; crime and

local community (unit of study)
87–92; limestone landscapes,
teaching 82–7; as political and
moral process 93
curriculum development 29–30
curriculum planning 74–6, 95;
phenomenological thinking 99;
pupil involvement 86–7; rational
74–5; 'valuable educational
activity' 80
Curry, M. 117

Daly, C. 170
Darwin, Charles 18, 19, 21
Davis, W. M. 19
Dear, Michael 51–5
degree, geography 175, 177
demographic transition theory 46
Department for Education and
Skills (DfES) 165, 204
dependency school 78
'desocialising of geography' 142
development: birth rate,
relationship with 46; definition
76–82; indicators of 77; partial
accounts of 78; post-
development debates 80; QCA
unit on 95; underdevelopment,
and 78
Development Education 32
Dewey, John 139
Dickenson, J. 77–8
Dictionary of Development
(W. Sachs) 80
Divided Britain (R. Hudson and
A. Williams) 14
Down on the Farm (simulation
package) 121
Drury, L. 146
Dubliners 126
Duncan, J. 51, 55

Earle, Steve 124–5
earth, origin of 18
'earth-writing' (literal meaning of
geography) 102

ecological studies: crime
rates/environmental measures
88–9; 'tropical rainforests' 145
economic development 77
economic literacy 33–4
economics, changes in (UK) 13–14
economic space, mapping 110–11
Education Reform Act (1988) 165
empiricist science 44, 50–1, 74, 118;
see also positivism, in geography
England and Wales, relief of 83
enterprise, and geography 33–4
Environmental Education 32
environmental ethics 62–5
environmental geography:
evaluating 145–9; mapping 113;
people–environment approach,
geography teaching 61
Environmental History of Great
Britain (I. Simmons) 21–2
equilibrium concept 145, 146
erosion, cycle of 19
ethics: environmental issues 62–5;
geography teaching 156; morally
'careless' geography teaching
157–8
evaluation of geography education
133–52; assessment, role of
150–2; environmental geography
145–9; human geography 142–5;
practical considerations 142–9;
progress 134–42; purpose 133,
149–50; see also school
geography; teaching of geography
Everson, J. 28
evolutionary theory 18–19, 46
Explanation in Geography
(D. Harvey) 10

feminist geographers 15–16, 52–3,
66, 100, 143
Fielding, Michael 162, 166
fieldwork 34
Fien, J. 99
films and video 127–9
Fitzgerald, B. 28

fluvial erosion 19, 20
folk music 125, 126
Fordist/post-Fordist economic
    system 13
Frank, Andre Gunder 78
Freidmann 77–8
freshwater species, halting
    extinction of 62–5
Friel, Brian 109
Friere, P. 98
Full Monty (film) 128–9

GA (Geographical Association): on
    curriculum issues 39; *Geography,
    Schools and Industry* collection
    33; independence 198;
    membership 195; origins 195;
    role 154, 195; Sir Keith Joseph's
    address to (1985) 37; strengths
    205–6; vision of *196–8*
gender: language use, and 103; role
    of 15–16, 52–3, 66
General Teaching Council for
    England (GTCE) 172, 195;
    professional code *185*
Geographical Association *see* GA
    (Geographical Association)
Geographical Imaginations
    (D. Gregory) 8
geographical inquiry, 'poetics' of 55
Geographical magazine 113
geographical scales 49
Geographies of Exclusion
    (D. Sibley) 17
geography: as academic discipline 5,
    26, 31; crime, of 88; cultural 16,
    17; doing 5–23; 'earth-writing', as
    literal meaning 102; education *see*
    geography education; enterprise,
    and 33–4; environmental 145–9;
    feminist 15–16, 52–3, 66, 100,
    143; human *see* human
    geography; as 'humanities' subject
    39; 'ideosyncratic' 105;
    'intentional' 48; media, and *see*
    media, and geography; 'new' *see*

'new' geography; new
    opportunities, and 38–40;
    organising concepts 6; as personal
    response 47, 128; physical *see*
    physical geography; positivism in
    see positivism, in geography;
    postmodernism, and 43, 51–8;
    progressivism *see* progressivism,
    in geography teaching; radical
    development 79–80; regional
    science, and 8, 9, 27–8, 29;
    relevance of *174*; school *see*
    school geography; as science 47;
    socially critical education, and
    35–6; spatial science, and 8, 9,
    27–9, 44, 58; status, disciplinary
    26–7, 28–9; teaching *see* teaching
    of geography; technocratic 120;
    welfare approach to 30
Geography, Schools and Industry
    Partnership (GSIP) 34
*Geography, the Media and Popular
    Culture* (J. Burgess and J. Gold)
    122
*Geography and Geographers:
    Anglo-American human
    geography since 1945*
    (R. Johnston) 7
Geography and Geographers
    (R. Johnston) 51
geography education: evaluation *see*
    evaluation of geography
    education; human geography
    44–51; importance of 173;
    people–environment approach
    60–1; physical geography,
    purposes 59–65; postmodern
    turn, and 43, 51–5; purposes
    42–3, 58; *see also* school
    geography; teaching of geography
Geography for the Young School
    Leaver (GYSL) project 29–30
Geography National Curriculum
    Working Group 37–8
Geography of Urban Crime
    (D. Herbert) 88, 91

geological column (identification of
rocks) 83
Geomorphology (B. Sparks) 19
Geomorphology in Deserts
(R. Cooke and A. Warren) 20
Gibson, C. 124
Gilbert, Rob 103–4
Glaciers and Landscape (D. Sugden
and B. John) 20
Global Casino (N. Middleton) 21
Global Environmental Change
(A. Mannion) 21
globalisation, 'neo-liberal' 16
global warming 61
GNP (gross national product) per
capita 57–8
Gold, J. 122, 123
Goodson, Ivor 26, 28, 117–18
Graceland (P. Simon) 127
gradient (spatial concept) 137
*Graphicacy and Geography
Teaching* (D. Boardman) 108
Graves, Norman 74, 75, 200
gravity model 44, *45*
Gregory, Derek 5; on geographical
inquiry, 'poetics' of 55; on
'hegemony of spatial science'
22–3; on human geography 7, 15,
40, 138–9; on progress in
geography 140, 141; on
schematic development of
geography 8, 13
Gregory, Ken 18, 20–1
Gritzner, C. *157*
Grosvener, I. 142

Haggett, Peter 5, 9, 27, 139
Hall, David 27, 30, 37–8
Hamnett, Chris 17
Hardy, Jules *168*
Hargreaves, David 188, 192, 193
Harley, Brian 113–14
Harvey, David 10–11, 17, 28, 42,
43, 97, 101
Hassell, D. 116, 118
Healey, M. 47, 128

Heffernan, M. 7
Henley, R. 104, 105
Herbert, David 88, 89, 90, 91
heuristic models 8
Higher Education Study Group 204
Hirst, Paul 75
histories: human geography 7–13;
physical geography 18–22; school
geography 26–7
HOD (head of geography) 189
Hodson, D. 169
Holloway, L. 17, 110
Holloway, S. 6
homeostasis *145*
Horizons in Human Geography
(D. Gregory and R. Walford)
138–9
Hoyle, E. 161, 166
Hoyt, Homer 44
Hubbard, P. 17, 56, 110
Huckle, J. 31, 35, 119–20
Hudson, R. 14
Human Development Index 77
human geography: evaluating
142–5; histories 7–13; knowledge
and education 44–51; physical
geography, and 84; recent
movements 13–18; in schools 6;
in universities 6
humanistic geography/sciences:
development, and 81; Johnston's
schema 47–8, 118, 119;
knowledge and education 43, 46;
language, and 104–5
'humanities' subject, geography as
39
Eliot-Hurst, M. 138
Hutton, James 18–19
hydrology 20

ICT (information and
communications technology), and
geography teaching 114–22;
assumptions, questioning 134–5;
Down on the Farm (simulation
package) *121*; effectiveness of

technologies 116; growing
importance 117; historical phases
115; problems 116; software
packages 119–20
ideology 103–4
Ideology and Curriculum
(M. Apple) 73
'ideosyncratic geography' 105
Impotent Image (R. Gilbert) 104
industrial location theory
(A. Weber) 45
information and communications
technology *see* ICT (information
and communications technology),
and geography teaching
Inglis, Fred 24, 25, 32
Institute of British Geographers *see*
RGS-IBG (Royal Geographical
Society with Institute of British
Geographers)
*Intellectual Life of the British
Working-Classes* (J. Rose) 102
'intentional geography' 48
*Introduction to Coastal
Geomorphology* (J. Pethick) 20

Jacks, G. 20
Jackson, Peter 5–6, 16, 143
Jenkins, Simon 109
'Job Ghettos' (map) 112
John, B. 20
John, P. 161, 166
John Ruskin College, J. Callaghan's
speech at (1976) 33
Johnston, Ron 7, 14; on science
types 44–51, 58, 118–19
Jones, Graham (story of) 49–50
Jones, Ken 32, 36–7
Joseph, Sir Keith 37
*Justice, Nature and the Geographies
of Difference* (D. Harvey) 11

Kent, A. 104
Kenway, J. 130
Key Concepts in Geography
(S. Holloway *et al.*) 6

Key Stage (KS) 3 Strategy 39, 162,
164, 165, 201; 'Knowledge and
Understanding' Standard *176*;
'Thinking Skills' 134
Kincheloe, J. 96, 129–30, 141
Klein, Naomi 130
knowledge: fields 75; forms 75;
geographical, critique of 97–8;
geography as field of 75;
humanistic geographical 43;
partial nature of 55; postmodern
critique *see* postmodernism;
practical theories 75; progress as
accumulation of 151; 'pure'
formal 76; re-presentation to
pupils 79; of soil 60; structure of
75; subject 39, 175, 177–9, 182;
'technocratic' 60; *see also*
geographical education
knowledge society 192
'Knowledge and Understanding'
(government Standard) 175,
176–7
Kuhn, Thomas 7–8

Lambert, D. 114–15, 123, 125,
151
landscapes, limestone *see* limestone
landscapes, teaching of
land use models 10, 44
language: critical approaches to
(in geography) 101–8; of
deconstruction 131; of education
162; geographical 128; ideology,
and 104; linguistic turn 55;
neutrality, lack of 103; of
'scientism' 104
leadership, and professional
development 189–90
league tables 160–1
Learning and Teaching Support
Network (LTSN) 204
Learning Through Enquiry
(M. Roberts) *163*
Learning Through Geography
(F. Slater) *163*

least cost location, spatial concepts
137, 140
Leat, David 135, *163*
Leaving Safe Harbors (D. Carlson)
67
LEDCs (Less Economically
Developed Countries) 58, 77
Lee, Alison 40, 105
Lee, E. 123
Lee, R. 94
Lee, Roger 138
Lewis, J. 14
Leyshon, Andrew 17
limestone landscapes, teaching of
82–7; formation of landscapes 83;
formation of limestone 83–4; key
words 83; 'landscape', as human
construction 85; pair work 84;
protection concerns 85; tourist
leaflets 84
linguistic turn 55
literacy: classification of types 106;
critical 106; critical approaches to
(in geography) 101–8; cultural
106, 107
Literacy in Geography document:
critical approaches to
language/literacy 101–2, 103,
105, 107–8; progressivism in
education 135, 136
Living Geography (textbook) 106–7
Livingstone, D. 26
local education authorities (LEAs)
160, 161
location theory 136, 137, 140–1
London Board (A Level examination
syllabus) 59–60
Lyell, Charles 19
lyrics, musical 124, 125

McDowell, Linda 65–6
McEwen, N. 47–8
MacGowan, Shane 125
Machon, P. 36
McKay, H. 88
Maguire, D. 115, 117, 118

Making Movies Matter (British Film
Institute report) 127–8
Management of Ignorance
(Fred Inglis) 24
Mannion, A. 21
*Man's Role in Changing the Face of
the Earth* (W. Thomas) 20
mapping 108–14; crime patterns 89,
90; data collection problems 112;
economic space 110–11;
environmental 113; social class,
and 108; social space 111–12;
theoretical issues 113–14
Maps and Politics (J. Black) 113
Marxism: Harvey on 10, 11;
Structuralist 16
Masterman, Len 122–3
Master of Teaching, on-line
discussion forum 169–70
materialism, historical 11
MEDCs (More Economically
Developed Countries) 77
media, and geography 122–30; films
and video 127–9; musical
geographies 123–7; products of
media, as 'social constructions'
123
Meinig, D. W. 85–6, 96
Mercer, D. 120
Middleton, N. 21
migration 104; as cultural
experience 126
minority groups, and geography 1
Modern Dictionary of Geography
(M. Witherwick) 76–7
modernisation theory (W. Rostow)
46, 77, 78
Mohan, J. 15
Moore, A. 95, 106, 156
Moore, P. *146*, *147–8*
moral carelessness, avoiding 62–5
moral education *156*
More Thinking Through Geography
(A. Nichols) 99–100
Moving Images in the Classroom
128

musical geographies 123–7
Myrdal, Gunnar 77–8

A Nation Dividing? (R. Johnston
et al.) 14
national anthems 125
National College for School
Leadership (NCSL) 195
National Curriculum 36–8;
citizenship requirements 88;
descriptions, vague nature of
151; earth science 82;
Education Reform Act (1988),
and 165; exemplar schemes of
work 87–92; geography, and 47,
118, 161; Geography Association,
and 198; Geography National
Curriculum Working Group
37–8; 'orders' 161; social and
cultural development, promotion
in pupils 92; *see also* curriculum
National Curriculum Framework
176
National Curriculum Handbook
176
National Literacy Strategy 101
natural sciences, legacy on
geography teaching 45–6
Nature of Physical Geography
(K. Gregory) 18
nearest neighbour index 44
neighbourhoods 45
neo-Marxism 79
network, spatial concepts 137
networked society, concept of
192
'new' geography: curriculum
planning 74; 'dehumanising'
tendencies of 11–12; 'issues-
based' approach 30;
progressivism 136; science, and
9, 13, 29, 51, 117; status of
geography 28; student types 31
New Horizons in Human
Geography (D. Gregory and R.
Walford) 40

New Labour government (1997)
38–9
Newman, O. 89
'New Model Army', history 28
New Thinking in School
Geography (Department of
Education and Science) 28
Nichols, A. 99–100
No Logo (N. Klein) 130
'north–south' divide, economic
prospects 13–14; *North–South*
Divide (J. Lewis and
A. Townsend) 14
nuclear power plants, maps of
111

Ofsted 164, 165, 201
Ogden, P. 138
oil crisis (1973) 16
Olson, A. 112
On Human Geography (R.
Johnston) 44
Ordnance Survey maps 108–10
Origin of Species (C. Darwin) 19

Park, R. E. 10
Peet, R. 91
peneplain (eroded base-level
surface) 19
people–environment approach
(geography education) 60–1
Pepper, David 59–60, 84
personal response, geography as
47, 128
Peters Projection 114
Peters, Richard 75
Pethick, J. 20
PGCE (Post-Graduate Certificate of
Education) students 186
phenomenology, ideas 47, 48, 99
Philo, Chris 142
physical geography: histories
18–22; human geography, and
84; in schools 6, 59–65; soil,
knowledge of 60; in universities
6, 59

Piaget, Jean 108
Place and Placelessness (E. Relph)
12
planning, stages of 74
poetics, defined 55
Pogues, The 125
Policy and Change in Thatcher's
Britain (P. Cloke) 14
political correctness 131
political economy models 8
pollution 61
population studies (ageing) *143–4*
positionality 53, 55
positivism, in geography: crime,
study of 90; curriculum
planning, and 74; decision-
making exercise 100; domination,
in teaching of 47, 48, 50–1;
Harvey on 10; human geography,
post-positivist turn (1970s) 12;
'new' geography 31; science,
positivist 44; *see also* empiricist
science
postmodernism: as attitude 53, *54*;
Condition of Postmodernity
(D. Harvey) 11; definition 53; on
difference 53–4; geography, and
43, 51–8; as object of study 53
postmodernity, definition 53
post-structuralism 56; structuralism,
and *57*
Power of Development (J. Crush)
56–7
Principles of Geology (C. Lyell) 19
Proctor, James *62–65*
professional development 188–99;
ambition 156; career
development, as 189; community
of practice, belonging to 190,
193; CPD (continuous
professional development) 159,
165, 190, 191, 195; definition
188–94; leadership, and 189–90;
professional learning 191–3;
'scholarship of teaching' 193–4;
subject associations, role 194–8

professional identity 155
professionalism: accountability 165;
autonomy 161, 162, 163, 166–7,
173; case study 169–71;
competence 169; definitions
160–9; responsibility 163, 166;
standards *see* standards,
professional; teachers' knowledge
166; teaching of geography
160–9, 183–187, *185*;
terminology problems 155; values
and practice *185*
progressivism, in geography
teaching 31–2, 134–42;
evaluation of progress 140–2;
progress of geography/progress in
geography 134, 135–6, 140;
spatial concepts 137
Punjabi folk music 126

QCA (Qualifications and
Curriculum Authority), exemplar
schemes of work for National
Curriculum 87, 91, 95
QTS (Qualified Teacher Status)
155; Knowledge and
Understanding (subject
knowledge) 175, *176–7*;
Standards 75, 159, *184*, *185*

race, language use, and 103
Rape of the Earth (G. Jacks and
R. Whyte) 20
rap lyrics 124
Rawling, Eleanor 5, 29, 30, 31, 32,
38, 161, 165
reading, importance of *102–3*
realist science 49, 118, 119
real/representation, distinction
between 123
Rediscovering Geography (National
Research Council) 57
regional science, and geography 8,
9, 27–8, 29
relief maps 83
Relph, Edward 12

RGS-IBG (Royal Geographical Society with Institute of British Geographers) 195, 196, 203–5

'rhetorical constructions', geographical accounts as 55

Rhoads, B. 21

Richardson, Robin 158

Roberts, M. 47, 48

Roberts, Margaret *163*

Roberts, N. 21, 38

'rock cycle' 18

Rose, Jonathan 102, 103

Ross, A. 37

Rostow, W. *46*, 77–8

Royal Geographical Society *see* RGS-IBG (Royal Geographical Society with Institute of British Geographers)

Sachs, Wolfgang 80–1

Sarup, Madan 99

SATs (Standard Assessment Test) 165

scale, geographical 49

'scholarship of teaching', target of 193–4

school geography: curriculum *see* curriculum; histories 26–7; humanistic influences, and student centredness 29–33; making 24–41; phenomenologically based approach 47, 48, 99; physical geography in 6, *59*–65; pupils' needs 30; 'radical' 36; skills, basic 34, 39; university education, and 28, 40; *see also* geography education; teaching of geography

school-industry initiatives 33

Schools Council 29; Geography 16–19 Project 9, 30–1, 60–1

Schulman, L. 166

science: applied 44; biological *45*; dominant ideas 7–8; empiricist 44, 50–1, 74, 118; geography as 47; humanistic *see* humanistic geography/sciences; natural *see*

natural sciences; 'new' geography, and 9, 13, 29, 51, 117; 'real', geography's position as 29; realist 49, 118, 119; regional 8, 9, 27–8, 29; spatial 8, 9, 27–9, 44, 58

'scientism', language of 104

Seager, J. 112, 113

sector model (H. Hoyt) 44

SEN (special educational needs) 180

Shaw, C. 88

Short, John Rennie 134, 135, 138, 142

Shuker, R. 127

Shurmer-Smith, P. 16

Sibley, David 17

Siemens semiconductor factory, closure (1997) 49–50

Simmons, I. 21–2

Simon, Paul 127

Sims, P. 20

Slater, Frances 47, 103, 163

Small, R. 19

Smith, D. 138

Smith, Susan 16, 143

social class: mapping abilities 108; 'rainforest', attitudes to *147*

social constructivism 62–5, 97; media products as 'social constructions' 123

Social Justice and the City (D. Harvey) 10–11

socially critical education, and geography 35–6

social space, mapping 111–12

sociology: of education 99; influence of 8

soil, knowledge of 60

song lyrics 124, 125

Spaces of Hope (D. Harvey) 11

Sparks, B. 19

spatial science, and geography 8, 9, 27–9, 44, 58; progressivism in teaching 137

special educational needs (SENs) 180

sporting events, anthems at 125

Springsteen, Bruce 124
Standards and Effectiveness Unit 194
standards, professional 172, 183–7; QTS (Qualified Teacher Status) 75, 159, *184*, *185*
State of the Earth (J. Seager) 113
Steinberg, S. *96*, 129–30, 141
Stott, Philip *146*
structuralism, post-structuralism and *57*
Study of Landforms (R. Small) 19
subject associations, role 194–8
subject knowledge/specialism 39, 175, 177–9, 182
Sugden, D. 20
sustainability 39, *146*

Tansley, Arthur *145*
Taylor, Peter 49–50
teacher, learning to be 180–3
Teacher Training Agency (TTA) 172, *184*, 195, 204
teaching of geography 155–71; approaches 48, 98–101; 'banking model' 98, 99, 144; case study 169–170; critical teaching 130–1; curriculum, and teaching approach 48; development issues 78–82; ethical issues *156*, *157*–8; learning to teach 174–80; mapping of meanings *see* mapping; natural sciences, legacy of *45*–6; people–environment approach 60–1; professionalism 160–9, 183–7, *185*; progressivism *see* progressivism, in geography teaching; purpose 40; Qualified Teacher Status *see* QTS (Qualified Teacher Status); quality issues 164; re-presentation of knowledge to pupils 79; role of teachers 25, 41; 'scholarship of teaching' 193–4; shortage of teachers 164; subject knowledge 39, 175, 177–9, 182; syllabuses 34;

teacher, learning to be 180–3; technoliteracy, and 114–22; training 158, 174–5; *see also* curriculum; geography education; school geography
Teaching the Media (L. Masterman) 122–3
technocratic geography 120
technoliteracy, and geography 114–22
textbooks, geography 46–7, 77–8, 104; coal industry 106–7
Thatcherism 14, 160
Theory of the Earth (J. Hutton) 18
'Thinking Skills' 100, 134
Thinking through Geography (D. Leat) 135, *163*
Thomas, W. 20
Thrift, Nigel 15
Times, The 109
tinkering 193
Topophilia (Y.F. Tuan) 21
Townsend, A. 14
Trans-Amazonian Highway 113
Translations (B. Friel) 109
travel patterns *45*
tropical rainforests *145*–8
Tuan, Yi-Fu 21

underdeveloped nations 58, 77
Understanding Popular Music (R. Shuker) 127
United States, 'scholarship of teaching' 193
universities: human geography 6; physical geography 6, 18, *59*; school geography, and 28, 40
upland areas 83
Urban, M. 21
urban residential structure theory 10, *45*

Varignon frames principle *45*, 141
videos, geographical 127–9
Von Thunen, Johann 9, 10

Walford, Rex 28, 40, 117, 138–9
Warren, A. 20
Weber, Alfred 9, 44, *45*, 140–1
White, John 100
Whyte, R. 20
Williams, A. 14
Williams, Raymond 25, 104
Wilson, Harold (Prime Minister) 28
Witherwick, M. 76–7
women, and geography 15–16, 52–3, 66, 100, 143

Women in the World Atlas (J. Seager and A. Olson) 112
Wookey Hole, tourist leaflet usage 84, 85
World Studies 32
Wright, David *86*
Writing Worlds (T. Barnes and J. Duncan) 55
Wynette, Tammy 124

Yapa, L. 57–8

Zipf, G. *45*

eBooks – at www.eBookstore.tandf.co.uk

A library at your fingertips!

eBooks are electronic versions of printed books. You can store them on your PC/laptop or browse them online.

They have advantages for anyone needing rapid access to a wide variety of published, copyright information.

eBooks can help your research by enabling you to bookmark chapters, annotate text and use instant searches to find specific words or phrases. Several eBook files would fit on even a small laptop or PDA.

NEW: Save money by eSubscribing: cheap, online access to any eBook for as long as you need it.

Annual subscription packages

We now offer special low-cost bulk subscriptions to packages of eBooks in certain subject areas. These are available to libraries or to individuals.

For more information please contact webmaster.ebooks@tandf.co.uk

We're continually developing the eBook concept, so keep up to date by visiting the website.

www.eBookstore.tandf.co.uk